BUDDHISM IN SRI LANKA

BUDDHISM IN SRI LANKA

KANAI LAL HAZRA

BUDDHIST WORLD PRESS
Delhi - 110 052

Cataloging in Publication Data--DK
Courtesy: D.K. Agencies (P) Ltd. <docinfo@dkagencies.com>

Hazra, Kanai Lal, 1932-
Buddhism in Sri Lanka : / Kanai Lal Hazra.
p. cm.
Includes bibliographical references (p.)
Includes index.
ISBN 9788190638821

1. Buddhism--Sri Lanka--History. 2. Monasteries, Buddhist--Sri Lanka. I. Title.

DDC 294.309 549 3 22

Printed and Published by:
Buddhist World Press
425, Nimri Colony
Ashok Vihar, Phase-IV
Delhi - 110 052
Ph.: 011-2325 9196, 011-2325 9648
e-mail: *brpc@vsnl.com*

First Published, 2009

ISBN : 978-81-906388-2-1

To

All the People of Sri Lanka

To my friends I owe a debt so profound, so sublime, so deep, so touchy and so great that this book shows as much theirs as it indicates mine. I love Sri Lanka and its people with all my heart. To me it is my second mother-land.

Preface

In this study an attempt is made to trace the introduction and the development of Buddhism in Sri Lanka from the earliest times up to the present day. The history of Sri Lanka began with the colonization of the island by Prince Vijaya from Bengal in the 5th Century B.C. It would not be unreasonable to think that Vijaya helped to introduce the elements of Buddhism in Sri Lanka, but the religion, however, until the time of Devānampiya Tissa (3rd century B.C.), did not obtain any wide popularity in the Island. Devānampiya Tissa was a contemporary of the Maurya a ruler Asoka of India. He had friendly relations with the Indian ruler. He received warmly Thera Mahinda and other Buddhist monks who were despatched by Asoka to introduce Buddhism in Sri Lanka. Devānampiya Tissa then sent a mission to India to bring a branch of the Bodhi tree under which santama Buddha obtained enlightenment. With due pomp and ceremony he planted it in Anurādhāpura when it reached Sri Lanka. He also created the Mahāvihāra and the Thupārāma at Anurādhapura. After Devānampiya Tissa, for a time the kingdom went into the hands of the Tamil rulers. But Duṣṭhagamana Abhaya reoccupied it. He was a follower of Buddhism. He constructed the Lohapāsāda, and the Mahāthupa or Ruvamawali dāgoba at Anurādhapura. When the foundation stone of the dāgoba was laid, many monks from different regions of India arrived in Sri Lanka. In the history of Buddhism in Sri Lanka the reign of Duṣṭhagamana Abhaya was an important period. The Tripiṭakas which were kept so long in memory were committed to writing by the monks of the Mahāvihāra.

A new monastery at a dāgoba known as the Abhayagiri vihāra was built by Abhaya and it became a prominent centre of

Buddhism and Buddhist culture. According to Fa-Hien, the Chinese traveller, about five thousand Buddhist monks used to live there. He also stated that about three thousand Buddhist monks stayed at the Mahāvihāra. Sri Lanka's monasteries as great centre of learning got the attention of the Buddhist scholars from far and wide. During the rule of king Mahānāma in the fifth century A.D. Buddhaghosa, the celebrated Buddhist scholar, visited Sri Lanka from India. For some time he had studied in the Mahāvihāra. Then he devoted his time to undertake the translation of the Sinholese commentaries. In the 8th Century, A.D. due to political reason arriving from the Tamil invasion, Polonnaruva became the capital of Sri Lanka. It was shifted from Anurādhapura. The political, cultural and religious activities then began to move round the new capital. King Parākramabāhu I of the 12th century A.D. was a great ruler. He ruled from Polannaruva and he was a devotee of Buddhism. During the subsequent times in spite of opposition due to changes in political situation, Buddhism was able to survive in Sri Lanka. It became the religion of the people. Still today it was able to manage its existence. It has attained wide popularity and has become the religion of the country. Chapter Two (II) deals with Mahayanism in Sri Lanka and the important role played by sacred Buddhist monks and some Kings of Sri Lanka for the introduction and progress of Mahāyānism in the Island. Chapter Three (III) discusses Buddhist Education in Sri Lanka. Chapter Four (IV) gives an account of Buddhist Art, Architecture and Sculpture of Sri Lanka. Chapter Five (V) narrates Buddhist Festivals of Sri Lanka. Chapter Six (VI) describes Buddhist Literature of Sri Lanka. Chapter Seven (VII) mentions the Buddhist Monastery of Sri Lanka: Its Administrative System. Chapter Eight (VII) throws light on the life of the Arahants in Sri Lanka.

I express my deep gratitude to Prof. Dr. Mrs. Sirima Kiribamnne, and Dr. Daya Amarasekera of the University of Parademiya, Sri Lanka, and Prof. Dr. M.K. Ganguly and Dr. Mrs. Manikuntala Halder (De) of the University of Calcutta for taking personal interest in my work. My thanks are also due to my brother Mr. Subodh Kumar Hazra, my niece Mrs. Pratima Haldar, my niece Mrs. Malaya Paul and her son Mr. Biswarup Paul, and my another niece Mrs. Chandrima Ojha and her husband Mr. Benoy Ojha for their keen interest in the publication of this book. My thanks are also due to the librarian and the deputy librarian Mr. Chitta Patra of the Indian Museum Library Calcutta for helping me to use books in this library. I must be thankful to my publisher for the publication of this book.

KANAI LAL HAZRA

Contents

Abbreviations

CHAPTER ONE

1. BCPP = Buddhism in Ceylon, It Past and Its Present, H.R. Perera.
2. Mhv = Mahāvaṃsa, W. Geiger.
3. HBC = History of Buddhism in Ceylon, Walpola Rahula.
4. DPV = Diparaṃsa, H. Oldenberg.
5. MN = Majjhima Nikāya.
6. BIA = Buddhism in India and abroad, A.C. Banerjee.
7. AN = Aviguttara Nikāya.
8. Rsv = Rasavāhinī.
9. AA = Aviguttara-nikāyaṭṭhakathā (Manoratha-purāṇī). Commentary on the Aviguttara-nikāya.
10. VbhA = Vibhaṅgatthakathā (Sannohavimodanī) commentary on the Vibhaṅga.
11. Nks = Nikāyasaṅgrahaya.
12. Hiuen Tsiang = Buddhist Records of the Western World, translated from the Chinese to Hiuen Tsiang by Samuel Beal.
13. MT = Mahavaṃsa-Tīkā, Vaṃsatthappakāsinī.
14. EZ = Epigraphia Zeylanica.
15. HIL = A History of Indian Literature, M. Winternitz.
16. Dāṭhā = Dāṭhāvaṃsa ed., by Silalaṅkāra Thera.
17. Fa Hien = A record of Buddhist kingdom: An account of the Chinese Monk Fa Hien

			of his Travels in India and Ceylon translated by J. Lesse.
18.	HTBSEA	=	History of Theravāda Buddhism in South East Asia with special reference to Ceylon, Kanai Lal Hazra.
19.	CV	=	Cūlavaṃsa, W. Geiger.
20.	CCMT	=	Culture of Ceylon in Mediaeval Times, Heinz Bechart.
21.	Sās	=	Sāsanavaṃsa, ed., M. Bode.
22.	GPC	=	Glass Palace Chronicle, tr. By Pe Money Tih and G.H. Luce.
23.	EI	=	Epigraphia Indica.
24.	PV	=	Pūjāvaliya, ed. B. Gunasekera Mudaliyar.
25.	IA	=	Indian Antiquary.
26.	DPRD	=	The Decline of Polonnaruwa and the Rise of Dambadeniya, Amaradasa Liyanagamage.
27.	CV. TR.	=	Cūlavaṃsa (Translation).
28.	Ep. Zeyl	=	Epigraphia Zeylanica.
29.	Ktk. Sng	=	Katikavat Saṅgara, ed. by D.B. Jayatilaka.
30.	UCHC	=	University of Ceylon History of Ceylon, ed., by H.C. Ray and S. Paranavitana.
31.	RJV	=	Rājāvaliya.
32.	RJV Tr.	=	Rājāvaliya (Translation)
33.	Dal. S.	=	Daladā Sirita, ed. by Valivitiye Sorata.
34.	JRAS, Cey Br., NS.	=	Journal Royal Asiatic Society, Ceylon Branch, New Series, Colombo.
35.	CHC	=	A Concise History of Ceylon, C.W. Nicholas and S. Paramavitana.
36.	Dmb. A.	=	Dambadeni Asha, ed. Kirialle Ñāṇavimala Thera.
37.	Sinh. Lit.	=	Sinhalese literature, C.E. Godakumbara.
38.	UCR	=	University of Ceylon Review, Colombo.
39.	HVU	=	Hatthavanagallaviharavaṃsa.

40. Bell	= Report on the Kāgalla district of the Province of Safaragamnva, H.C.P. Bell.
41. PLC	= Pali Literature of Ceylon, G.P. Mahalasekera.
42. PRC	= Portuguese Rule in Ceylon, 1594-1612, Colombo, 1966.
43. CPE	= Ceylon, the Portuguese Era, P.E. Pieria.
44. JCBRAS	= Journal of the Ceylon Branch of the Royal Asiatic Society, XX, II.
45. SK	= Sandeśakathā, Prof. Minayeff.
46. AHSEA	= A History of South-East Asia, D.G.E. Hall.
47. BEA	= Buddhism in East Asia, Sukumar Dutt.

CHAPTER TWO

1. Paramavitava	= Mahāyānism in Ceylon, S. Paramavitana.
2. Gunawardana	= Buddhist Nikāyas in Mediaeval Ceylon, R.A.L. H. Gunawardana.
3. Mhv	= Mahāvaṃsa, W. Geiger.
4. CHC	= A Concise History of Ceylon, C.W. Nicholas and S. Paramavitana.
5. HBC	= History of Buddhism in Ceylon, Walpola Rahula.
6. Pañca A.	= Pañcappakaraṇaṭṭhakathā (Kathāvatthuppa-Karaṇavaṇṇmā)
7. DPV	= Dīpavaṃsa, H. Oldenberg.
8. Vibh A	= Vibhaṅgaṭṭhakathā
9. MA	= Majjhima-Nikāyaṭṭhakathā
10. Geiger	= Mahāvaṃsa, W. Geiger.
11. Nks	= Nikāyasaṅgrahaya
12. MIB	= Manual of Indian Buddhism, H. Kern.
13. Pradhan	= Abhidharma-Samuccaya, ed. Pradhan.
14. CJSc.G	= Ceylon Journal of Science, II.
15. HIL	= History of Indian Literature, M. Winternitz.

16.	HB	=	Hinduism and Buddhism, Charles Eliot.
17.	JBAS	=	The Journal of the Bengal Asiatic Society, Calcutta, 1915, Plate XX.

CHAPTER THREE

1.	HBC	=	History of Buddhism in Ceylon, Walpola Rahula.
2.	AIE	=	Ancient Indian Education, Radha Kumud Mookerji.
3.	DN	=	Dīgha Nikāya, Walitara Siri Ñānarāsa Thera.
4.	Vsm	=	Visnddhimagga.
5.	DA	=	Dīgha-Nikāyaṭṭhakathā (Sumaṅgalavilāsinī), commentary on the Dīgha-Nikāya.
6.	Smp	=	Samantapāsādikā, Vinaya commentary.
7.	Mhv	=	Mahāvaṃsa, W. Geiger.
8.	VbhA	=	Vibhaṅgaṭṭhakathā (Sammohavinodanī).
9.	Ma	=	Majjhima-Nikāyaṭṭhakathā (Papañcasudani), commentary on the Majjhima Nikāya.
10.	MSA	=	Mediaeval Sinhalese Art, Ananda K. Coomaraswamy.
11.	EZ	=	Epigraphia Zeylanica, Oxford University Press.
12.	Clvg	=	Cullavagga.
13.	Tennant	=	Ceylon, Sir J.E. Tennant.
14.	Koṭahane	=	Srī Dharmāloka Caritaya, Koṭahame Prajñākirti.
15.	AA	=	Aṅguttara-Nikāyaṭṭhakathā (Manorathapūraṇī), commentary on the Aṅguttara-Nikāya
16.	DhpA	=	Dhammapadaṭṭhakathā, commentary on the Dhammapada.
17.	Paramavitana	=	Sīgiriya Graffiti by S. Paramavitana.

18. Beal	=	The life of Hiuen Tsiang, S. Beal.
19. BPE	=	Buddhist Perspectives on Education, Nathan Katz and Judith Simmer.

CHAPTER FOUR

1. Pachori	=	The splendours of Buddhist Art in Asia, Dr. L.N. Pachori.
2. CHC	=	A Concise History of Ceylon, C.W. Nicholas and S. Paramavitana.
3. Ceylon	=	The Ceylon Tourist Board.

CHAPTER FIVE

1. DA	=	Dīgha-nikāyaṭṭhakathā.
2. MA	=	Majjhima-nikāyaṭṭhakathā.
3. VbhA	=	Vibhaṇgaṭṭhakatha.
4. A	=	Aṅguttara-nikāyaṭṭhakatha.
5. Dpv	=	Dīpavaṃsa, H. Oldenberg.
6. Mhv	=	Mahāvaṃsa, W. Geiger.
7. HBC	=	History of Buddhism in Ceylon, Walpola Rahula.
8. RSV	=	Rasavāhini, Saraṇatissa Thera.
9. EZ	=	Epigraphia Zeylanica.
10. SA	=	Sanuattanikāyaṭṭha Katha.
11. A	=	Aṅguttara-nikāya, ed. By Devamitta Thera (Samayawardhana Press, Colombo).
12. Fa Hien	=	A Record of the Buddhist Kingdom: An Account of Chinese Monk Fa Hien of his Travels in India and Ceylon (A.D. 399-414) by J. Legge, Oxford, 1886.
13. Vsm	=	Visuddhimagga.
14. SnA	=	Suttanipātaṭṭha Katha (Paramatthajotikā) commentary on the Suttanipāta.

15. Cbha = Catubhāṇavāraṭṭhā Kathā (Sāratthasamuccaya), commentary on the Catubhāṇavāra.
16. Clv = Cūlavaṃsa.
17. Miln = Milinda-pañha.
18. Dāṭhā = Dāṭhāvaṃsa, Sīlālaṅkara Thera.
19. Dhātu = Dhātuvaṃsa.
20. Hiuen Tsiang = Buddhist Records of the Western world translated from the Chinese of Hiuen Tsiang by Samuel Beal.

CHAPTER SIX

1. CHC ≠ A Concise History of Ceylon, C.W. Nicholas and S. Paramavitana.
2. BC = Buddhism in Ceylon, H.R. Perera.
3. BACSEA = The Buddhist Annals and Chronicles of South-East Asia, K.L. Hazra.
4. BIA = Buddhism in India and Abroad, A.C. Banerjee.
5. PLC = The Pali Literature of Ceylon, G.P. Mahalasekera.
6. OCC = On the Chronicles of Ceylon, B.C. Law.
7. DV = Dīpavaṃsa, B.C. Law.
8. DPV = Dīpavaṃsa, ed. and tr. By H. Oldenberg.
9. HIL = A History of Indian Literature, M. Winternitz.
10. DIPMAH = The Dīpavaṃsa and the Mahāvaṃsa and their Historical Development in Ceylon by Wilhelm Geiger and tr. E.M. Coomaraswamy.
11. DPRD = The Decline of Polonnaruwa and the Rise of Damba-Deviya by Amaradasa Liyanagamage.

12. Wickramasinghe = Catalogue of the Simhala Manuscripts in the British Museum, D.M. Dez Wickramasinghe.
13. Dtv = Dāthāvaṃsa ed. by Rhys Davids and R. Morris.
14. HPL = A History of Pali Literature, B.C. Law.
15. SHVGV = A Study on the Hattavamagallavihara-vaṃsa by Manikuntala Haldar (Dr).
16. HTVGV = Hattavanagallavihāravaṃsa by C.E. Godakumbara.
17. HC = History of Ceylon, by H.C. Ray and S. Paramavitana.
18. DA = Dombadeni Asha, Kirialle, Namavimala Thera.
19. SL = Sinhalese Literature, C.E. Godakumbara.

CHAPTER SEVEN

1. AA = Aṅguttara-nikāyaṭṭha Katha (Mansrathapūraṇī), commentary on the Aṅguttara-nikāya.
2. EZ = Epigraphia Zeylanica, 4 vols., Oxford University Press.
3. Smp = Somantapāsādikā, Vinaya commentary, 3 parts (SHB).
4. SBE = Sacred Books of the East.
5. SHB = Simon Hemavitarne Bequest Series (Colombo).
6. HBC = History of Buddhism in Ceylon, Walpola Rahula.
7. CJSC = Ceylon Journal of Science.
8. VbhA = Vibhagaṭṭha Katha (Sammohavinodanī), commentary on the Vibhaṅga.
9. Fa Hien = A Record of Buddhist Kingdom: An Account of Chinese Monk Fa Hien of his Travels in India and Ceylon (A.D. 399–414) by J. Lesse.

10. Hiuen Tsiang	=	Buddhist Records of the Western World, translated from the Chinese of Hiuen Tsiang (A.D. 629) by Samuel Beal.
11. Mhv	=	Mahāvaṃsa.
12. Mhvg	=	Mahāvagga.
13. DN	=	Dīgha-Nikāya.
14. MA	=	Majjhima-nikāyaṭṭhakathā (Papañcasūdanī), commentary on the Majjhima-nikāya.
15. AVDN	=	Anagatavaṃsadesanāva.
16. MN	=	Majjhima-nikāya.
17. DPPN	=	Dictionary of Pali Proper Names by G.P. Malalasekera.
18. Thera	=	Theragāthā.
19. Vsm	=	Visuddhimagga.
20. RSV	=	Rasavāhinī, ed. By Saranatina Tissa.
21. Pācit	=	Pācittiya-Pāli (of the Vinaya).
22. CHI	=	The Cultural Heritage of India, vol. I, Nalinaksha Dutt.
23. DA	=	Dīgha-nikāyaṭṭha Katha (Sumaṅgala-vilasinī), commentary on the Dīgha-nikāya, 2 parts (SHB).
24. DhpA	=	Dhammapadaṭṭha Katha, Commentary on the Dhammapada.
25. MT	=	Mahavaṃsa-Ṭīkā, Vaṃsaṭṭhappakasini, ed. by G.P. Mahalasekera (PTS), 2 vols.
26. Prmj	=	Paramathajotika.
27. EHBC	=	Early History of Buddhism in Ceylon, E.W. Adikaran
28. CLv	=	Cūlavaṃsa, tr. By G. Geiger.
29. Dpv	=	Dīpavaṃsa by H. Oldenberg.

CHAPTER EIGHT

1. HBC	=	History of Buddhism in Ceylon, Walpola Rahula.

2. Sat. Br	=	Śatapatha Brāhmaṇa.
3. SBE	=	Sacred Books of the East.
4. MA	=	Majjhima-nikāyaṭṭhā Kathā (Papañasadamī), commentary on the Majjhima-nikāya.
5. DA	=	Dīgha-nikāyaṭṭha Kathā (Sumañgalavilāsinī), commentary on the Dīgha-nikāya.
6. SA	=	Saṃyutta-nikāyaṭṭha Kathā (Sāratthappakasinī), commentary on the Saṃyutta-nikāya.
7. VbhA	=	Vibhaṅgaṭṭha Katha (Sammohavinodanī), commentary on the Vibhaṅga.
8. AA	=	Aṅguttara-ṇikāyaṭṭha Katha (Maharathapuraṇī), commentary on the Aṅguttara-nikāya.
9. Smp	=	Samantapāsādikā.
10. Vsm	=	Visuddhimagga.
11. Clvg	=	Cullavagga (of the Vinaya) ed. by Saddhātissa Thera.
12. MhV	=	Mahāvaṃsa, ed. by W. Geiger, Ed. by Sumaṅgala and Batuwantudawa.

Maps

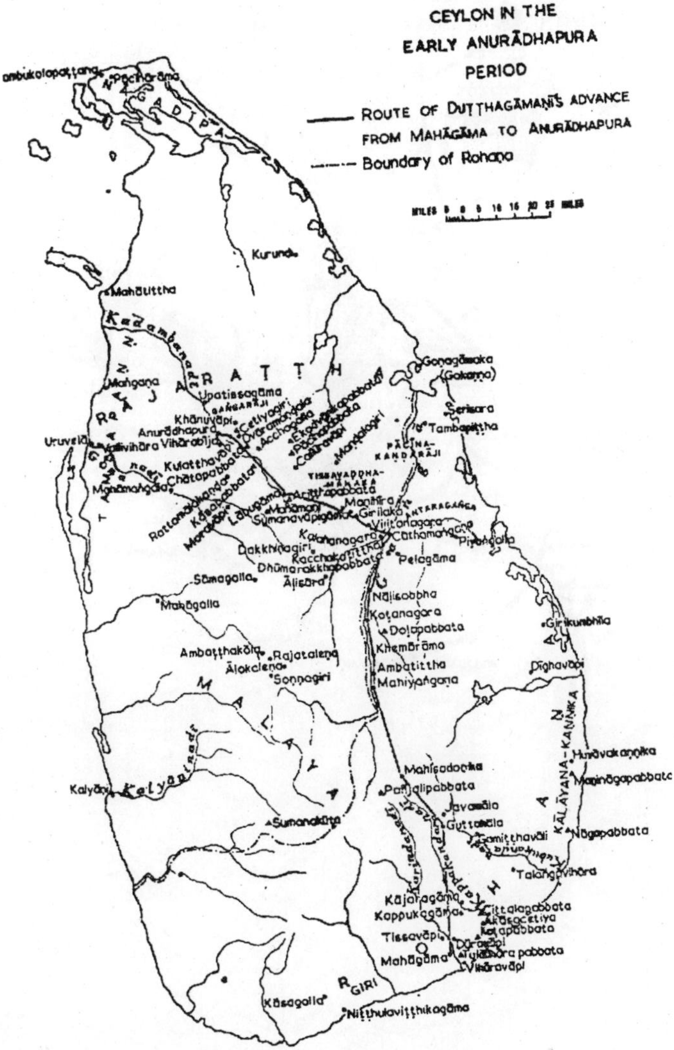
CEYLON IN THE
EARLY ANURĀDHAPURA
PERIOD
ROUTE OF DUṬṬHAGĀMAṆI'S ADVANCE
FROM MAHĀGĀMA TO ANURĀDHAPURA
Boundary of Rohaṇa
Kurundi
Mahātittha
Anurādhapura
Uruvelā
Gonagāmaka
(Gokaṇṇa)
Serisara
Tambapiṭṭha
Sāmagalla
Mahāgalla
Ambaṭṭhakōla
Rajatalena
Ālokalena
Sonnagiri
Girikumbhila
Dīghavāpi
Kalyāṇi
Sumanakūṭa
Mahiyaṅgaṇa
Nāgapabbata
Talaṅgavihāra
Tissavāpi
Mahāgāma
Kāsagalla
Nitthulaviṭṭhikagāma
M A L A Y A
R O H A Ṇ A
GIRI

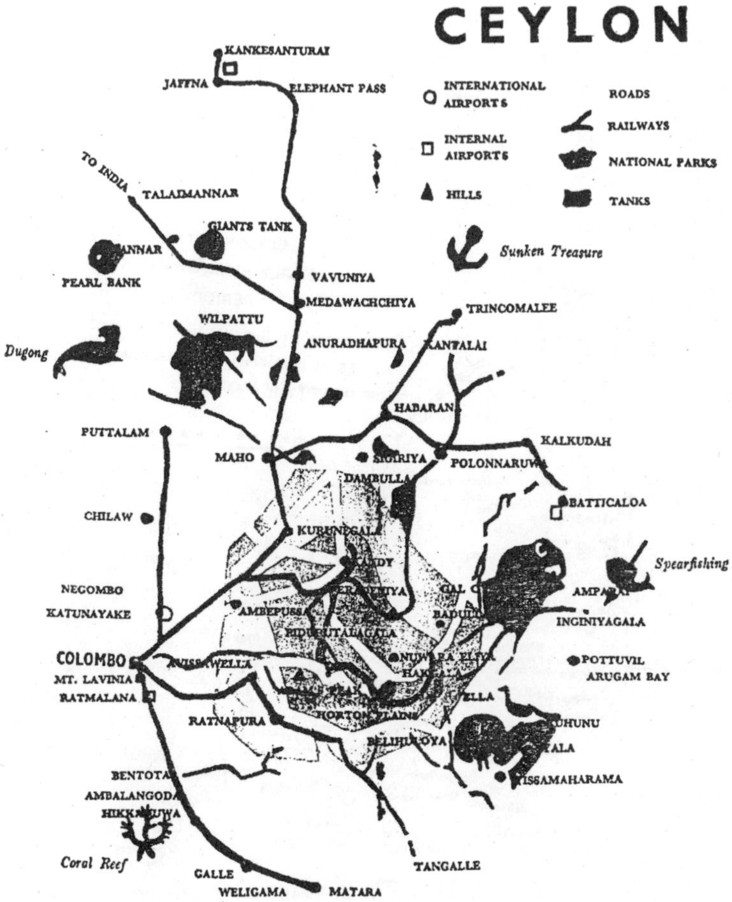
CEYLON
INTERNATIONAL AIRPORTS
INTERNAL AIRPORTS
HILLS
ROADS
RAILWAYS
NATIONAL PARKS
TANKS
Sunken Treasure
KANKESANTURAI
JAFFNA
ELEPHANT PASS
TO INDIA
TALAIMANNAR
GIANTS TANK
PEARL BANK
VAVUNIYA
MEDAWACHCHIYA
WILPATTU
TRINCOMALEE
Dugong
ANURADHAPURA
HABARANA
PUTTALAM
KALKUDAH
MAHO
POLONNARUWA
DAMBULLA
BATTICALOA
CHILAW
Spearfishing
NEGOMBO
KATUNAYAKE
INGINIYAGALA
COLOMBO
MT. LAVINIA
RATMALANA
POTTUVIL
ARUGAM BAY
ELLA
RATNAPURA
BELIHULOYA
BENTOTA
AMBALANGODA
TISSAMAHARAMA
Coral Reef
TANGALLE
GALLE
WELIGAMA
MATARA

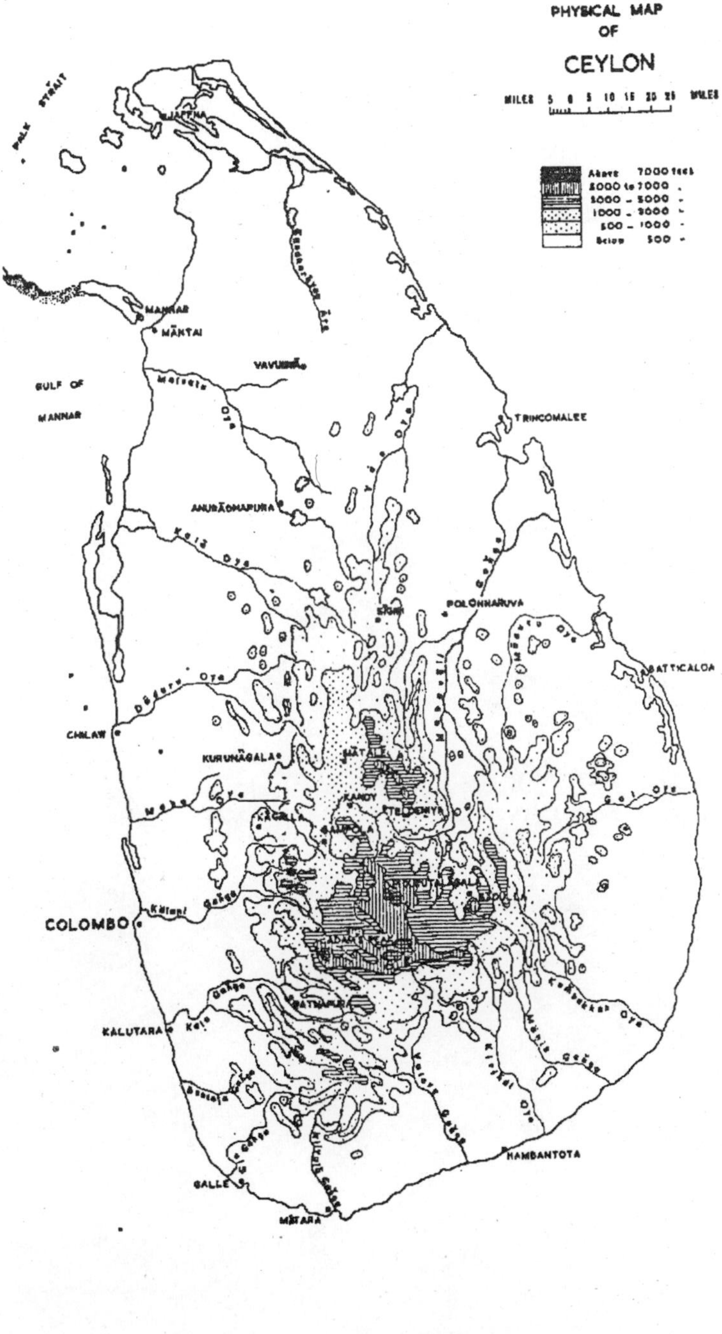
PHYSICAL MAP
OF
CEYLON
PALK STRAIT
JAFFNA
MANNAR
MĀNTAI
GULF OF
MANNAR
TRINCOMALEE
ANURĀDHAPURA
Kala Oya
POLONNARUVA
BATTICALOA
CHILAW
KURUNĀGALA
MĀTALE
KANDY
GAMPOLA
Maha Oya
Gal Oya
COLOMBO
ADAM'S PEAK
RATNAPURA
KALUTARA
GALLE
MĀTARA
HAMBANTOTA

1

Buddhism in Sri Lanka

The history of Sri Lanka begins with the colonisation of the island by Prince Vijaya from Bengal in the fifth century B.C. A prince named Vijaya and his followers arrived in Sri Lanka from India on the day of the Paribhāna of the Buddha. At that time the island was occupied by Yakkhas (demons), Nāgas etc. They were the aborigines who occupied the island before the arrival of Prince Vijaya and his followers. These aborigines were a primitive tribe and they used to live by hunting. The present Veddas were their descendants.[1] Vijaya was a Kshatriya. He established his friendly ties with an aboriginal princess named Kuveni and married her and soon became the master of the country. Later Kuveni was driven away by him and a princess from Madura became his queen. Vijaya died after a rule of 38 years.[2] He had no son. Then his nephew Paṇḍuvāsudeva became ruler of the country and he ruled for 30 years and his eldest son Abhaya succeeded him and he ruled for 20 years.[3] The next ruler was Paṇḍukābhaya, who was the son of his sister Ummādacitta.[4] He established himself as a great ruler and in his reign Anurādhapura became well-known as a great city with well-marked boundaries. He ruled for 70 years. Then his son Muṭasiva succeeded him and he ruled for 60 years. His second son Devānaṁpiya Tissa succeeded him in 250 B.C.[5] Before the introduction of Buddhism in the reign of king Devānaṁpiya Tissa there was no single religion which was established as the national religion of the country. There were various religious beliefs and practices and they were different from one another and each individual according to his belief observed his religion.[6] The pre-Buddhist religion of Sri Lanka was a mixture of the aboriginal cults and the beliefs of the Aryan new-comers.[7] This was the feature of the pre-Buddhist religion of Sri Lanka. A widely prevalent aboriginal custom of pre-Buddhist Sri Lanka was the worship of Yakkhas and Yakkhinīs. Devānampiya Tissa's grand-father was Paṇḍukābhaya. He built shrines for many of these spirits and he arranged sacrificial offerings annually for them. Some of these Yakkhas and Yakkhinīs became known by their names and they were Kālavela, Cittarāja, Vessaraṇa, Valavāmukhī and Citta.[8] Vyādhadeva, Kammāradeva and Pacchimarājiṇī were aboriginal spirits. Tree-worship was also prevalent and the banyan and palmyrah were also mentioned as the cults of these spirits.[9] Several nigaṇṭhas (Jainas) such as Giri, Jotiya and Kumbhaṇḍa lived in the reign of Paṇḍukābhaya and hermitages were built for them.[10] Other ascetics like the ājivakas, brāhmaṇas and the wandering mendicant monks used to live in his reign. Several families of heretical beliefs used to live near the city of Anurādhapura.[11] People used to worship Śiva. In society the brāhmaṇas had an important place. Śaivism existed in Sri Lanka at that time.[12] In Anurādhapura there was a dwelling place for the brāhmaṇas (brāhmaṇa-vatthuṃ).[13] Probably it was an arama or monastery for the brāhmaṇas.[14] Paribhājakas and ājīvikas, pāsaṇḍas and pabbajitas and many other ascetics, known as Samaṇas, were found in the island. The Mahāvaṃsa records that Paṇḍukābhaya constructed a monastery for paribhājakas and a house for ājīvikas.[15] Various pāsaṇḍas and samaṇas used to live in the area where the Nigaṇṭhas Giri and Jotiya used to live.[16] In pre-Buddhist Sri Lanka the paribhājakas and the pabbajitas were numerous and popular. A religious sect called Tāpasa existed at that time.[17] The cult of astrology also became popular in pre-Buddhist Sri Lanka.[18]

Buddhism was introduced into Sri Lanka in 236 B.E. (cir. 250 B.C.) and from that time it became the national religion of the people of Sri Lanka. From the Sinhalese chronicles it was known that king Aśoka of the Maurya empire on the advice of Moggaliputta Tissa sent religious missions to the different regions of India and abroad to propagate the teachings of Gotama Buddha. He sent his son Mahinda along with six other companions to preach the doctrine of the Buddha in Sri Lanka. The theras Iṭṭhiya, Uttiya, Sambala of Bhaddasāla, Sumana Sāmaṇera, the son of Sanghamitta and Bhaṇḍuka Upāsaka (lay disciple), the son of the daughter of his aunt were his companions,[19] Devānaṁpiya Tissa received them at Mihintale which was about eight miles east of Anurādhapura, on the full-moon day of the month of Jeṭṭha.[20] Mahinda was very much impressed after his talk with the king and he knew that the king was intelligent and he would be able to understand the Buddha's teachings, well. He then preached the Cūla-hatthipadopama-sutta to the king.[21] It discusses the training of monks with a simile of an elephant's foot. It refers to the fundamental teachings of Buddhism and it speaks of the Buddha, Dhammạ and Saṃgha and the ideal life of a Buddhist monk. It mentions in detail "the simple and holy life of a monk. The subline qualities he practices and possesses, the things from which he abstains, the various stages of development of his life and his attainment of arahantship which is the final fruit of Buddhism.[22] As a result, the king along with his followers embraced the religion of the Buddha. On the invitation of the king next morning Mahinda and his companions arrived at Anurādhapura from Mihintale and the king received them with great honour. After-taking meal, Mahinda preached the Petavatthu, the Vimānavatthu and the Sacca-Saṁyutta to the royal household.[23] At first he delivered discourses to the ladies of the royal household and afterwards to the general public. He had told them "how dreadful was samsara, the cycle of births and deaths to which they were subject endlessly."[24] Many of those who listened to the sermon accepted the new faith. He then preached the Devadūta-sutta which discusses the results of good and bad actions, the misery that awaits criminals and the descriptions of the tortures of hell. It helped men to desist from wrong-doing for fear of evil consequences.[25] He then preached the Balapaṇḍita Sutta which informs "how through folly men commit evil and suffer both here and hereafter. The wise man, on the contrary, abstains from evil, does good and attains to happiness in both worlds."[26] Thousands of men and women embraced the new religion. Many men became Buddhist monks. King Devanampiya Tissa then offered the Mahāmeghavana of Anurādhapura to the Buddhist Samgha for the residence of monks. In later times it became the Mahāvihāra monastery, "the great centre of Buddhist culture and learning in the island, the stronghold of the Theravada."[27] After accepting the Mahāmeghavana Mahinda preached the Aggikkhandhopama-Sutta[28] which says that "a Buddhist monk should be virtuous and live a holy life, so that those who give him the necessities of life may be benefited and that he himself may attain Nibhāna—the ultimate goal. This is for his own benefit as well as for the benefit of others."[29] Mahinda spent twenty-six days in the Mahāmegha park and then for the rain-retreat (vassavāsa) he returned to Mihintale. This was the establishment of the Cetiyagiri-vihāra. It became very famous as a great monastic institution. King Devānampiya Tissa constructed monasteries, stūpas and other Buddhist establishments on all sides of the Mahāmeghavana and for their proper maintenance he made endowments. He built monasteries a yojana from one another. Of them the Isurumunivihāra and the Vessagirivihāra became very famous as important places of worship.[30] The king received the Buddha's alms-bowl, bone-relics and the collar-bone and over them he built the Thūpārāma cetiya which was the first cetiya in Sri Lanka.[31] Anulā, the wife of Mahānāga, the brother of the king and many women of Sri Lanka wished to join the Saṃgha as nuns (bhikkhunīs). Then at Mahinda's advice, king Devānaṁpiya Tissa despatched an embassy to the court of Emperor Aśoka to bring Saṃghamitta, the sister of Mahinda Thera along with the southern branch of the Bodhi tree. No monk was allowed to ordain a women. Woman should be ordained by the nun only. When Saṃghamitta arrived with the branch of the Bodhi tree in Sri Lanka, then Anulā and other women entered the order of the Bhikkhuṇīs.[32] Thus the Bhikkhuṇī Saṃgha (order of num) was established in Sri Lanka. The branch of the Bodhi tree was planted in the Mahāmeghavana of Anurādhapura and "up to this date it flourishes as one of the most sacred objects of veneration and worship for millions of Buddhists."[33] Separate residences were built for Saṃghamitta and her attendants. The planting of the Bodhi branch was performed with pomp and grandeur. Representations from all parts of the island—from the North as well as from the South attended this ceremony and they took part in it actively. Subsequently the saplings of this Bodhi were planted in Anurādhapura and its neighbouring regions, and in Jambukolapaṭṭana and in the village of Tivakka Brahmaṇa in the North, in Kājaragāma (Kataragama) in the South and in Candanagāma. Later some thirty-two saplings were planted all over the island.[34] The bringing of the Bodhi branch and the relics of the Buddha along with his pātra (alms-bowl) further contributed very much to establish the great cultural link between India and Sri Lanka. The planting of the Bodhi tree gave indication that Buddhist was not only established in Sri Lanka but Buddhist culture also found an important place in the cultural history of the island. "The relics of the Buddha were regarded as representing the Buddha himself and this enshrinement was as good as the Buddha's residence in Lanka."[35] The King's house was the place where the alms-bowl of the Buddha was kept. Besides the Mahāvihāra and the Cetiya Pabbata Devānampiya Tissa established several monasteries. The Mahāvaṃsa mentions that the place, where those who joined the order of Monks from noble families lived, became Issarasamaṇaka[36] (place of "noble monks"), and the place when those who entered the order from the Vaiśya center lived, became Vessagiri (Mountain of the vaiśyas).[37] Ariṭṭha, the king's nephew, joined the order of monks on his return from India.[38] Also five hundred men entered the Buddhist Saṃgha and they all became arahants. When all these acts of religious devotion were performed the king asked Mahinda Thera whether Buddhism had been firmly established in the island, to which Mahinda told that it had only been planted but would take firm root when a persa born in Sri Lanka, of Sinhalese parents, studied the Vinaya in Sri Lanka and expounded it in Sri Lanka. Thera Ariṭṭha was invited to deliver a discourse on the Vinaya in the presence of Mahinda. His exposition was very correct and there was great rejoicing because he fulfilled the condition which was required for the firm establishment of the Buddha's religion.[39] Mahinda's arrival in Sri Lanka can be regarded as the beginning of Sinhalese culture. He brought to Lanka not only a new religion but also a whole civilization then at the height of its glory. He introduced art and architecture into the Island along with saṅghārāmas and cetiyas. He can be regarded as the father of the Sinhalese literature. Buddhaghosa says that Mahinda brought to the Island of the Sinhalese the commentaries of the Tripistaka and put them into Sinhalese for the benefit of the people of the island. He then made Sinhalese a literary language and inaugurated its literature. It is probable that he introduced the Aśokan alphabet as well.[40]

Devānaṃpiya Tissa reigmed in Sri Lanka for forty years. Buddhism was introduced into Sri Lanka in the first year of his reign. He always tried to do something for the progress of the religion of the Buddha. He established several monasteries and Buddhist monuments. Apart from the Mahāvihāra, the Catiyapabbata-vihāra, the Thupārāma, the Issurumuni-vihāra, and the Vessagiri-vihāra, he constructed the Pathamaka-cetiya, the Jambukola-vihāra, the Pācinārāma and the nunneries upāsikā-vihāra and the Hatthālhaka-vihāra and the refectory.[41] Many men and women became Buddhist monks and nuns and they entered the Buddhist Samgha during his reign. Buddhism not only established in Anurādhapura but also became very popular in distant regions like Jambukola in the north and Kājaragāma and Cendangāma in the south under his patronage. Mahinda and Devānaṃpiya Tissa played very well for the development of Buddhism in Sri Lanka. The religion of the Buddha was firmly established in Sri Lanka during his reign. Saṃghamitta also played a great role for the welfare of women in Sri Lanka. The king showed his keen interest in the welfare of Buddhism. Thus under his patronage the people of the island accepted Buddhism as the religion of the country. Thus it became the state religion from the day of its introduction into the island.

After Devānaṃpiya Tissa's death, his brother Uṭṭiya became the ruler of the island. Mahinda died at the age of 80 years in the eighth year and Samghamita at the age of 79 years in the ninth year of the reign of king Uttiya.[42] The latter with great honour performed their funerals and over their relics he built stūpas. After a reign of ten years the king died in 286 B.E. Mahinda Thera was succeeded by Arittha and in turn Isidatta, Kālasumena, Dīghanāma and Dīghasumana succeeded him.[43]

After the death of Uttiya, the Tamil usurpers from South India captured Anurādhapura. Sena and Guttika reigned together for twenty-two years and Elāra, another Tamil usurper, ruled for forty-four years.[44] During their rule Buddhism suffered very much. Duṭṭhagāmaṇi, the son of Kīkavanna Tissa and Vihāramahādevī of Magama of the South-Eastern principality of Rohuṇa (Rohaṇa), defeated and killed Elāra in battle and became the ruler of Anurādhapura.[45] He established the sovereignty of the Sinhalese rulers of Anurādhapura. He ruled for twenty-four years. He played a great role for the progress, development and advancement of Buddhism in the island. His greatest work was the Ruvana veli or vali-saya, the famous stūpa or the Mahāthūpa in Sri Lanka. He constructed several edifices like the Mirisaveti or Vatiya-dagoba (Maricavāṭṭi), and the nine-storyed Lohapāsāda, "the Brazan Palace" for the use of the monks.[46]

He was a great supporter of Buddhism. The Pāli commentaries refer to him as a pious ruler. Several learned Buddhist monks under his patronage flourished in his reign. He was a devout Buddhist. It may be noted here that he was the greatest national hero of early Buddhist Sri Lanka. "He organized a great crusade to liberate Buddhism from foreign rule. His war-cry was "not for kingdom, but for Buddhism." "Pāragaṅgam gamissāmi jotetum sasanam ahaṃ."[47] "rajjasukhaya vāyāmo nāyaṃ mama kadāpi ca, Sambuddhasāsanasseva thapaṅāya ayaṃ mama."[48] The entire Sinahlese race was united under the banner of the young Gāmaṇī. This was the beginning of nationalism among the Sinhalese. It was a new race with healthy young blood, organised under the new order of Buddhism. A kind of religio-nationalism, which almost amounted to fanaticism, roused the whole Sinahlese people. A non-Buddhist was not regarded as a human being. Evidently all sinhalese without exception were Buddhists."[49] After the defeat of Elāra, Duṭṭha-Gāmaṇī felt sorry for the death of many thousands of people. Eight arahants from Piyaṅgudīpa gave him assurance that there was no cause for repentance, that only one and a half human beings had been slain—one who had taken refuge in the Buddha, Dhamma and Sangha and the other who had observed the five precepts—and that the rest who were wrong-believers (micchādiṭṭhi) and men of evil life (dussīlā) were equal to animals (pasusamā).[50] They told him, "but thou wilt illumine the doctrine of the Buddha in many ways, therefore dispel care from the mind."[51] The orthodox religious opinion encouraged to the people to develop their Buddhist nationalist ideas. For the first time in the history of Buddhism the Buddhist monks were allowed officially to join the field of political and mundane interests.[52] At the request of Duttha-Gāmaṇī they used to go with the liberating army, "since the sight of the bhikkhus is both blessing and protection for us."[53] Even the Buddhist monks for the welfare of the religion and the nation used to leave their roles and join the army. One of Duṭṭha-Gāmaṇī's ten generals, Theraputta Abhaya, formerly a Buddhist monk, gave up his robes and joined the army. After the war, this general re-entered the Buddhist Saṃgha and became an arahant.[54] Duṭṭha-Gāmaṇī used to put a relic of the Buddha into his spear.[55] In order to unite the people and to rid his motherland of foreign rule the king very much tried to exploit all the religious and national sentiments of the masses.[56] Under his patronage Buddhism became the pride of his people. Many people from foreign countries came to Sri Lanka to sea the dedication festival of the Mahāthūpa.[57] About twenty-four Vesākha-puja was performed by Duṭṭha-gāmaṇī.[58]

Buddhism flourished during the reign of Duṭṭha-gāmaṇī. There were orders of Bhikkhus (monks) and Bhikkhuṇīs (nuns) and many men and women joined the Buddhist Sangha. There were thousands of monks in some of the monasteries. Many people used to practice meditation in forests and rock caves. The Novices (sāmaṇera) Bhikkhus (fully ordained), Theras (elders) and Maha Theras (chief elders) were four classes of disciples. Under the rules of the Vinaya the Buddhist monks used to manage the affairs of the Buddhist Samgha. During the rainy season, the Buddhist monks used to live in their vihāras and at other seasons they travelled far and wide in the country, visited villages and other vihāras. They also used to go to Gayā in India to offer their prayers at the sacred Bodhi Tree there. The Buddhist monks learnt the Dhamma and many committed to memory the scriptures or parts of them and by frequent rehearsal they preserved the tradition. Each temple in a district once a year preached the Ariyavaṃsa Sutta and it continued for seven days. The crowds were so great that many people waited outside the hall for the whole night to listen to the Dhamma. The listeners were the bhikkhus and the laity. Even lay preachers well-versed in the Dhamma were employed by the king at halls of preaching to deliver discourses to the people.[59]

After the death of king, Duṭṭha-gamaṇī his younger brother Saddhātissa became king as he ruled for eight years. He worked hard for the progress of Buddhism. Many vihāra were constructed by him. The Dakkhiṇāgiri-vihāra was one of them.[60] It became very famous in the history of Buddhism in Sri Lanka. Saddhātissa was succeeded by his sons Thūlatthuna, Lañjatissa, Khallāṭa Nāga and Vaṭṭagāmaṇī Abhaya, in succession.[61] Vaṭṭagāmaṇī Abhaya's reign was an important period in the history of early Buddhism in Sri Lanka. The better part of the first century B.C. witnessed some very prominent events in the Buddhist history of Sri Lanka. A Brahmaṇa named Tiya (or Tissa) fresh Ruhuṇa (Rohaṇa) of South Sri Lanka revolted against Vaṭṭagāmaṇī Abhaya.[62] At the same time a Tamil army led by some Tamil chiefs landed at Mahātittha (Manes) and marched towards Anurādhapura and declared war against the king. The Tamil army vanquished Tiya and in battle defeated Vaṭṭagāmaṇī Abhaya. The blatter fled and lived in remote places for fourteen years.[63] For fourteen years the Tamils stayed at Anurādhapura and they ruled there in succession. Buddhism suffered very much during these fourteen years of Tamil domination. By an unprecedented famine, generally known as Brāhmaṇa-Tissa famine or Bamiṇiṭ iyāsāya, the whole country was ravaged.[64] During that time there was no food at all and there were cases of cannibalism. Many monks and laymen died of starvation. Many vihāras were deserted. The Mahāvihāra of Anurādhapura was abandoned and the Mahāthūpa was in a neglected condition. About 12,000 Arahants from the Tissamahārāma and another 12,000 from the Cittalapabata-vihāra died in the forests because there was no food for them. Many monks left the country and went to India.[65] The Mahātheras and the leader of the Sinhalese felt sorry for Buddhism. There was no good hope for the future of Buddhism. Its future was in danger and its existence was threatened. There was no Sinhalese King who came forward to play a great role as its patron. No one supported it. "The continuation of the oral tradition of the three Piṭakas, which had so far been handed down orally from teachers to pupil, appeared no longer possible under the prevailing adverse circumstances. The primary concern of the Saṃgha during this tragic period was to preserve the teaching of the Buddha which they valued above all else. Therefore, far-seeing Mahātheras, under the patronage of a local chief, assembled at Aluvihāra at Mātale and committed to writing the whole of the Tripiṭaka with the commentaries thereon for the first time in history "in order that the true doctrine might endure" (ciraṭṭhitatthaṃ dhammassa)."[66] The Mahāniddesa of the Sutta Piṭaka was known by only one monk at that time. Practically, it was on the verge of being lost. In order to preserve the teachings of the Buddha, the monks used to eat roots and leaves of trees, because they had no food. In this way, they maintained themselves and recited the scriptures. Because they feared that they would forget them. They sat down and recited the scriptures when they had the strength. But when they were unable to keep bodies erect, they then lay down and they tried to continue their recitation. In this way, the preservation of the texts and commentaries continued until the misery was over.[67]

After fourteen years of supreme struggle Vaṭṭagāmaṇī Abhaya (29-17 B.C.) recaptured Anurādhapura and he regained the throne. He demolished the Giri-monastery of the Nigaṇṭhas (Jains) and built over it a Buddhist monastery called the Abhayagiri-Vihāra.[68] He then gave it to a work named Kupikkala Mahā Tissa in gratitude for his friendship. This work had helped the king when the latter was in his exile.[69] After sometime, the monks of the Mahāvihāra on the charge of improper contact with lay families expelled Tissa. The latter's pupil Bahalamassu Tissa protected against this expulsion and as a result, he was also expelled from the Mahāvihāra. He then with his five hundred followers left the Mahāvihāra and lived at the Abhayagiri-Vihāra.[70] It may be noted here that this was the first record of a vihāra being offered to a work as a personal gift. Mahātissa at the special invitation of the king stayed at Anurādhapura and he made a great influence upon the ruling class. This no doubt disturbed the authority of the Mahāvihāra. The Mahāvihāra monks felt insulted and they charged Mahātissa Thera "with having frequented the families of laymen (Kulasaṃsaṭṭha) and imposed on him the punishment of expulsion known as Pabbājaniya Kamma".[71] Thus Mahātissa and his disciple

Bahalamassu-Tissa "Big-bearded Tissa" were expelled from the Mahāvihāra. This was the beginning of descension in the Buddhist Saṃgha. The monks of the Abhayagiri Vihāra used to live in a separate group from the Mahāvihāra but there was no difference between the two vihāras at the beginning either in theory or in practice. The Abhayagiri monks said that the Mahāvihāra monks did not take a good decision against Mahātissa. This was a wrong decision against him by them.[72] At that time, some monks, disciples of a teacher called Dhammaruci, belonging to the Vajjiputra sect in India, arrived in Sri Lanka and the monks of the Abhayagiri Vihāra received them.[73] In order to strengthen their position the monks of the Abhayagiri showed their friendly attitudes towards other monks and they wanted to win some allies. Tissa and his followers accepted the new monks and their teachings and the monks of the Abhayagiri became known as the Dhammaruci sect after the name of the great teacher in India.[74] The king was a great patron of this sect and he supported the works of this sect. In order to draw inspiration and strength the monks of the Abhayagiri Vihāra established contact with various Buddisht sects and movements in India. In their views they always showed their liberal attitudes and they appreciated new ideas from abroad and they were very progressive in their outlook. But the Mahāvihāra monks showed their conservative attitudes, studed the Theravāda and they were against the Mahāyāna. But the Abhayagiri monks studied both the Theravāda and the Mahāyāna and "widely diffured the Tripiṭakes".[75] The Mahāvihāra monks mentioned the Abhayagiri monks as unorthodox and heretical. From this time the Abhayagiri remained as a separate sect opposed to the Mahāvihāra.

Towards the beginning of the first century B.C. Vaṭṭagāmaṇī Abhaya reigned in Sri Lanka. According to tradition and custom, the members of Buddhist Saṃgha learnt the various parts of the Piṭaka and committed to memory and those were preserved as oral traditions. But when the famine broke out in the time of king Vaṭṭagāmaṇī Abhaya it was very difficult for the monks to continue this form of preserving the teachings of the Tripiṭaka. They had hitherto been committed to memory and handed down from teachers to pupils. The monks then knew that the continuation of oral tradition was not possible and part of the scriptures might be lost. They then decided that this was the right time for committing these teachings to writing, so that for further generations they might be preserved in a nice way. They then convened a council. This council was held at Āluvihāra at Mātale and about 500 monks assembled there. They then recited the teachings and the scribes were busy to commit to writing, on palm leaves, the Pāli cannonical texts (the Tiripiṭaka) consists of Vinaya, Sutta and Abhidhamma and the Sinhalese commentaries. They completed the work assigned to them and for the first time the teachings of the Buddha in book form brough out.[76]

The first centre of Buddhism in Sri Lanka was the Mahāvihāra. It was established by Mahinda himself. Its monks not only guarded the honour and the authority of their vihāra but they always felt proud of the great traditions. They had received the respect, loyalty and support of the state and the public and they disliked new elements and ideas in their fields to take their privileges and to divide the affection. But they were unable to stop the new developments. "The discussions in the Saṃgha were by no means a symptom of decay and degeneration, but a sign of movement and progress".[77]

Vaṭṭagāmuṇī's son Coranāga destroyed eighteen vihāras. Because during the days of his rebellion against his cousin Mahācūlika Mahātissa, he had not given shelter in the vihāras. Because of his hostile activities, Buddhism suffered and the Buddhist monks felt disturbed. The damage was very great and the another of the Mahāvaṃsa remarked "the evil-doer was reborn in Lokantarika-hell."[78] King Bhātikābhaya supplied requisites for Buddhist monks "engaged in ganthadhura "occupation with books", that is study."[79] Bhātikābhaya followed the tradition set up by Duṭṭha-gāmaṇī and held twenty-eight vesak festivals.[80] Bhātikābhaya's successor Mahādāthika Mahānāga worked hard for the development of Buddhism. He introduced the Giribhaṇḍa-pūjā.[81] His son Āmaṇḍgāmaṇī followed the example of Aśoka and gave the order of māghāta or non-killing of animals all over the Island.[82] Kaṇīrajānu-Tissa, his brother or successor, ordered that about sixty bad monks to be thrown down the precipice of a rock in Cetiya-pabha (Mihintale).[83] They ignored his decision in a case relating to some monostic dispute and they planned to kill the king within the uposatha house itself. This incident had damaged the prestige of the Buddhist Saṃgha. King Vasabha impartially patronised all vihāras and worked for the development of Buddhism. He helped the preachers of Dhamma and constructed new cetiyas and images and repaired old monasteries.[84] During his reign vihāras were built even in Nāgadīpa (modern Jaffna peninsula) in the North.[85] He celebrated forty-four vesāk festivals. The country's civic, economic and health condition, were improved by the King.

In the third century A.D. Vohārika-Tissa ruled in Sri Lanka. During his time a new school of thought known as the Vetullavāda or the Vaitulyavāda appeared in Sri Lanka. The names of the Abhayagiri-vihāra adopted it. The monks of the Mahāvihāra rejected the vaitulya doctrines "as being opposed to traditional doctrine." The king patronised the two vihāras—the Mahāvihāra and the Abhayagirivihāra but he suppressed the Vaitulyavāda doctrine with the help of his minister Kapila, "who was well-versed both in the law of the Buddha and in that of the land."[86] Thus he purified the religion. Despite the suppression by Vohārika Tissa, the Vaitulyavādins or the Vaitulyakas again appeared in the reign of Goṭhābhaya. Buddhism was in a bad state and the Saṁgha was corrupt. King Vohārika Tissa paid three hundred thousand and freed many Buddhist monks who were in debt.[87] He established alms-giving at all places over the island where the Ariyavaṃsa sutta was preached.[88] Now the preaching of the Ariyavaṃsa was a sign which indicated that Buddhism was in an unsatisfactory state.[89] Vohārika-Tissa abolished the infliction of physical pain as penalty and a great vesak festival was held by him.[90] Under his patronage Buddhism prospered.

Goṭhābhaya became the ruler of the island in the fourth century A.D. He was a strong ruler and he contributed very much to the progress of Buddhism in the island. He improved the material conditions of Buddhism "by providing an abundance of requisites for bhikkhus." He repaired old monasteries, constructed new ones and he held popular festivals such as the Vesākha Pūjā.[91] He suppressed the Vaitulyavādins or the Vaitulyakas, burnt their books and expelled the Vaitulya monks. Sixty of them left for the Chola country in South India.[92] It was about this time Araṅga's Yogācāra school and Vasubandhu became very powerful in India and mystic and magical practices were introduced into the Buddhist system.[93] Sri Lanka's Buddhist monks who were in exile in Kāveri established their close contact with Sanghamitra, a powerful and able young monk. He later played a great role for the development of Mahāyānism in Sri Lanka. The Mahāvaṃsa refers to him as one "who was versed in the teachings concerning the exorcism of spirits and so forth" which was quite in keeping with the trend of religious development in India at the time."[94] Saṅghamitra came to Sri Lanka and became the tutor of the king's two sons. He made a great influence upon his younger pupil, Mahāsena and instilled into him the new doctrine and Mahāsena became a follower of his views. When Mahāsena became king after his brother Jeṭṭha-Tissa, then Saṃghamitra became very powerful in Sri Lanka's religious world. The king, at the advice of Saṃghamitra there, gave order that no one should give food to the monks of the Mahāvihāra. As a result, for about nine years the Mahāvihāra was a deserted place. No one was there. None lived there. Saṃghamitra's supporters destroyed the buildings of the Mahāvihāra and took away their material to build new buildings for the Abhayagiri-vihāra.[95] The new king Mahāsena, occupied in Sri Lanka's history "not only as a strong and able king who did a great deal for the country, but also as a man who had the courage of his conviction to stand against the mighty authority of the Mahāvihāra, which no ruler ever before dared to attempt."[96] Saṃghamitra used to live at the Abhayagiri-vihāra. He with the approval of the king and with the help of a minister named Soṇa completely destroyed the seven-storeyed Lohapāsāda and many other buildings of the Mahāvihāra. The grounds of the Mahāvihāra were ploughed and sown with beans.[97] On seeing the action of the king against the Mahāvihāra, the whole country was shocked and felt sorry to see the plight of the Mahāvihāra. The Mahāvihāra's popularity was very great and the public opinion was against the king. The king then understood the Mahāvihāra's influence over the people. His most intimate friend, Meghananṇa-Abhaya, the minister, went to Malaya, raised an army and declared war against the king. The king then knew his error and tried to restore the Mahāvihāra.[98]

A minister and a queen of the king helped to suppress the vaitulyavāda and saved the Mahāvihāra. Saṃghamitra was killed by a carpenter and Saṃghamitra's friend, Soṇa, the minister, was killed also. Maghavaṇṇa-Abhaya, the minister, worked hard for the restoration of the Mahāvihāra.[99] Even then, the king constructed the Jeta-Vana-Vihāra within the boundaries of the Mahāvihāra and gave it to a Thera named Tissa of the Dakkhiṇārāma or Dakkhiṇāgiri.[100] Tissa there was charged in the assembly of monks with having committed an offence of the gravest kind.[101] The Minister of Justice by his order disrobed Tissa but he did it against the wish of the king, who was Mahāsena.[102] The latter was the secular head of the religion but his power was greatly weakened by his acts which were against the religion of the Buddha. Even a minister showed his courage to ignore the king's wishes and dissolved a mark who was highly honoured by the king. This thing happened because the Mahāvihāra and the public opinion were against the king.[103] The Dāṭhāraṃna says that the Tooth Relic of the Budha from India was sent to the king of Sri Lanka for protection, but, by the time it reached, Mahāsena, Sri Lanka's king, was dead.[104] For the first time in Sri Lanka's history of Buddhism reference to an image of Bodhisatva was found during this period and it clearly indicates that Mahāyānism made a great influence in Sri Lanka's religion world at that time. This beautiful image of Bodhisattva by the order of Mahāsena was made by Jeṭṭha-Tissa II, who was Mahāsena's younger son and he was a well-known corner in ivory.[105]

Sirimeghavaṇṇa was Mahāsena's elder son. He ascended the throne after his father Mahāsena in the middle of the fourth century A.D. He felt very sorry for all his father's ill-advised deeds against the Mahāvihāra and in order to win back the goodwill of the Mahāvihāra and the people he worked hard for the progress of Buddhism in Sri Lanka. He made a golden statue of Mahinda and in order to commemorate Mahinda's arrival in Sri Lanka he inaugurated a Buddhist festival and a procession which lasted for several days. From all parts of the island both laymen and Buddhist monks took part in it. The king gave order that succeeding kings should do something to hold the festival annually. The king took keen interest to hold the festival annually so that this would help to forget the bitter memory of the evil days of the past.[106] The left eye-tooth of the Buddha was brought from Damtapura in Kalinga in India to Sri Lanka in the ninth year of king Sirimeghavaṇṇa.[107] It was kept in a special building and for public exhibition the Buddhist monks used to take annually to the Abhayagiri.[108] It may be remarked that in the worship of the Tooth Relic the Mahāvihāra did not take part in it. During the days of Mahāsena, the Abhayagiri vihāra as a great center of Mahāyānism because well-known in India. The prince and the princess who brought the Tooth Relic from India to Sri Lanka were no doubt Mahāyānists and they established their contact first with the monks of the Abhayagini monks. For this reason the monks of the Abhayagiri-vihāra took the charge of the Tooth Relic. The monks of the Mahāvihāra did not take part in it.[109] It was known from records that king Sirimeghavaṇṇa dispatched an embassy to Samudra Gupta of

India. The former wanted to take permission from the latter to construct a monastery at Buddhagayā for Sinhalese pilgrims.[110]

Buddhadāsa ruled in the beginning of the fifth century A.D. During his reign Fa-Hien, the famous Chinese pilgrim, visited Sri Lanka. He stayed at the Abhayagiri-Vihāra. According to him, there were 5,000 monks at the Abhayagiri-vihāra and about 3,000 monks lived at the Mahāvihāra.[111] It shown that the Abhayagiri-Vihāra was flourishing at that time. Buddhadāsa was a well-known physician king. He was a religious person. He honoured the learned people and he tried to spread the teaching of the Buddha. He fixed payments for the maintenance of preachers.[112] During the time of Upatissa I, a son of Buddhadāsa, Gaṅgzārohaṇa, a new festival, was inaugurated.[113] At the suggestion of the Buddhist monks the king introduced this festival. He did this in order to overcome a famine which occurred early in the fifth century A.D. He gave order that whenever there was a famine this festival should be held. He worked hard for the progress of Buddhism. He used to receive his food from the Mahāpātā, the common refectory of the Buddhist Saṇgha.[114]

Mahānāma, a brother of Upatina I, ascended the throne of Sri Lanka. The latter was killed by his queen. Mahānāma was a Buddhist monk. But he disrobed himself and he became king of Sri Lanka. Mahānāma showed his learning trends the Abhayagiri-vihāra. He took his interest in the affairs of this vihāra. But his queen turned her attention towards the Mahāvihāra. She was devoted to it.[115] During the reign of Mahānāma, Buddhaghosa, the great commentator, arrived in Anurādhapura from India and resided at the Mahāvihāra and he translated the Sinhalese commentaries on the Tripiṭka into Pāli.[116] The Visuddhimagga, his well-known work, was written in Sri Lanka. It was his first work in Sri Lanka.

After Mahānāma, six Tamil usurpers in succession ruled at Anurādhapura. The country was in chaos. Not only the development of the religion was disturbed but also the cultural and economic progress of the nation suffered very much at the hands of the foreign invaders. Many Sinhalese families left Anurādhapura and went to Rohana. But some influential Sinhalese stayed at Anurādhapura and served the Tamil invaders.[117] The next ruler was Dhātusena. He liberated the country from the rule of the foreign invaders. Originally, he was a monk, but he gave up his robes, killed the Tamils and re-established the Sinhalese ruler, under his patronage Buddhism prospered. The progress of the country took place during the reign.[118] He was a great follower of the Mahāvihāra and he constructed eighteen great vihāras and tanks and he gave them to the monks of the Theriya sect. Many smaller vihāras and tanks were built by him and gave them to the same sect. He helped the Buddhist monks and encouraged the spread of the teaching of the Tripiṭaka.[119] He also gave necessary help for the improvements at the Abhayagiri-vihāra.[120] He repaired the Ambaṭṭhala-vihāra on the Cetiya-pabbata (Mihintale) and gave it to the Dhammarucika sect.[121] Several statues of the Buddha and the Boddhisattvas were made by him and for them he constructed houses.[122] He himself took interest to make an image of Mahinda and at the cremation ground of the Thera a great festival was held and on this occasion the Dīpavaṃsa was recited and explained.[123]

After Dhātusena his patricide son Kassapa I ascended the throne of Sri Lanka. Then his brother Moggallāna fled to India.[124] At first the monks of the Theriya sect did not like to accept king Kassapa I's offer of the Issarasamaṇārāma which was enlarged and enriched with new endowments by the king. But later on, they allowed it to offer to the image of the Buddha and indirectly they accepted it.[125] The Dhammarucikas received a vihāra which was built by Kassapa I.[126] His brother Moggallāna I returned from India and defeated Kassapa I and captured the throne of Sri Lanka. After his victory he paid homage to the Buddhist Saṃgha and he visited both vihāras.[127] The monks of the Mahāvihāra after cleansing the place, and after wearing the robes, stood in order of rank to receive the new king Moggallāna, who then entered the vihāra, worshipped the Buddhist Saṃgha, offered them as a mark of homage and gratitude the state-parasol "which was duly returned back to him."[128] During Moggallāna's time, the Kesadhātu, the Hair Relic of the Buddha, was brought from India to Sri Lanka. In an image house the Hair Relic was placed in a crystal casket and a great festival was held on this occasion.[129] During the troublesome days of his brother Kassapa I the Buddhist Sāsana was disorganised. But Moggallāna I purified it.[130] Kumāra-Dhātusena ascended the throne after his father Moggallāna I. He held a dhammasaṅgīti or "recital of the sacred texts" and purified the Sāsana.[131] The next ruler was Silākāla. He gave the order of non-killing, māghāta, over the island, maintained hospitals, and the usual religious activities were performed.[132] In his reign a Vaitulyan book called the Dharmadhātu was brought to Sri Lanka from India and it was kept at the Jetavana-vihāra.[133] The Abhayagiri-vihāra honoured the Dharmadhātu. Its monks paid homage to it. But the Mahāvihāra and some of the citizens of Anurādhapura stayed away altogether from these activities. They did not like to associate themselves with the works of the Abhayagiri-vihāra and the Dharmadhātu.[134] During the reign of Culla-Moggallāna or Moggallāna II, Buddhism prospered and the king took steps to promote learning. He rewarded the preachers by offering abundant gifts and asked them to preach the Tripiṭaka along with the commentaries.[135] He also took steps to write down books and he made arrangements for this purpose. He also composed a religious poem and he gave sweetmeats to children to study the dhamma.[136]

The next ruler was Aggabodhi I. During his reign many poems in Sinhalese were composed by twelve great poets.[137] Under the guidance of his advisor called Dāṭhāsiva Mahāthera the king did some good work for the welfare of the state and Buddhism.[138] Towards the end of the sixth century A.D. a great Thera named Jotipāla came from India and in a public controversy he defeated the followers of the Vaitulyavāda or the Vetulyavāda.[139] The Nikāyasaṃgraha mentions that after this public defeat the

Vaitulya doctrine had lost its popularity and there were no more converts to the Vaitulya doctrine and the monks of the two nikāyas—the Abhayagirivihāra and the Jetavana-vihāra dismissed pride and lived in submission to the Mahāvihāra. The monks of the Abhayagirivihāra and the Jetavanavihāra were followers of the Vaitulya doctrine. But since that time they abandoned their pride and tried to follow the Mahāvihāra doctrine.[140]

The next king Aggabodhi II (601-611 A.D.) wanted to do something for the Abhayagiri Vihāra and the Jetavana Vihāra and he did more for these two vihāras than for the Mahāvihāra. His queen also showed her interest in the affairs of the Abhayagiri Vihāra.[141] The king built the Thūpārāma Dāgaba.[142] For the monks of the Sāgaliya sect he constructed the Veluvana vihāra.[143] During this time the king of Kaliṅga, on account of some political disturbances in his country, came to Sri Lanka and under Jotipāla there he became a monk. His queen and his ministers also came to Sri Lanka and joined the Buddhist Saṃgha. The royal Thera died in Sri Lanka.[144]

The next ruler was Dalla-Moggallāna or Moggallāna III (611-617 A.D.). In his reign a grand recital of the Thera Piṭakas was held and he honoured the learned and encouraged the spread of religious knowledge.[145] In his reign a Kaṭhina-ceremony was held. He purified the Sāsana. During the reign of his successor, Silāmeghavaṇṇa (617-626 A.D.) a great disturbance occurred at the Abhayagiri vihāra. A monk called Bodhi resided at the Abhayagiri vihāra. He asked the king to take necessary steps against the undisciplined behaviour of many monks in that vihāra and requested the king to hold a dhamma-kamma, regulative act.[146] The king asked Bodhi to do something for the purification. But all the undisciplined monks acted together and killed Bodhi. The king took necessary steps against them and expelled about hundred monks from the vihāra and he purified the Sāsana. The king was very much worried and he wanted to bring about a settlement between the two vihāras and he requested the monks of the Mahāvihāra to hold the uporatha ceremony together with those of the Abhayagirivihāra. But the monks of the Mahāvihāra did not like it and ignored the king's request.[147] During the next fifteen years the country was disturbed by civil wars between rulers. The Mahāvihāras and the Abhayagiri vihāra were plundend. The cetiyas like the Thūpārāma were damaged. Golden images, pinnacles and other movable things of the monasteries were stolen and in order to maintain the armies of different rebels they were sold.[148] Some rulers Aggabodhi III and Dāṭhapatissa took the help of evil practices and they robbed monasteries of their gold images, precious gems and other valuables which for centuries had kept there. They did it for the purpose of financing their military operations when the royal treasure became empty.[149] Dāṭhopatina I removed the gold finial of the Thūpārāma and the gem-studded umbrella of the cetiya. Relic chambers of stūpas were opened and valuable offerings were taken away.[150] Many Tamil soldiers burnt the monastic buildings like the Tooth Relic Temple and they took away the valuable articles. The Pāṇḍya and the cola invaders from South India attached Sri Lanka several times during this period and they took away vast treasures from the monasteries.[151]

After these troubles Kassapa II (640-650 A.D.) occupied the throne.[152] He took steps to repair the buildings that had been destroyed. He felt very much for his evil actions in the past and for this reason he was busy with many religious activities and he performed those works.[153] Under his patronage the monks used to go different places to preach the dhamma and he caused a compendium (saṅgaba) of the Pāli texts to be composed.[154] He also asked the Buddhist monks to recite the Abhidhamma alogn with the commentaries.[155] During this time the people took keen interest in the study of the Abhidhamma. It became "an outstanding feature of the intellectual class of the period"[156] Jeṭṭhatissa III told his general to request the queen to study the Abhidhamma, to preach it and to transfer its merits to him.[157] Mahinda II also made arrangements for preaching the Abhidhamma on an elaborate scale.[158] In Dāṭhopatina II's time

(650-658 A.D.) there were some disagreements between the king and the Mahāvihāra. Dāṭhopatina wanted to construct a vihāra for the Abhayagiri vihāra, but the Mahāvihāra objected it on the ground that it was within their boundaries. But the king used force to carry out his plan. The monks of the Mahāvihāra became very angry with the king and they applied the patta-nikkujjana-kamma "the turning down of the alms-bowl" to him, "which was considered the excommunication of a layman".[159] The king did not take any steps against the Mahāvihāra. The next ruler was Aggabodhi IV, the younger brother of Daṭhopatina II. He ruled from 658 A.D. to 674 A.D. His adviser was Dāṭhāsiva. All the three nikāyas got same treatment from him. He gave them maintenance-villages, servants and attendants and all other comforts. "To the Three fraternities he gave a thousand villages with large and assured revenues"[160] It may be noted here that the whole country tried to follow the example of the king. Even the Tamils who used to work and to hold high offices in the king's service showed their eagerness to follow the king in religious activities. The queen for bhikkhuṇīs (nuns) constructed a nunnery and all comforts were provided for them.[161] During the reign of Aggabodhi IV the chanting of paritta (Sin. pirit) as a ceremony became a regular feature of later Buddhist practices.[162] He also announced the order of māghāta (non-killing).[163] Kassapa III (711-724 A.D.) not only decreed the order of māghāta but also in two fords reared fish.[164] Mahinda II (772-792 A.D.) and Sena I (831-851) made provision for fish, beasts and birds while Udaya I (Dappula II) (792-797 A.D.) gave corn to cattle and rice to crows and other birds.[165] The latter's queen built a nunnery for bhikkhuṇīs (nuns).

At the time of Mānavamma (676-711 A.D.) ascetic monks known as the Paṃsukūlikas became very prominent.[166] The king patronised them. Aggabodhi V (711-717 A.D.) gave the fine garments worn by himself to the paṃsukūlika monks for robes.[167] Aggabodhi IV (658-674 A.D.) was the first king who occupied Polonnaruva temporarily. He was a religious person and his ashes were used by the people as medicine.[168] Anurādhapura became more of a holy city than the seat of government. It gradually was growing old.[169] Aggabodhi VII (766-772 A.D.) purified the Sāsana. He hot only supported the Paṃmkūlikas but also he patronized monks of all three fraternities.[170] At this time Polonnaruva became an important place as a capital and this king occupied it as his capital. He was the first to occupy it.[171] Mahinda II "restored many dilapidated temples of gods (devakula) here and there and had costly images of the gods made, and also he gave the Brāhmaṇas delicious foods such as the king received and gave them milk with sugar to drink in golden goblets".[172]

During the reign of Sena I (831-851 A.D.) a member of the Vajraparvata sect in India came to Sri Lanka and played a role for the spread of the Vājiriyavāda or Vajrayāna in the island and he stayed at the Vīrāṅkura-ārāma in the Abhayagiri-vihāra.[173] At this time a sect known as the Nilapaṭadarśana appeared in Sri Lanka's religious history.[174]

The Nikāya-saṅgraha mentions that king Matvala-Sen rejected such powerful sūtras as the Ratana-sutta and the secret teachings of the Vājiriyavāda was accepted by him.[175] From the time of Matvala-Sen the Vājiriyavīda was "prevalent among the foolish and ignorant people of this country because it was protected and practised secretly as a mystic teaching"[176] At this time the king of Pāṇḍya country invaded Sri Lanka with a large army. He destroyed the king's palace, towns and monasteries and took away all valuable things including the golden images of the Buddha and "caused the island of Laṅkā to be deprived of her valuables, leaving the splendid town in a state as if it had been plundered by the yakkhas."[177] The next ruler was Sena II (851-885 or 887 A.D.). He sent a Sinhalese army to invade the Pāṇḍya country. The Pāṇḍya king, who plundered Sri Lanka, was defeated by the Sinhalese army and the army brought back all the treasures that had belonged to the Sinhalese. Under the able rule of Sena II the whole island was again united.[178] Many old vihāras and monasteries were restored by him. He gave endowments literally, held religious festivals such as a grand pirit ceremony as a Vesak festival. Under his instruction and advice, the Ratanasutta was written on a gold plate and he made offerings to it. A recital of the Abhidhamma was held by him.[179] In the twentieth year of this king the Paṃsukūlikas took their separation from the Abhayagiri Vihāra and formed a separate group.[180] The king purified the three fertinities together[181] after" they were disorganized during the preceding period."[182] Buddhist and Hindu practices came close together and Sena II "had a thousand jars of gold filled with pearls and on the top of each placed a costly jewel and presented them to a thousand Bhahmaṇs whom he had fed with milk rice in jewelled goblets, and also he gave them golden threads. He clothed them also, as a friend of meritorious deeds, with new garments to their hearts' desire and gladdened them with festive pomp"[183] At that time Anurādhapura as a seat of Government had lost its position after nearly twelve centuries. King Udaya II ascaded the throne after Sena II. He was the last king of Anurādhapura. Sena II repaired the Lohapāsāda. About 32 monks resided there at that time.[184]

Not long after, Kassapa IV (898-914 A.D.) expelled indisciplined monks from the three fraternities and purified the Buddhist Saṃgha.[185] He built a Pariveṇa. It was the Samuddagiri Pariveṇa in the Mahāvihāra and he offered it to the Paṃsukūlikas.[186] The Paṃsukūlikas used to wear rag-robes. The word Paṃsukūla means rags found in dust-heaps and paṃsukulin is a bhikkhu whose garments were made of such rags patched together. The name is merely a symbol of the utmost poprness.[187] Kassapa IV patronized the Dhammarucika and the Sāgalika sects and he also helped the Mahāvihāra.[188] The Dhammarucika belonged to the Abhayagiri vihāra. A Mahāthera named Sagala of the Dakkhināgiri vihāra taught religion there and from that time this now group became known as the Sāgalika.[189] King Kassapa IV's general Rukkha and the grand scribe Sena gave services to the Mahāvihāra.[190] Kassapa V (929-939 A.D.) reformed the whole Buddhist Saṃgha.[191] During the reign of Mahinda IV (956-972 A.D.) a recital of the Abhidhamma was held.[192] Two inscription of Mahinda IV discovered at Mihintale mention this king's important role to popularise the study of the Abhidhamma.[193] Sena V ascended the throne in the last quarter of the tenth century A.D. He tried to give good services to the Buddhist Saṃgha. He protected it.[194]

The facts mentioned above clearly inform that the Mahāvihāra contributed very much to the development of Theravāda Buddhism in Sri Lanka. In the history of Buddhism in Sri Lanka the rise of the Abhayagiri-vihāra was an important phenomenon. Several rulers showed keen interest in the affairs of the Abhayagiri-vihāra, and it received favoured treatment from them, but it could not do anything to overshadow the Mahāvihāra ultimately. In religious texts there are many references to the rise of new sects. These new sects disturbed the progress of the Mahāvihāra very much. But, even then, the Mahāvihāra, the citadel of orthodoxy, as the main centre of Theravāda Buddhism, remained very prominent during this period. It may be noted here that the political situation in Sri Lanka from about the middle of the fifth century A.D. until the third quarter of the eleventh century A.D. was not very good to help Buddhism for its smooth progress in Sri Lanka. It was not favourable at all towards its development. In this period of Sri Lanka's history there were continuous disturbances and wars between the reiging king and his rival claimants or the foreign invaders. The rulers from such a political situation did not get an opportunity to work for the religion and for this reason the Buddhist Saṃgha and the monasteries were neglected. Some rulers even took away gold images, precious gems and other valuables from the monasteries for the purpose of financing their military operations. The Tamil soliders were allowed to burn down monastic buildings like the Tooth Relic Temple and took away the valuables. During this period the Pāṇḍya and the

Cola invaders from South India attacked Sri Lanka several times. They not only destroyed the monasteries but also took vast treasurers from these places. These condition becames very bad when the Coḷas from South India captured Sri Lanka and it remained a part of the Coḷa expire until 1070 A.D.[195]

Vijayabāhu I in A.D. 1070 became the ruler of Sri Lanka after defeating the Coḷas. For several years (A.D. 993-1070)[196] Sri Lanka was ruled by foreign rulers and for this reason her sufferings took place for some time. She suffered very much due to this reason. The eleventh century A.D. saw that Sri Lanka had fallen upon evil days. Her progress was checked by political crises and there were confusion and disorder everywhere. Vjayabāhu I resided at Polonnaruwa and it became his capital. After his accession to the throne Buddhism once again got its life in Sri Lanka. He then engaged himself to reform the Buddhist Saṃgha which had fallen into decay during the period of foreign rules and war. The Cūlavaṃsa[197] mention that at that time the member of ordained monks were very few in Sri Lanka and King Vijayabāhu I was unable to convene a chapter of five monks to perform an ordination ceremony in Sri Lanka. He worked hard to put an end to this state of affairs. He then sent an embassy to King Anoratha (or Anuraddha) of Myanmar for his help to revive Buddhism in Sri Lanka. He not only wanted to re-establish the Buddhist Saṃgha in Sri Lanka but also he wished to secure a chapter of five monks for the ordination ceremony. He despatched a religious mission in 1071 A.D. to king Anuraddha in the Rāmañña country in Myanmar and requested him to send Buddhist monks who were well-versed in the three Piṭakas, who were a format of moral discipline and other virtues and who were well-known as theras and also he expressed his desire to receive Buddhist texts from him.[198] King Anuraddha of Myanmar sent a number of distinguished monks from Myanmar to reform the Buddhist Saṃgha and to help to perform the ordination ceremony in Sir Lanka. He sent ordained monks and also Buddhist texts to Vijayabāhu I. The Sāsanavaṃsa and the Glass Place chronicle say that there was a religious contact between Sri Lanka and Myanmar at that time.[199] The Poḷonnaruva inscription of Vijayabāhu I and the Poḷonnaruva Slab inscription of the Velaikkaras (circa 1137-1153 A.D.)[200] describe the purification of the Buddhist Saṃgha of the three Nikāyas in Sri Lanka with the help of the monks from Arumaṇa during the time of Vijayabāhu I. The Mahāvihāra, the Abhayagiri and the Jetavana sects were the three Nikāyas or Fraternities into which the Buddhist Saṃgha in Sri Lanka was divided.[201] Arumaṇa (Sinhalese Aramaṇa) in another form of Pāli word Rāmañña. It is identified with Rāmaññadesa or the district of Thaton in Lower Myanmar. The Nikāyasaṅgrahava says that the king of Laṅkā Vijayabāhu I from Anuraddha got twenty senior ordained monks and sacred texts.[202] The Pūjāvaliya mention monks the same story.[203] Vijayabāhu I re-established the valid ordination in Sri Lanka with the help of the Buddhist monks from Rāmaññadesa. Under his patronage Buddhism flourished in Sri Lanka.[204] King Anuraddha in return requested the king of Sri Lanka to give him the sacred Tooth Relic of Buddha which Sri Lanka proudly possessed.[205] The king of Sri Lanka complied with his request and he despatched a duplicate Tooth Relic to Myanmar. King Anuraddha was not happy with the copies of the Tipiṭaka brought from Sudhammapura (or That on) in lower Myanmar. He then sent religious missions to Vijayabāhu I for Tipiṭaka of Sri Lanka, when the religious mission reached Myanmar from Sri Lanka with the copies of the Tipiṭaka, king Anurādha with the help of his religious teacher Shiv Arahana studied, examined and compared the copies brought from Sri Lanka with that of Thaton.[206] The sending of the copies of the Tipiṭaka from Sri Lanka to Myanmar and the purification of the Buddhist Saṃgha of Sri Lanka with the help of the monks from Myanmar clearly show that Sri Lanka or Myanmar, the two Buddhist Theravāda countries, came very close to each other and religious intercourse became very frequent between these two countries in the eleventh century A.D. under the patronage of Vijayabāhu I and Anuraddha.

King Vijayabāhu I was a powerful ruler. At the same time he was quite well-known for his great devotion to Buddhism. During his time Buddhism prepared. Many men joined the Buddhist Saṃgha and several monasteries and stūpas were built. The religious revival inaugurated by King Vijayabāhu I led to a great intellectual re-awakening and a large number of religious literary works in Pāli and Sanskrit were composed.[207] Many learned men got encouragement from King Vijayabāhu I to come to Sri Lanka to do works on Buddhism. But these activities suffered very much with the death of King Vijayabāhu I in 1110 A.D.

The period between the death of Vijayabāhu I (A.D. 1070-1110) and the ascendancy of Parākramabāhu I (1153-1186 A.D.) can be mentioned as a dark chapter in the history of Buddhism in Sri Lanka. After Vijayabāhu I's death there were internal troubles and political crises disturbed the country's progress. The kings of this period were extremely busy in their petty personal politics. They were two weak to stop disturbances in the country. As a result, there was no king to devote his time to the development of Buddhism. For this reason, it was on the decline again. After a great struggle with rival claimants King Parākramabāhu the great occupied the throne in A.D. 1186. He suppressed many rebellions even after his accession.[208] He was a great ruler and he restored order and as a conqueror he carried his prowess even to South India and Myanmar.[209] He reconstructed the city of Polonnaruwa and rebuilt vihāras and monasteries there. Many new religious edifices were built by him in Polounaruwa. He also turned his mind to restore the ancient capital city of Anurādhapura. After the occupation of the Coḷas it had been neglected and abandoned.[210] King Parākramabāhu I restored all the important monuments at Anurādhapura and also the Mihintale monastry.[211] Under his patronage Buddhism prospered and Sri Lanka established itself again as a great centre of Thèravāda Buddhism. He was mentioned as one of the greatest kings of Sri Lanka. His reign was regarded as a glorious one for many reasons. In the history of Buddhism in Sri Lanka he contributed very much to the development of Buddhism. He unified the Buddhist Saṃgha in Sri Lanka. He established Buddhism in its former purity, unity and glory.[212] His most important work was that the king purified as well as unified the Buddhist Saṃgha in Sri Lanka. Although Vijayabāhu I worked hard for the welfare of the Buddhist Saṃgha, yet there were some monks of the Buddhist Saṃgha who were quite unfit to lead the monastic life. Some of the monks had wives and children. At the advice of a learned Thera named Mahā Kassapa of Udumbaragiri Vihāra (Dimbulagale near Polonnuruwa) King Parākramabāhu I convened a council of the leading monks of the dissentient schools and they all agreed that "the teachings of the Mahāvihāra were correct and their claims were in keeping with the Dhamma".[213] Many of the unworthy monks were requested to leave the order and many monks were expelled from the Buddhist Saṃgha. After that the king united the Mahāvihāra, the Abhayagiri-vihāra and the Jetavana-vihāra.[214] With the help of the leading monks king Parākramabāhu I proclaimed for the guidance of the Buddhist monks in Sri Lanka a code of regulations.[215] The code of regulations introduced by the king of Sri Lanka became a royal proclamation. It mentioned the proper observance of the Vinaya rules and discussed the procedure that should be followed by his subjects who wanted to become lay pupils, novices and subsequently ordained monks.[216] King Parākramabāhu I engraved the proclamation on the rock surface of the Uttārarāma or the Gol-vihāra. It became known as Polounaru-Katikāvata or the Parākramabāhu-Katikāvata.[217] It may be noted here that in spite of political differences between Sri Lanka and Myanmar during Parākramabāhu I's reign, strong religious and cultural relations existed between these two countries. The Cūlavaṃsa mention that it was the mediation of the Buddhist monks of Sri Lanka by which the war between the two countries—Sri Lanka and Myanmar—was brought to an end. The monks of Sri Lanka played a great role to bring about a peaceful settlement with the kings of Myanmar. King Parākramabāhu I became very happy after hearing the friendly words of the Sinhalese Buddhist monks and the friendship was established between Sri Lanka and Myanmar.[218] Parākramabāhu I took keen interest in the affairs of Buddhism. He brought internal peace and security. During his reign a revival of Buddhist learning took place. Many scholars produced Buddhist literature as well as Buddhist philosophical works. During the reign of Parākramabāhu I religious ties between Myanmar and Sri Lanka were strengthened by the visit of Uttarajiva Mahathera of Myanmar to Sri Lanka. He was the preceptor of the king of Pagan of Myanmar. He came to Sri Lanka with Chapata and many other disciples of the Myanmarese Saṁgha in A.D. 1170 or 1171 in order to worship at holy shrines.[219] Chapata received the ordination in Sri Lanka and he was admitted into the Sinhalese Saṁgha and he spent in there about ten years in the island. Chapata's visit to Sri Lanka, his admission into the Sinhalese Saṁgha, his arrival in Myanmar with four other monks from Sri Lanka and the introduction and the establishment of the Sīhala Saṁha at Pagan in Myanmar in the twelfth century A.D. were important religious events in the history of Buddhism in Myanmar and Sri Lanka.[220] All these facts throw flood of light on the important role played by Sri Lanka in the introduction, establishment, growth and development of Sīhala Buddhism in Myanmar in the twelfth century A.D. All these events took place in the reign of Parākramabāhu I. This shows his great contribution to Sri Lanka's Buddhist World.

After the death of Parākramabāhu the Great, Sri Lanka again had suffered very much due to rivalry to the throne and foreign invasions. There was much internal disturbance and Buddhism again fell into evil days. It declined again. Parakramabāhu I's immediate successor was Vijayabāhu II (1186-1187 A.D.). He re-established friendly ties between Myanmar and Sri Lanka. He promoted trade and religious relations between these two countries.[221] The Cūlavaṃsa says that under royal patronage during this period in Sri Lanka the religion of the Buddha was flourishing.[222] The Sāsanavaṃsa mentions the purification of the religion in Sri Lanka in the reign of Vijayabāhu II. "... The religion having become stainless ...".[223] But Vijayabāhu II was killed by an usurper after a year's reign. The next ruler was Mahinda VI. He belonged to the Kuliṅga class.[224] But he was however killed by Nissankamalla five days later. Then Nissankamalla became Sri Lanka's ruler and he ruled for nine years (1187-1196 A.D.).[225] He was a great patron of Buddhism. He constructed several religious edifices in Polonnaruwa, his capital and they were like the Ruvanaveli-dāgaba (now called Rankot-Vehera), the beautiful Vaṭadā-ge, the Tooth-Relic Temple (Hetadāge) and the Nissankalatā-maṇḍa.[226] Even to this day they exist. King Nissankamala used to go to the Sumana-Kūṭa (Śri Pāda or Adam's Peak), the Dambulu-vihāra and other religious places.[227] At several important places he constructed alms-houses. He expelled corrupt Buddhist monks from the Buddhist Saṃgha and he purified the Dāsava.[228] His reign was mentioned as "a bright spot in the troubled history of this period. The most remarkable aspect of his rule, apart from his service to the laity and the order, was the large number of epigraphs he set up—the largest number of inscription credited to any individed King in Ceylon (Sri Lanka)."[229] The Satmahal Pāsāda in Polonnaruwa was built by this ruler.[230] But some people think that the original construction was not the work of this ruler. In the Jambokola-vihāra (Dambulla) he has left an epigraph. That vihāra was built "resplendent with walls and pillars shimmering in gold and silver, where the floor was of red lead, and the bricks of the roof, were of gold, the wise (monarch) had rebuilt and placed therein seventy-three golden statues of the master."[231] His inscription engraved on a rock at the site describes his embellishment of these caves and they became known as Suvaṇṇagiriguhā. This shows that this ruler has restored that vihāra.[232] In order to win the godd-will of the people he visited places of religious importance such as Kalaṇiya,

Mahāgāma, Mahiyaṅgana and Samanoḷa.[233] Some of his inscriptions say that he tried to unify the Buddhist Saṃgha.[234] It may be noted here that Vijayabāhu I or Parākaramabāhu I purified the Buddhist Saṃgha, but their efforts brought temporary results.[235] Thus Nissaṅkamalla worked hard to help the Sāsana when it needed the patronage of the king.[236] Some scholars think that "these services to help the course of Buddhism were not without a political motive is hinted at, when he appeals to the inhabitants of the country not to allow non-Buddhists such as the Coḷa and Kerala princes to aspire to the throne of Ceylon (Sri Lanka). The position is even clearer when he brushes aside the claims of the people of Govikula and declares that the Kalinga line alone had a rightful claim to the throne of Ceylon (Sri Lanka)".[237]

Nissaṅkamalla was succeeded by his son Vīrabāhu. He "ruled for one night and fell to the power of death."[238] General Tāvuru, having killed Vīrabāhu, raised Niśśaṅkamalla's younger brother Vikramabāhu to the throne.[239] The latter's reign was very brief. He was on the throne only for three months.[240] He was put to death by a prince called Coḍagaṅga.[241] He was a sister's son of Nissaṅkamalla.[242] Coḍagaṅga ruled for only nine months.[243] He was put to death by general Kitti. The latter than placed Līlāvati—the first mahesi (queen) of Parākramabāhu I on the throne.[244] She reigned for three years. But general Kitti in the name of Līlāvati ruled the country. The Cūlavaṃsa describes that she ruled 'without mishap'[245] and her inscriptions mention that the people and the Buddhist order were in a 'peaceful state'.[246] But some scholars remark that her reign was disturbed by foreign invasions, quite apart from the threats of the factions who wanted to place a Kaliṅga prince on the throne.[247] Most probably, Līlāvati ruled between the year 1197 and 1200.[248] Her successor was Sāhasamalla. Then Kalyāṇavatī, the first queen of Niśśaṅkamalla, ascended the throne.[249] The Cūlavaṃsa informs that she ruled for six months only.[250] Both the Pūjāvaliya and the Rājāvaliya describe that she reigned for six years.[251] According to the Pūjāvaliya, she was deposed and a five months old infant Dharmāsoka was raised by Eḷulu Ābo Senevirat (Āyasmanta) to the throne.[252] The Cūlavaṃsa mentions that Dharmāsoka's reign lasted one year. But the Rājāvaliya says that he reigned for six years only.[253] The Cūlavaṃsa says that one Mahādipāda Anīkaniga came from the Coḷa country and killed the ruler Dharmāsoka and general Āyasmanta and took over the reigns of the government.[254] Anīkaṅga was put to death by general Vikkanta-cāmūnakka, who placed Parākramabāhu's queen Līlāvati on the throne for the second time.[255] It may be noted here that the rise of Līlāvatī to the throne for a second time and later for a third time, and a Pāṇḍya prince called Parākrama Pāṇḍya's ascendancy on the throne of Rājaraṭṭha some time before Māgha's invasion would indicate that the Pāṇḍya faction became powerful at the expense of the Kaliṅgas.[256] Queen Līlāvatī was deposed by Lokissara. But his reign was very brief. He was put to death by a general named Pasākrama and Līlāvatī ascended the throne for a third time.[257] All these facts mentioned above clearly indicate that the political condition of Sri Lanka during these periods was not very good for the progress of Buddhism in Sri Lanka.

The period of two decades that followed king Nissaṅkamalla's death was one of the most disturbed years in Sri Lanka and during this time several rulers were assassinated and several foreigners invaded the country. In A.D. 1214 a foreigner named Māgha attacked Sri Lanka, defeated the Sinhalese ruler and ruled for 36 years (1215-1251 A.D.)[258] In his reign Buddhism declined. Māgha destroyed many monasteries and he built houses there and asked his soldiers to dwell in.[259] Many people in Sri Lanka got ill-treatment from him. He asked the people to adopt a different religion and for this reason he used force. Many libraries with valuable books were destroyed by him.

Vijayabāhu III established himself as the ruler of Māyāraṭṭ ha and he ruled from A.D. 1232 to A.D. 1236.[260] He recovered the Tooth Relic and the Alms Bowl of the Buddha.[261] This no doubt helped to strengthen his position in Māyāraṭṭha. At that time when Rājaraṭṭha was ravaged by Māgha's forces, the Mahātheras of the time headed by Vācissara for the safety of these relics took them from Pulatthinagara to Māyāraṭṭha. They buried these relics in the earth at Kotthumala mountain and these monks then crossed over to the Coḷa and Pāṇḍya countries.[262] Vijayabāhu III asked these monks to come to Māyāraṭṭha from South India and he took their help to recover and to remove the relics from the spot where they buried and then he brought these relics to Jambuddoni amidst great festivity and celebrations.[263] "By this time the Tooth Relic had acquired such great veneration among the Buddhists in Ceyla (Sri Lanka) that its possession seems to have become a sine qua non to justify the claims of the Sinhalese Kings to the throne of Ceylon (Sri Lanka).[264] King after king made generous endowments and paid great homage to it. Kings like Vijayabāhu I, Parākramabāhu I and even Nissaṅkamalla, if his claims are to be accepted, each built a Tooth Relic Temple, usually located close to the royal Place.[265] We have seen that one of the reason for Parākramabāhu's campaigns in Rohaṇa was his desire to recover the Tooth Relic which was then in that province in the possession of queen Sugata ...... Shattered in combat the foe is in flight. They have seized the splendid sacred relics of the alms-bowl and the Tooth Relic and are fain, though fear to cross the sea. So have I heard. If this is so, that the island of Lanka will be desolate. For, though here on the Sīhala inland various jewels and pearls and the like and costly kinds of various precious stones are found, yet of quite incomparable costliness are the two sacred relics of the Lord of the truth, the Tooth and the Alms-bowl."[266] For the reception of these relics in Poḷonnaruwa at the end of these compaign, a great religious festival ceremony was held by Vijayabāhu III. For the purpose he constructed a temple in Poḷonnaruwa and he deposited the relic in it.[267] These facts show the importance of the Tooth Relic during this period in the religious life of the people as well as in the political life of the country. Because its possession helped the ruler to have a distinct advantage.[268] Vijayabāhu III did not build a Tooth Relic Temple in his capital, Jambuddoṇi because there was the threat of Māgha's forces and it brought an air of insecurity in the political atmosphere of his time. For this reason on the top of the Billasela mountain he erected a Tooth Relic Temple and this was situated not very close to the enemy's camp. It was far away from the enemy.[269] Billasela was identified with the present Beligala in the Otara Pattu in the Kagalla district of the Sabaragamuva province.[270] Vijayabāhu III thought that Beligala was less vulnerable than Dambadeniya in the event of an attack by Māgha's armies. The king not only recovered the Tooth Relic but also he erected a Temple for this relic. The Buddhist Saṃgha and the lay Buddhists supported and admired his religious work. He got the support of the Buddhist Saṃgha heeded by such leading mahātheras as Saṃgharakkhita and Dimbulāgala Araṇyarāsi Medhaṅkara and this helped him very much to win the confidence of the people.[271] It is known from the Dambadeṇi Kātikāvat and the Nikāya Saṃgrahaya that Saṃgharakkhita was the head of the Buddhist order (Śāsanānuśāsaka) and he was the chief monk of the Grāmavāsī sect and a pupil of Śāriputta Mahāsāmi, a leading mahāthera, who flourished in the reign of Parākramabāhu I.[272] Dimbulāgala (Pāli: Udumbaragiri) Madhaṅkara Mahāsāmi was the head of the varanāsi sect.[273] Then Mahātheras had a great influence upon the Buddhist population and this co-operation and goodwill had helped to strengthen Vijayabāhu III's position as the ruler of Māyāraṭṭha.[274] The Vanavāsī and the Grāmavāsī sects and their respective heads were great supporters of this ruler. In this way Māyāraṭṭha became an important place of the Buddhist Saṃgha. The king and the people became very religious and they engaged themselves to do work for the progress of the religion of the Buddha. The king wanted to establish Buddhism in the country in its former glory. He repaired the dilapidated monasteries, some of which suffered very much at the hands of the invaders. He erected new vihāras. He unified and purified the Buddhist Saṃgha. He gave encouragement to the study of the Dhamma. The Buddhist Saṃgha and the lay Buddhists advised him for his important role for the study of Dhamma and for the development of learning.[275] The Rājāvaliya describes: "Raising a Simhalese army, he (Vijayabāhu III) went out and caused the forts of the Tamils in the various villages to surrender, and the forts of the Tamils at Poḷonnaruva to surrender; attacked, expelled and destroyed the Tamils who dwelt in the Vanni districts. Thereafter he (re)built the Thūpārāma, Ruvanavalisāya, crowned them with pinnacles and made great offerings. He cleared the jungle on the sites of the vihāras broken down by the Tamils in every port of illustrious Laṅkā .... brought Māyā and the other two countries under one canopy and received tribute".[276] The places at which Vijayabāhu III erected new religious edifices or repaired old ones indicate that he exercised effective power over the territory. Apart from Dambadeṇiya and Beligala, Vattala, Kalaṇiya, Attanagalla and Toṭagamuna near Hikkaḍuva were the places where he built religious edifices.[277] This shows that the south-western sea-board, which was the principality of Rohuṇa, owed allegiance to him. When he died after a reign of four years (1232-1236), his body was cremated at Attanagalla and over the ashes a stūpa was erected.[278] The Cūlavaṃsa and the Pūjāvaliya refer to the reign of Vijayabāhu as four years.[279] But the Rājāvaliya mentions that he ruled for 24 years.[280] It is stated that "although Vijayabāhu cherished the desire to bring about the welfare of the world and the Sāsana, he realized that he had but a short time left to fight the Tamils in order to bring peace to Lanka, and to restore the dilapidated vihāras, due to fact that he attained kingship when his youth had passed. The short reign of four years is in keeping with this statement in a contemporary work and confirmed by the Cūlavaṃsa, in preference to the version given in a late chronicle."[281]

Vijayabāhu III had two sons, of whom the elder, named Parākramabāhu, succeeded his father as king.[282] On the death of Vijayabāhu III, Parākramabāhu ascended the throne and received his first consecration in Jambuddoni in A.D.1236.[283] At the time of his accession Rājaraṭṭha was still under the control of Māgha and he ruled from Poḷonnaruva.[284] Parākramabāhu II reigned from Dambaduniya from 1236 A.D. while Māgha was still very powerful and made his great influence in north Srī Lanka.[285] Parākramabāhu II was a ruler of great learning. He got his training in all the arts and sciences. The Pūjāvaliya says that this training included dharma-nīti (moral precepts), rāja-nīti (statecraft), the art of letters and so forth.[286] The Dambadeṇī Asva refers to the branches of learning in which Parākramabāhu II became proficient and mentions that he knew many languages including Demaḷa, Siṃhala, Saṃskṛta and Māgadha (Pāli).[287] Similarly, he learnt the Buddha Dhamma in its three Piṭakas, Vinaya, Sutta and Abhidhamma, grammar (vyākaraṇa) in the two systems, namely Moggallāyana vyākaraṇa and Kāyisan vyākaraṇa, the three Vedas, prosody (chandolaksṣṇa), astrology (nakśatraya) and so forth.[288] He was very good in sword-fighting (kadu-śilpaya), archery (dhanuśilpaya), law (nītiśāstraya), logic (tarkaya), and other branches of learning included in the eighteen crafts (aśṭādaśa-śilpaya) as well as those of sixty-four arts (sūsāṭa kalā).[289] He received his education under the supervision of a learned thera named Saṃghankkhita. For this reason he earned a high degree of proficiency in languages such as Sanskrit, Pāli and Sinhalese, in the Buddha Dhaṃmma or other branches of traditional learning.[290] On account of his learning he received the title Kalikāla Sāhicca-sahaññu-paṇḍita (Skt. Kalikāla Sāhitya Sarvajña Paṇḍita), "the scholar who is omniscient in the literature of Kali Age."[291] The Visuddhimagga Mahāsannaya and the Vanavinisa Sanaaya mention his scholarship or learning. The former informs the profound knowledge of the author in Buddhist philosophy and other schools of thought, "inaccessible to him unless he had mastered the Sanskrit language in addition to Pāli", which the latter refers to his high attainments in the rules of the discipline of the Buddhist clergy.[292] Some scholars believe that the Kavsiḷumiṇa was the work of Parākramabāhu II.[293] This informs Parākramabāhu II's poetic gifts, his mastery of the canons of Sanskrit poetics and prosody. Prior to waging war with Māgha, Parākramabāhu II brought Tooth Relic to Beligala from Jambuddoṇi where Vijayabāhu III had kept it for greater safety.[294] He built a Tooth Relic Temple near the royal palace and he used to worship the relic 'in the three periods of the day' whenever he wanted to do so.[295] In honour of the Tooth Relic a great festival was held by Parākramabāhu II in the city and on that occasion he took the relic on his palm and "resorted to an act of faith (Skt. Satya Kriyā)."[296] "It is stated that the island of Laṅkā was sanctified by the visits of the Buddha on three occasions and that, therefore, it was not possible for kings of a 'false faith' to hold sway there. Each of the foreign invaders was defeated by successive Sinhalese Kings."[297] "We are made to believe that Parākramabāhu II was similarly determined to defeat the Damiḷas, who were in occupation by force. It is stated that Parākramabāhu claimed that, if he had been chosen by the Buddha to be included among the heroic kings of old in Laṅkā, and was similarly destined to conquer the foreign enemies and establish order in Laṅkā and promote the welfare of the world and the Sāsana, the Tooth Relic should perform a miracle and demonstrate it.[298] He claimed also that, in the past when the Buddha was living, many far-famed monarchs heard his sermons and saw the miracles, and so did other kings like Asoka, Devānampiya Tissa and Duṭṭhagāmaṇī, who lived when the Buddha had passed away, but had the fortune to see such miracles. Parākramabāhu wished the Tooth Relic to perform a similar miracle.[299] We are told that the Tooth Relic instantly rose to the sky and appeared in the life-like form of the Buddha, radiating the six-coloured effulgence which lit the whole city. Having satisfied the wish of the king, the Tooth Relic descended and rested on the palm of the king."[300] In honour of the relic, festivals and celebrations were held and the king took part in them and they indirectly helped to strengthen the sympathy and support of the people toward the king at a time when Buddhism at the hands of foreign invaders in Rājaraṭṭha had suffered very much.[301] Parākramabāhu II restored the Sāsana by bringing over monks from the Coḷa country in South India and held a festival to admit monks to the higher ordination.[302] The monks of the whole island gathered at Sahassatittha for the performance of the ceremony of admission to the Buddhist Saṃgha.[303] The Vanni kings of Patiṭṭhāraṭṭha (Rājaraṭṭha) and Rohaṇa brought with them the requisite provisions of alms for the assembly of monks who came at Sahassatittha.[304] Many monks received the higher ordination at this ceremony which was held at Sahassatittha. The deserving theras received the different ranks such as that of the Grand Master (Mahāsāmipadaṃ), chief thera (mūlapadaṃ), Grand Thera (Mahāthera Padaṃ) and Parivaṇa thera (parivara therapadaṃ).[305] The ceremony continued for a period of half a month. At the conclusion of the ceremony, "he (Parākramabāhu) sent many remaining articles of use to the bhikkhus settled in the Pandu and Coḷa countries."[306] It shows that the cordial religious ties existed between Sri Lanka and the Damila country. Parākramabāhu II brough about the purification of the Buddhist Saṃgha but the results were not lasting as had been the case when his predecessors in this direction tried to do it. Parākramabāhu II worked hard to improve the discipline of the Buddhist Saṃgha in Sri Lanka and he wanted to see the progress of Buddhism in the island. After these ceremonies of admission to the order at Sahassatittha, Parākramabāhu II returned to Dambadeniya and he entrusted the administration of the Northern Province to Vīrabāhu who stayed at Polonnaruwa.[307] Parākramabāhu II erected several monasteries and parivaṇas and encouraged learning. Under the leadership of the great thera Āranyaka Madhankara a great Council of monks was held during his reign and he purified the sāsana.[308] For the proper conduct of the monks the king formulated rules and the code of these rules became known as Daṁbadeni Katikāvata.[309] For the hermit-monks he built a great monastery at Palābatgala.[310] Many writers flourished during his reign under his patronage and they praised him. His contribution to religion and literature were no doubt outstanding, but his achievement was not very glorious one in the political field.[311] He failed to bring the whole island under his rule. He was unable to present the establishment of the independent kingdom in the Jaffna Peninsula. He was very powerless to do so. After nearly two hundred years it come under Sinhalese control. But that was only for a short period.[312] He could not check the decay of the Rajaraṭa (Rājarattha) or its elaborate irrigation system. The misrule of Māgha had brought its decay and its elaborate irrigation system.[313] Parākramabāhu II's reign lasted thirty-five years. The Pūjāvaliya mentions that in his thirty-fifth regnal year the upasampadā ceremony at Sahassatittha was held, but it does not mention his death.[314] Most probably, his death occurred in his thirty-fifth regnal year, though the Rājāvaliya refers to this event in his thirty-second year.[315] One inscription of Parākramabāhu II was found at Nāranbādda, a village situated at a distance of two miles from the Ramlukkana Railway Station in the Deyāladahamnna Pattuva, Kiṇigoda Korale of the Kāgalla District.[316] It describes Parākramabāhu II's defeat of the Damiḷas who wanted to destroy the Māyā kingdom, and the recovery of the Tooth Relic and the Alms Bowl. It also says that helpful services were given to these relics to protect them from the enemies.[317] It also narrates the erection of the Sela-vihāra (Rock Monastery) which was named after him as Parākramabāhu Pirivaṇa and certain lands were given to it.[318] The record is undated, but it belongs to Parākramabāhu II. Bell remonks: "The allusion to the Tamil invasion, and the recovery of the Relics, together with the style and character in which the inscripti is written justifies its ascription to Parākramabāhu II."[319] The Cūlavaṃsa records: "Thereupon the king erected a parivaṇa that was called by his name Parākramabāhu, adorned with lofty pāsādas, granted the vihārs diverse objects of use suited to it as well as rich maintenance villages and celebrated a great sacrificial festival."[320] Parākramabāhu II appointed his brother Bhuvanakabāhu to look after the ecclesiastical affairs of the Saṃgha and asked his brother to encourage and to supervise the instruction of the Buddhist monks in the doctrines.[321] We also know further that: "with the reflection that Theras who were acquainted with the sacred texts were rare in the island, he had all books brought from Jambudīpa, had many bhikkhus instructed in the sacred texts, as also in all sciences such as philosophy and grammar and the like and made of them cultivated people."[322] King Parākramabāhu II also invited learned monks from the Coḷa country.[323] Such measures had helped to promote learning and scholarship in the order. For this reason, several Buddhist vihāras of the time, such as those at the Puṭabhattasela, Vālāgiri, and the Vijayasundarārama in Jambuddoṇī became very prominent as centres of learning and productive intellectual activity.[324] Many commentaries, and subcommentaries and glossaries were written in order to facilitate a better understanding of the sacred texts. The Visuddhimārga Mahā Sannaya, a Sinhalese translation of the Visuddhimagga, was written by Parākramabāhu II himself.[325] This was an example of the vigorous intellectual activity in this period. Apart from works of philosophical nature, several writers of this period wrote voluminous works of a popular nature extolling the virtues of the Buddha. The Rasavāhinī is a compilation of Buddhist stories of an earlier date by the Vedeha Thera and it is a work written in the Dambadaṇi period.[326] The Hatthavanagallavihāravaṃsa is a hali poem. At the request of Anomadassi Mahāsāmi it was composed during the reign of Parākramabāhu II.[327] Buddhappiya's Pajjamadhu was also written during this period.[328] The writers of this period took interest in grammar, prosody, medicine and astrology. Among the medical works of this period, mention may be made of the Pāli Bhesajja mañjusā (Casket of Medicine), written by the Pañcamūla Pariveṇadhipati (Pasmula Mahāsāme).[329] The authors of this period wrote many grammatical works dealing with the grammar of both Pāli and Sinhalese.

Prince Vijayabāhu ascended the throne at Dambadeniya after the death of his father Parākramabāhu II. He was Vijayabāhu IV.

He was mild and humane in his character and had the surname of Buddhisattva.[330] He was the idol of the people. But his general named Mitta had assassinated him in the second year of his reign.[331] He ruled from A.D. 1270 to 1272.[332] Then Bhuvanckabāhu, a younger brother of Vijayabāhu, became king of Dambaḍeniya. He was Bhuvanakabāhu I.[333] He patronised the Buddhist Saṃgha and his rule was acceptable to the people. He showed keen interest in establishing trade relations with the Arab power which at that time controlled the sea-lanes. He dispatched an embassy to the Sultan of Egypt at Cairo in April 1283.[334] King Bhuvanakabāhu I died in or about A.D. 1284 in the twelfth year of his reign.[335] The Sinhalese sources refer to an interregnum, i.e. an interval without a legitimate ruler, after him. The next ruler was Parākramabāhu III. He was the last king of reign from polonvaruma. He occupied throne in or about 1287 A.D. and he ruled up to A.D. 1293. Under his patronage Buddhism flourished in his Kingdom.[336] The next ruler was Bhuvanakabāhu II. He ascended the throne in A.D. 1293 and his reign lasted for nine years.[337] He brought the Tooth Relic to Kuruṇagala and declared himself as king and Kuruṇagala was his capital.[338] He was succecded by his son Parākramabāhu IV or Paṇḍita Parākramabāhu II as he is mentioned in Sinhalese writings.[339] He continued to reign from Kuruṇagala but a Tamil poem refers to him as guardian of Dambai, i.e., Dambadeniya.[340] The same source mentions that his accession took place in 1302 A.D. But a sinhalese literary work says that he was on the throne in 1326 A.D. This king patronized scholars and writers. Under his patronage many literary works were written. He erected many religious edifices, religious buildings and monasteries. In his reign there was a rebellion headed by a personage called Bodā-māpāṇan-dā and forced the monks in the capital to disperse. Most probably, this rebellion had disturbed his reign very much and for this reason his kingdom had suffered and his reign came to an end.[341] He was mentioned as the last king of the dynasty established by Vijayabāhu III.[342]

Bhuvanakabāhu IV of Gaṁpala began his reign in 1341 or 1342 A.D.[343] Two inscriptions refer to 1344 A.D. as the Third year of Bhuvanakabāhu IV of Gaṁpala. Between Parakramabāhu IV and Bhuvanakabāhu IV of Gaṁpala there were two rulers: Bhuvanakabāhu III, called Vanni Bhuvanakabāhu and Vijayabāhu V. The epithet of Savuḷu is attached to the latter's name.[344] A complete change took place in the political scene in the island during the interval of sixteen years and the available sources do not say anything on it. The seat of Government was shifted from Kuruṇagala on the plains to Gaṁpala in the highlands. Bhuvanakabāhu IV was the first king who ruled from this city.[345] Most probably, Kuruṇagala was the capital of his two prodecessors. Bhuvanakabāhu III constructed the Kuruṇagala tank. He also built temples in the Vanni Hatpattu.[346] Vijayabāhu V was the founder of a new dynasty, "which was connected by later eulogists with the ancient Sinhalese royal stock of Lāmāni (Lambakaṇṇa)."[347] Vijayabāhu V ruled for atleast eleven years. It was not known that the eleventh was his last regnal year and that Parākramabāhu IV "ceased to reign after the last date known of him", Bhuvanakabāhu III, who came between the two, had a very brief reign.[348] He belonged to the Dambadeniya dynasty and he made a great influence in some part of the island contemporaneously with Vijayabāhu V. Parākramabāhu V with Bhuvanakabāhu IV exercised joint sovereignty and Dādigama was his residence.[349] Parākramabāhu V's date of his accession was 1344 A.D. and this was about three years later than that of Bhuvanakabāhu IV.[350] Parākramabāhu V was compelled to leave Dādigama as well as Gaṁpala. The Ariyan of Singai-nagar (the Ārya-cakravarti), who has left an inscription at Koṭagama, thirteen miles north-east of Dādigama, drove Parākramabāhu V to the wilds of Ruhuṇa.[351] The new king was Vikramabāhu III. He ascended the throne in A.D. 1356 or 1357 A.D.[352] He was a nephew (sister's son) of Parākramabāhu V and also of Bhuvanakabāhu IV. The Rājāvalīya says that at that time there were three centres of political power in the island. At Gaṁpala was the nephew of Parākramabāhu V, i.e., Vikramabāhu, at Rayigama was Alakeśvara and at Yāpāpaṭuna (Jaffna) ruled the Ārya-cakravarti.[353] Among these three rulers, the Ārya-cakravarti in military power and material resources excelled the other two.[354] Vikramabāhu III ruled for at least eighteen years and his successor was Bhuvanakabāhu V, "whose fifteenth year has been equated with 1929 of the Buddhist era, i.e. 1386."[355] Bhuvanakabāhu V's date of accession was 1371 or 1372 A.D. and this was the fifteenth year of Vikramabāhu III. Alakeśvara (Aḷagakkonāra) established himself as the prominent figure among the Sinhalese. He wanted to control the profitable foreign trade, conducted mainly by Arab seamen, which passed through Colombo and other harbours on the western coast. For this reason he built up his military power and he increased his power in a strategic position in the vicinity of Colombo.[356] Aḷagakkonāra became known as Prabhurāja. Alakeśvara is called Śrī-Lankādhiśvara, "the Lord of Śrī Laṅkā" and he and his brother Arthanāyaka" are eulogised in superlative terms."[357] For about twenty years he occupied an important position in Sri Lankā's political world. He became well-known in Sri Lanka at this time for his military and political activities. He was also a benefactor of the Buddhist Saṃgha and was a great patron of learning. He belonged to the Gaṇavāsi family on the mother's side and he belonged to the Meṇavara family through his father.[358] He died between 1382 and 1392 and Kunāra Alakeśvara (Aḷagakkonāra IV), his son, succeeded him. Kumāra Alakeśvara was a brother of the reigning king, Bhuvanakabāhu V. Vira Alakeśvara (Aḷagakkonāra V), the son of a sister of the great minister, ousted Kumāra Alakeśvara and occupied the throne.[359] Then Vīrabāhu-ādipāda, the younger brother of Vīra Alakeśvara, wanted to capture power from his brother and in a battle fought at Rayigama he defeated his brother Vīra Alakeśvara and became the de facto ruler of the Sinhalese.[360] For the progress of Buddhism he played an important role and Buddhism flourished during his reign. He was a great patron of learning. Most probably, he died in 1396 A.D. Vira Alakeśvara captured power in 1399 and he for twelve years occupied it.[361] It may be noted here that throughout this period of the struggle for power among the people of the Aḷagakkonāra family, Bhuvanakabāhu V continued to remain as the de jure king at Gaṁpala. An inscription dated 1415 mentions his thirty-sixth year, i.e. 1408 A.D. [362]

The next ruler was Parākramabāhu VI. "His long reign was last glorious period of Sinhalese history, with notable achievements in peace as well as in war."[363] Several contemporary writings and official documents of his reign mention dates in the Buddhist and Śaka eras, corresponding to 1410, 1412 and 1415 A.D., as the year of the accession of Parākramabāhu VI.[364] Of these, most probably 1410 was the date on which he first intimated the assumption of sovereignty, in 1412 he came back from China with the seals of his office and in 1415 he defeated all his enemies and he had consecrated himself.[365]

He had been crowned at Rayigama. He stayed three years at that place and then he made Jayavardhanapura or Koṭṭe his capital. He constructed a new palace and erected a Temple of the Tooth-Relic at Koṭṭe. He was a devout Buddhist. His efforts were responsible for the progress of Buddhism and Buddhist Saṃgha in Sri Lanka. Under his patronage a number of poets and scholars flourished and their works throw light on his reign. During his reign many religious edifices were built. He supported the Buddhist Saṃgha and many religious institutions. He was a religious person and he received the epithet of Bodhisatvāvatāra.[366] His reign may be mentioned as an important period in the history of Buddhism. He offered grants to Brāhmaṇas and his raputation as a liberal patron helped to draw to Sri Lanka a learned Brāhmaṇa from Bengal.[367] Parākramabāhu VI was one of the greatest kings of island. His reign may be mentioned as an important period in the history of Buddhism. He earned the love and respect of his subjects and he died at a ripe old age after a reign of fifty-five years.[368] According to scholars, he ruled from A.D.1412 to 1468 A.D.[369] His long reign was free from internal trouble but towards its close the ruler of Udaraṭa tried to disturb his reign.[370] Most probably, the sons of Parākramabāhu VI predeceased him or it was the custom in the family to continue the succession through females. A son of his daughter Ulakuḍaya-devī was selected for the succession.[371] In the thirty-fifth year of Parākramabāhu VI the son of Ulakuḍaya-devī was born. Therefore he was twenty years of age when he occupied the throne. He took the title of Jayavīra Parākramabāhu, but he became known as Jayabāhu (the second).[372] He had a brief reign.

From the tradition it was known that prince Sapumal reached Koṭṭe from Jaffna when he knew the accession of Jayabāhu II and the latter was killed by him and he himself occupied the throne as Bhuvanakabāhu VI.[373] A Sinhalese poem composed in his reign says that the third year of Bhuvanakabāhu VI was 2015 B.E. i.e., 1472 or 1473 A.D.[374] According to the Rājāvaliya, he ruled for seven years. But an inscription of his gives the eighth regnal year.[375] Several scholars inform that Bhuvanakabāhu VI reigned from A.D. 1470 to 1478.[376] "Possibly the Rājāvaliya has given only the number of completed years, without taking into account the year current at his death or it has given the actual number of years he ruled after he assumed power at Koṭṭe, which the official document counted his regnal years from the death of Parākramabāhu VI, treating him as that king's legitimate successor and omitting Jayabāhu II from the list of Kings".[377] Bhuvanakabāhu VI's reign was a troubled one. The entire country between the Kalu Gaṅga and the Valare Gaṅga under the leadership of two leaders, Śrīvardhana Patirāja of Kalani-dola in Pasdun Korale and the Lord of Kuragama revotled and declared war against him.[378] This revolt is called Siṃhala-peraḷiya (the revolt of the Sinhalese) in the Rājāvaliya and Siṁhala-saṃga (the Sinhalese war) in the Dādigama inscription.[379] "It was an upsurge of national sentiment in opposition to a ruler who, on his father's side, was of non-Sinhalese extraction."[380] The revolt had broken out before the sixth year from the coronation of the King. The latter imprisoned the two rebel leaders. Buddhism flourished in Sri Lanka at that time. The reputation of the Buddhist Saṃgha became well established in Sri Lanka. In 1476 A.D. King Dhammaceti of Myanmar sent twenty-two Buddhist monks to Sri Lanka to obtain ordination and to bring back the tradition of Sri Lanka to Myanmar.[381] He sent these Buddhist monks with presents and two ministers, citradūta or Rāmadūta took charge of them. King Bhuvanakabāhu VI received these deputation and he gave a reception. He ruled at Koṭṭe, six miles from Colombo. These Buddhist monks from Myanmar were ordained in the sīmā in the Kalyāṇī river near Colombo. After their ordination they went back to Myanmar from Sri Lanka. At this period Sri Lanka and Myanmar came very close to each other. It brought good results no doubt. Many books that kept in Sri Lanka were taken to Myanmar, Thailand and Cambodia and these countries established the Mahāvihāra Nikāya there. At the subsequent period when the ordination had disappeared in the island and the books were lost, then Sri Lanka got back the books and the ordination. According to the advice of the king of Sri Lanka the twenty-four prominent and well-ordained monks such as Dhammakitti Mahāthera, Vanaratava Mahāthera, Paṃcaparivenavāsīmaṅgala thera and Sīhlarāja-juvarājacarriyathera formed a chapter under the leadership of Mahāthera Vidāgama and the monks of Myanmar received the Sinhalese form of the upasampadā ordination from these monks within a consecrated boundary on the Kalyāṇī river near Colombo. It took four days to confer the upasampadā ordination on all the forty-four theras from Myanmar from July 17 to 20, 1476 A.D.[382] King Bhuvanakabāhu VI conferred titles on the theras of Myanmar. He then invited the monks of Myanmar to a meal and he gave many gifts to each of them. Myanmar established direct contact with the Mahāvihāra fraternity in Sri Lanka. Under royal patronage the Sīhala Saṃgha was established in Myanmar. It may be noted here that the reigns of Parākramabāhu VI and Bhuvanakabāhu VI were important periods in the history of Buddhism in Sri Lanka. These two rulers were zealous Buddhists and they showed keen interest in the affairs of Buddhism. Under their patronage not only Buddhism prospered but the Buddhist Saṃgha of Sri Lanka was well-established at that time. King Parākramabāhu VI erected a shrine and a collage for monks in the Pappata Grove and named it the Sunetrā Devī Parivaṇa after his mother.[383] Under his patronage the Tīpiṭaka with Aṭṭhakathā and tike were inscribed and he granted villages to scribes who gave their services.[384] Several educational institutions were established at this time. There were the Padmāvati Parivaṇa at Kavagala under the presidency of Rājaguru vanavatam Saṃgharāja, the Āranayaka at Paṭabatgila, the Vijayabāhu Pariveṇa at Totagamuva under Srī Rāhula, the Irugalkula Pariveṇa at Mulgirigala and Srī Gaṇānanda Pariveṇa at Rāyigama under Maittreya Mahāthera of the Mahā Netra vihāra.[385] The Saṃgharāja of Parākramabāhu VI was Vanaratana Mahāsāmi.[386] Parākramabāhu VI patronised Buddhist scholars and religious institutions in his Kingdom. His reign witnessed regular religious intercourse with neighbouring Buddhist countries in South-East Asia. Like Parākramabāhu VI, Bhuvanakabāhu VI also was a great patron of Buddhism and Buddhist scholars. They played important roles for the progress and development of Buddhism in the island. Most probably, because of the flourishing condition of Buddhism and of the existence of several well-organised educational and religious institutions in Sri Lanka, many Buddhist monks from foreign countries used to come to Sri Lanka to study Buddhism, Buddhist literature and Buddhist philosophical works under the able guidance and supervision of the Buddhist scholars in Sri Lanka during the reigns of Parākramabāhu VI and Bhuvanabāhu VI of Sri Lanka.

The Portuguese arrived in Sri Lanka in the beginning of the sixteenth century A.D.[387] At this time there were three kingdoms in the island, Koṭṭe, Kandy and Jaffna. The full name of the kingdom of Kandy was Kaṇḍa Udarata, the country of the hills. The Portuguese referred it to Caṇḍea, and used that name for both the kingdom and the capital Seṇkadagalanuwara.[388] Among the three kingdoms, Koṭṭe was the most important one. But suzerainty of Koṭṭe over the other two was only nominal.[389] After their arrival in Sri Lanka, the Portuguese first established contact with the ruler of the kingdom of Koṭṭe, Vīra Parākramabāhu VIII was the king of Koṭṭe. He was also known as Jayavīra Parākramabāhu and he reigned for three years.[390] The Rājāvaliya says that he ruled for twenty years. According to scholars, Parākramabāhu VIII's reign must have lasted for more than twenty years.[391] His sons and successors were Dharma Parākramabāhu IX and Vijayabāhu VI. Their respective reigns began in 1508 A.D. and 1510 A.D.[392] They reigned in Koṭṭe. Among the sons of Vijayabāhu VII (A.D. 1509-1521) this Kingdom was divided in A.D. 1521. Bhuvanakabāhu, Māyādunve and Madduma Bandāra were his three sons.[393] Bhuvanakabāhu VII (1534-1551 A.D.) reigned in Koṭṭe. He received the capital city of Koṭṭe. Māyādunne received Sītāwaka and Madduma Baṇḍāra ruled in Rayigama.[394] But the latter died shortly after his accession to the throne. Bhuvanakabāhu VII wanted to maintain his position against the aggressive policy of his brother Māyādunne and for this reason he made pact with the Portuguese and he took their help. Māyādunne established his contact with the ruler of Calicut who was busy in war with the Portuguese at that time.[395] Bhuvanakabāhu VII had no son. His successor was his grandson and he was the son of his daughter Samudradevī.[396] Mahā Baṇḍāra was the name of his grandson. In Sri Lanka's history he was known as Dharmapāla (A.D. 1551-1597).[397]

Parākramabāhu II and his successors until about the fifteenth century A.D. tried to maintain the political stability of the island but towards the end of that century it began to weaken. The Sinhalese king who reigned at Koṭṭe at this time was the leader of a very small territory. Several petty chief who controlled the country's internal regions had no faith in the religion and did not turn their attention to do something for the welfare of the country and of the people. The trade of the coastal regions was controlled by the moors. The country's economic condition was very bad. Food production was not very good and the island took the help of India to send food for its people.[398] Such was the economic and political condition of Sri Lanka when the Portuguese landed in Sri Lanka in 1505 A.D. Towards the close of the reign of Vira Parākramabāhu or Parākramabāhu VIII (1484-1508 A.D.) the Portuguese first arrived in Sri Lanka and their arrival had a great effect upon the Koṭṭe Kingdom and a new era began in the history of Sri Lanka.[399] King Parākramabāhu VIII at that time ruled at Koṭṭe. The Portuguese against his rivals promised to give him military help and in return they wanted great riches from the trade which they wished to do in Sri Lanka. They erected a fortress in Colombo and many trading settlements were established by them. In course of time the entire coastal region came under the control of the Portuguese and the kings of Koṭṭe were at the mercy of their allies. The Portuguese became very powerful at that time. They wanted to bring the whole island under their control and for this reason they attacked the interior regions of the country several times.[400] Gradually they occupied all maritime provinces and they stayed there up to 1658 A.D. They arrived in Colombo in A.D. 1505. The chronicles of Sri Lanka and several historians mention the Portuguese as cruel, inhuman, rapacious, bigoted and savage persecutors of Buddhism in their efforts to establish Roman Catholicism in Sri Lanka.[401] They wanted to impose their faith upon the people of Sri Lanka. Bhuvanakabāhu VII (1534-1551 A.D.) took the help of the Portuguese to ensure the succession of his grandson Dharmapāla to the throne. For this purpose Dharmapāla's ivory image was sent to Portugal where the Portuguese emperor arranged and coronation of the effigy.[402] Then a party of Fransiscans arrived in Sri Lanka with the Sinhalese ambassadors who returned from Portugal. These

Fransiscans under the direction of the Portuguese emperor or with the permission of the king of Koṭṭe began to preach the Christian Gospel in Sri Lanka and for the first time in the maritime provinces of Sri Lanka the Christian Communities were organized.[403] Dharmapāla became a Christian and took the name of Don Juan Dharmapāla in A.D. 1557. After his accession to the throne he gave them a deed of gift and transferred the Daladā Māligāra (i.e. the temple of the Tooth) and the temple of Kelaniya to them and all temple revenues in the island were used for the maintenance of the Christian missionary establishments.[404] The rulers of Koṭṭe gave necessary help to the Portuguese to suppress the progress of Buddhism, the national religion of the Sinhalese, and to propagate their own religion—catholicism. The Portuguese used force to convert the people to their faith. Where inducement failed brutal punishment was given to the Sinhalese people. In order to receive high offices under them and to earn the goodwill of those in power many people of Sri Lanka adopted the new faith and became Christians and they had their new names. But some people were punished who wanted to remain with their national faith and resisted it very much. Many men were thrown into rivers and they were enter by crocodiles. Many babies, children and mothers were tortured to death. Those who wore the yellow rote and offered prayer in public were put to death. Many Buddhist monasteries and institutions were destroyed and the Portuguese took away their treasures. Many libraries were burnt to ashes.[405] During the rule of the Protuguese, Buddhism fell on evil days. Their rule can be mentioned as one of the darkest periods of Buddhism in Sri Lanka. In A.D. 1564 Bayin Naung (A.D. 1551-1581) of Pegu in Myanmar sent a mission to king Don Juan Dharmapāla of Koṭṭe who was then living in Colombo.[406] The king of Myanmar in order to marry a princess of Sri Lanka's royal blood sent ambassadors to the king of Koṭṭe. But the latter was childless. So he sent a daughter to his minister as his own daughter.[407] Many Myanmarese Buddhist monks came to Sri Lanka with the ambassadors and they visited Śri Pada. Then in 1566 A.D. the king of Pegu again sent a mission to the king of Koṭṭe for the Tooth Relic and the mission returned to Pegu with it.[408] A minister of Sri Lanka from the tire of a stag made a tooth just like the genuine one and the king of Koṭṭe sent it to the Peguan King. The latter promised to send him a million of gold and annually a ship laden with rice and other provisions. The king of Pegu and his nobles received this Tooth Relic with great honour.[409] The king of Kandy knew Dharmapāla's contact with the Peguan king, and he also knew that the latter had sent valuable presents to the king of Koṭṭe. The king of Kandy sent ambassadors to the court of Pegu to tell that the princess was not the daughter of the king of Koṭṭe and the Tooth Relic was not the genuine one.[410] He said through his ambassadors that he was the possessor of genuine Tooth Relic and he wanted to give his daughter in marriage to the king of Pegu. The king of Kandy was Karalliyadde Baṇḍāra during this period. He ruled from A.D. 1565 to 1582.[411] The Portuguese source mentions that the king of Kandy claimed that the genuine Tooth Relic was kept under his supervision. He possessed the genuine Tooth Relic. But the relic at this time was at Sītāwaka. The Buddhist monks of Sītāwaka in great secrecy had kept it. The relic was kept hidden in the Labujagāma Vihāra at Delgamuwa, close at Kurnwita in Sabaragamnna in the kingdom of Sītāwaka during the closing years of the reign of Rājasinha.[412] When Vimaladhamma Suriya I (A.D. 1592-1604) had built a temple for the relic, he then took it to Kandy from there.[413]

King Rājasinha I (1581-1592 A.D.) who was the son of Māyādunne, a brother of Bhuvanakabāhu VI, ruled from Sītāwaka when Koṭṭe was under the control of the Portuguese.[414] He was a great warrior. He gained the confidence of the Sinhalese who were against the Portuguese rule and he won several battles against the Portuguese. The battle at Mulleriyawa was the most famous.[415] But his popularity was very short-lived. In his thirst for power, he killed his old father with his own hands.[416] Later, he became nervous for his crime and he was very much afraid for this crime. He then met the Buddhist monks and sought their advice for making himself free from the sin.[417] But the monks told him that it was not possible for them to do anything for this sin. It was a great crime. The king then became very angry. He became a worshipper of Śiva.[418] The Cūlavaṃsa says that Rājasinha I once told the elder Theras, "How can I undo the crime of my father's murder?" They stated him, "To undo the committed crime is impossible."[419] He then became follower of Śaivim. He became an enemy of Buddhism. The Chief Buddhist Elder was stoned to death. Many other monks were buried neck-deep in the earth and there heads ploughed off. The sacred edifices and the monasteries were destroyed and the sacred books were reduced to ashes. The lands which had been given to the monastic establishments in earlier times were taken away, and the king handed over the charge of the Sacred. Foot Print of the Buddha on Adam's Peak to the Śaivites. Many monks in order to escape from the king's wrath disrobed themselves and they left the place.[420] The Cūlavaṃsa describes, "He annihilated the order of the victor, slew the community of bhikkhus, burned the sacred books, destroyed the monasteries....... He placed miscreant ascetics of false faith on the Sumaṇa Kūṭa to take for thousands all the profile accruing therefrom .... At that time through fear of the king, bhikkhus left the order ...."[421] All these facts mentioned above show that the Portuguese were not the only enemies of Buddhism at this period. King Rajasinha I also showed his hostile attitude towards Buddhism. At the end of the sixteenth century A.D. Buddhism had suffered very much and was decaying in Sri Lanka. Both the Cūlavaṃsa and the Sāsanavaṃsa narrate the arrival of the Sinhalese envoys in Rakkhaṅgapura and the restoration of the Buddhist Saṃgha and the re-establishment of Buddhism in the island with the help of the monks of Rakkhaṅgapura.[422]

In 1592 A.D. Rājasinha died. Vimala Dharmasūriya I or Vimala Dhammasuriya I occupied the throne of Kandy and he ruled for twelve years. He was educated by the Portuguese and he was favoured by them. But after his accession to the throne the king worked hard for the country and he played a great role for the progress of Buddhism in Sri Lanka. He was a great patron of Buddhism. He built several Buddhist monasteries and he restored many Buddhist monuments. At that time it was very difficult for him to find a single monk in the island who was properly ordained. He in order to restore ordination in Srī Lanka sent an embassy to the country of Rekkhaṅga (Arakan in Myanmar).[423] In the last quarter of the sixteenth century A.D. in Sri Lanka the number of the ordained monks had decreased very much and it was not possible for Vimaladhamma Suriya to find five monks to form a chapter for properly constituted acts of the Buddhist Saṃgha. The king wanted to purify and to strengthen the religion sent ministers to the Rekkhaṅga country. The king invited Nandicakka and other Theras of the Rekkhaṅga country to come and to settle in Srī Lanka.[424] When they arrived they were received with great honour. Under the leadership of Nandicakka, the upasepadā ordination was held in the udakukkhapasīnā on the Mahāvalukagaṇga or the Mahāvali Gaṅga at Getamba near Peradeniya in A.D. 1596.[425] Several members of the royal family and noble families were ordained. Thus the upasepadā ordination was restored in Sri Lanka with the help of the Buddhist monks from the Rakkhaṅga country. King Vimala Dhamma Suriya I built a storyed pavilion and brought back the Tooth Relic from the Delgamu-vihāra where it was hidden and deposited it in the pavilion. He took the control of Srī Pāda from the Saivites and gave it to the Buddhist monks.[426] An ola leaf manuscript was found and it informs that "Buddhism in Sri Lanka was crumpled under the weight of the hostile attitude of Rājasinha towards Buddhism".[427] This document was found at the Kaḍadora vihāra which is located in the Gannava Korale of Uḍahavāhata in the district of Nuvara Eliya in the Central Province. Guṇālavikāra Dharmakirti Bhuvanakabā was the donor of the grant and mentions the repairs of the Kaḍadora vihāra after the death of King Vimaladhamma-Suriya II (A.D. 1687-1707). The grant was donated after A.D. 1707. This old leaf manuscript describes that under the supervision of the Buddhist monks of the Rekkhṅga Country, the upasepadā, ordination was held in Sri Lanka and Candavilāsa Nandicakka acted as their āceriya and upejjhiya represently.[428] Thus from this account it was known that during the sixteenth Century A.D. a strong religious tie existed between Sri Lanka and Arakan in Myanmar.

Vimaladhamma Suriya I was succeeded by senarat on the throne of Kandy.[429] He was a religious person. He contributed very much to the development of Buddhism. The Portuguese in his reign attacked Kandy and the king took away the Tooth Relic to Mahiyangana for its safety.[430] Rājasinha II (1634-1687 A.D.) was Senarat's son and successor.[431] He was a great warrior. He took the help of the Dutch for his war against the Portuguese. The Portuguese rule in the maritime provinces of Sri Lanka came to an end in his reign. He drove out the Portuguese from Sri Lanka in A.D. 1658 with the help of the Dutch.[432] The Dutch expelled the Portuguese and captured the Portuguese regions in Sri Lanka and they brought them under their control for 138 years.[433] From the king of Sri Lanka they got the full rights of the Cinnamon trade and they did their business very well. Their attitude towards the people of Sri Lanka was very friendly. During their rule the Sinhalese kings and their people worked for Buddhism and performed many religious acts. It may be noted here that in 1602 A.D. the Dutch visited the court of Kandy. In the reign of Vimaladhamma Suriya I they sought an alliance. In 1612 A.D. in the reign of king Senarat of Kandy a treaty was signed and was agreed upon between the Dutch and the king of Senarat.[434] Because of this agreement in 1638 A.D. Rājasinha II sought the help of the Dutch against the Portuguese.[435] From that time the Portuguese and the Dutch fought each other. They engaged themselves in bitter struggle to gain supremacy over the other and in 1658 A.D. the Dutch were able to expel the Portuguese from the island and after expelling them they occupied those regions which the Portuguese used to occupy and they stayed there up to 1796 A.D. In that year the British overthrew them from those places. The British drove them out from the island in A.D. 1796.[436] The Dutch people were the Protestant Christians. There was a great difference between them and Portuguese people. The Dutch wanted to do business in Sri Lanka. Their aim was to extend commerce. For this reason they need peace in the island. They tried to establish friendly relation with the Sinhalese people. They even helped the Sinhalese to send two missions to Siam (Thailand) and these missions were sent to get monks to establish higher ordination in Sri Lanka.[437] "The Dutch, however, had an established system of education throughout their territories. The school building was both church and school, the schoolmaster was both teacher and the representative of the religion. Services were held regularly at these places; births and marriages were registered according to Christian rites. When the agent of the church was so disposed, he was able to get those who did not attend church punished for the alleged offence. All civil rights and inheritance depended on a person's church affiliation. No person who was not a Christian could hold even a minor office under government, no person who was not a Christian could get married legally or register the birth of a child. There was, however, one redeeming feature of this system. The organization was so extensive that they had to employ Sinhalese as their teachers and agents of religion. The vast majority of these Protestant agents were at heart Buddhists, they were Christians only in the sense of their office. The people themselves followed their plan, they were Buddhists inwardly but were officially Christians, for the purpose of registering their marriages, the births of their children, for holding office etc. Thus the efforts of the Dutch in the propagation of their religion did not affect Buddhism much. On the other hand the Portuguese, where they had priests and where they had established churches under the direct control of these priests, were able to look after the congregations and gradually established their religion in such centres. Most of them were zealous and earnest in their duties and took a genuine interest in the welfare of their flocks."[438]

After Rājasinha II his son Vimaladhamma Suriya II (1687-1706) occupied the throne of Kandy.[439] He was a great patron of Buddhism. He erected a three storeyed pavilion for the Tooth Relic in Kandy. The king also on foot went to Sumanakūṭa (Adam's Peak). He was not very happy to see condition of the Buddhist Saṃgha in Sri Lanka. In the whole country not more than five ordained monks were found. The maritine districts of Sri Lanka were under the rule of the Portuguese and later the Dutch. Because of foreign rule Buddhism and its practices had suffered very much in Sri Lanka. The seventeenth century saw the establishment of the Buddhist Saṃgha in Sri Lanka by the monks of the Rakkhanga country.[440] The king sent an embassy to Rakkhaṅgapura (Arakan) and obtained monks from that country for an ordination ceremony. At his request ten monks from Rakkhaṅgapura arṛived in Sri Lanka. With their help an ordination ceremony was held at Getambe in Kandy. At this place a similar ceremony was held formerly in the reign of Vimaladhamma Suriya I. Thirty-three novices received their upasampadā ordination at the hands of the Buddhist monks from Rakkhaṅgapura at this ceremony. About one hundred and twenty persons were admitted to the Buddhist Saṃgha at this ceremony also. Thus with the help of the Buddhist monks from Rakkhaṅgapura, the upasampadā ordination was received in Sri Lanka for the second time.[441]

Sri Viraparākrama Narendrasinha (1706-1739 A.D.) a son of Vimaladhamma Suriya II, ascended the throne of Kandy. The former patronized Buddhism. He played a great role for the welfare of the religion. He built a two-storeyed building for the Tooth Relic. Many Buddhist laity joined the Buddhist Saṃgha during his reign. Many monks had resorted to scandalous practices in his reign.[442] Saramankara was a prominent figure in the history of Buddhism in Sri Lanka. He requested Sṛī

Vīraparākrama Narendrasinha to send a religious mission to Siam (Thailand) to bring Buddhist monks to Śrī Lankā. But the king ignored his request and he died after some time.[443]

The next ruler was Sri Vijay Rājasinha (1739-1747 A.D.).[444] He was a devout Buddhist. Many young persons entered the Buddhist Saṃgha in his reign. The king inspired them to do so. Several religious festivals were held. He showed his interest in the scholarly works of the monks. Scholastic activities in his reign were revived. He spent money for writing religious books and he built many preaching halls at several places of his kingdom. He also took measures to educate the people in the doctrine. He also discovered that the Buddhist Saṃgha in the island was almost extinct. For this reason he sent two missions to Siam (Thailand). The Dutch lent a ship for the voyage. Owing to shipwreck, the first expedition proved disastrous and the king died before the second mission returned. So his efforts for the restoration of the higher ordination in Sri Lanka were not successful. The king tried to restore it and to establish Buddhism in its former purity. But his efforts failed.[445] His reign saw religious ties between Sri Lanka and Thailand.

Kirti Srī Rajasinha (1748-1778 A.D.) ascended the throne of Kandy after Sri Vijaya Rājasinha.[446] His reign was one of the most inspiring periods for Buddhism in that century. He saw that the order of monks had sunk to a very low level of degeneracy. There was not a single monk in the whole island who had received the higher ordination. There were many novices but the majority of them led a life which was unbecoming to monks. They did not study the Dhamma and the Vinaya, but they took interest in the study of astrology, medicine and devil worship. They led scandalous lives and they remained busy in cultivation of land and in trade. The older sāmaṇeras ordamed only the sons of their relatives so that they could receive the immense wealth which many kings and ministers had given to the Buddhist Saṃgha.[447] King Kirti Srī Rājasinha determined to put an end to this state of affairs. The king sent an embassy to king Mahā Dhamarāja II or Dhammika (or Boromokot) of Siam (Thailand). The Dutch gave a vessel for the voyage. The king of Sri Lanka wanted Buddhist monks from Thailand for the re-establishment of the higher ordination in Sri Lanka. Several hundred persons were ordained. With the help of the Buddhists monks from Thailand, king Kirti Śrī Rājasinha purified the Buddhist Saṃgha and re-established the upasampadā ordination in Sri Lanka.[448] The Cūlavaṃsa says, "King Kirti Śrī Rājagiuha was mindful of the purity of the order. Amongst the Bhikkhus who were formerly present on the splendid island of Laṇkā, and amongst all the sāmaṇeras who had undergone the ceremony of world renunciation, were some who had fear of evil, respected the true doctrine, living in good moral discipline, in pure fashion. Others cherished evil, were of bad moral living, followed false doctrine, took pleasure in the maintaining of women and children and in domestic duties and devoted themselves to unseemly professions such as astrology, medical activity and the like. When the rulers heard findings of such unprincipled bhikkhus he sought out with care from among the pious bhikkhus who were on the side of the high principles...... with the reflection that this was the right thing to do, the ruler with his support, ordered according to precept, an investigation, took strong measures against them and had them seriously admonished that from now onwards those who had renounced the world should for ever avoid unseemly task, like astrology, medical activity and the like and should foster the study of the words of the Buddha. As the king was minded to further the order which had fallen into decay, he strengthened the influence of the high principled and in many ways gave the Order support. The ruler was appalled at the thought that with the lack of bhikkhus on whom the ceremony of admission to the Order had been performed, the pure Order of the victor should persist on the whole island and with the reflection: if a ruler like myself carried on the government in the island of Laṇkā, then the Order of the victor, ought not to perish .... further with the reflection: the furtherance of the Order which was not attained in the time of the former rulers in spite of their sending hither and thither for bhikkhus, this will I now bring to pass, the ruler of men, the Monarch, rich in merit, since he derived a continuance of the Order of the great Seer, when the year two thousand two hundred and ninety-three after the final nirvāna of the Prince of the Wise[449] had come .... sent messengers to whom he gave besides gifts of many kinds and many sacrificial articles, a splendid royal letter, to the superb town of Ayojjha, to fetch hither sons of the Buddha."[450] According to the Cūlaraṃsa, Dhammika was the king of Siam (Thailand).[451] It says that the king of Thailand sent a chapter consisting of a group of ten monks to Sri Lanka.[452] There were three ambassadors who came with them from Thailand. The king of Thailand sent a golden image of the Buddha, a superb golden book, a magnificent royal letter in Pāli and gifts of various kinds to the king of Sri Lanka who gave them a warm welcome when they arrived is Sri Lanka in A.D. 1753. King Kirti Śrī Rājasinha sent palanquins fitted with cushious and mattresses as well as a supply of robes of fine cloth, with sweetmeats and rice cakes for them. He also sent several elephants to go in front of the procession, and a group of trumpeters, drummers and other musicious. Ehelapola, Mahā Adikarama; Aṅgammana, Dissave of Matale; Hulangamuva, Dissave of uda Palata; Ellepola Kahande Mahottala, the Kodituwakku Lakama; Ellepola Mohottala, the Vedikkara Lakāma; Kahande Mohottala, the Kuruwe Lakama; Wiyalla Mohottala, Muhandiram, who was in charge of the Gabadagāma of Madulu and Harasgāma Muhaṇḍirām Rala, of the Vedikkara Lakama took part in the procession.[453] "From the sea as far as superb Sirivaddhanapura he (the King of Srī Lanka) had the road put in order and rest houses erected in many places. Then the ruler sent forth the Mahāsanāpati and dignitaries and made them fetch in the right order the golden image and the sacred books, the bhikkhu community and everything else. When with great pomp and great ceremony they making their way had reached the vicinity of Mahāvālukagṅgā which comes down from Sumanakūṭa, the ruler of the town Siriraddhana, the ruler of men desirous of gaining the reward accruing from the festive reception of the three sacred objects (a golden figure of the Buddha (Buddha), sacred books (Dhamma) and the Bhikkhus with upāli at the head (Saṃgha), the highly famed great king intent on merit, went forth with army in piety to meet them with elephants, steads and so forth. He showed revenues to the august Grand thera and to the others and at the same time greeted the great community. Having exchanged with them in the best way possible the customary speeches of welcome, he came with the three sacred objects at the head, to his town. In the fair Pupphārāma (Flower monastery, the now so-called Maharatuvihāra situated immediately on the lake of Kandy), in a graceful brick-roofed building erected by him, in this decorated monastery he the august community of monks take up their abode. Then he provided them in fitting manner with the necessaries and charged official to enquire day by day after their health or ill-health. The ruler of men accepted the splendid royal letter sent by the king of Ayojjha and he made the royal envoys who had arrived and other officials take up their abode in a fitting place and showed them all the distinction to which they were entitled."[454] The monks from Thailand stayed at the Malawatte vihāra in Kandy. Here lodgings had been newly erected and orders were given to provide them with all necessaries. After their arrival in Kandy Upāli Mahāthera gave upasampadā ordination to one of the sāmaṇeras who had accompanied him from Thailand. The king of Sri Lanka played a key role for the restoration of the upasampadā ordination in Sri Lanka. At the end of the ceremony Upāli Mahaithera and other monks worshipped the sacred Tooth Relic and the sixteen sacred places.[455] The Cūlavaṃsa also says that king Dhammika of Thailand again sent a group of more than ten monks to Sri Lanka for the furtherance of its Saṃgha.[456] Their leaders were Visuddhacariya and Varamuni and they stayed at Malawatte vihāra in Kandy. King Kirti Śri Rājasinta was very much happy to see the timely help of the king of Thailand. The latter sent monks to Sri Lanka twice and also sent books of every kind which were not found in Srī Lanka. The king of Sri Lanka in return also sent valuable presents such as a model of the Tooth Relic fashioned out of a costly jewel, a shell curved towards the right (such shells are very rare and precious and their possessor is supposed to be exceedingly lucky) and also various other things to the king of Thailand. Thus the Kirti Śrī Rājasinha purified the Buddhist Saṃgha in Srī Lanka with the help of monks from Thailand. At that time the Siyāma sect or the Siyāmagāma sect was established in Srī Lanka. This was no doubt an important event in Sri Lanka-Thailand relation. From the eleventh century onwards Srī Lanka and its Buddhist Saṃgha made a great contribution to the history of Buddhism in South-East Asia. But in the Eighteenth Century A.D. Thailand gave help to Srī Lanka and its Buddhist Saṃgha for the purification and the development of Buddhism in Srī Lanka. In this way Thailand repaid its religious debt which it owed to Sri Lanka. King Kirti Śrī Rājasinha proclaimed for the guidance of the Buddhist monks of Sri Lanka a code of conduct (Katikāvata).[457] The king was a devout Buddhist. He patronized Buddhism for its progress in his kingdom. In all his religious activities he was helped and guided by a sāmaṇera "who was distinguished for his piety, enthusiasm, learning at determination".[458] He was Velivita Piṇḍapātika Śrī Saraṇan Kera. He was a sāmaṇera when king Vimaladhamma Suriya II reigned. The king was very much happy to see his great devotion to Buddhism. The king made a gift casket set with seven hundred gems and presented it to Saraṇankera Sāmaṇera, with many books.[459] The king also inspired him to write several literary works. When king Śri Vijaya Rājasinha ascended the throne he also gave helpful services to the king for the progress of Buddhism in Sri Lanka. At his request king Vijaya Rājasinha sent two religious missions to Thailand. In the reign of king Kirti Śrī Rājasinha Velinita Śrī Saraṇakera played a great role in Sri Lanka for the revival of Buddhism in the country. He co-operated the king in his religious activities. The king for guidance, advice and inspiration very much depended upon him. According to his advice the king sent embassy to Thailand and he himself wrote the messages that were taken to the king of Thailand and the Saṃgharāja of Thailand. At his advice the king chose the ministers who went with the religious missions to Thailand. It was because of his great efforts the mission was successful.[460] After the return of the embassy Saraṇankara Sāmaṇera was given higher ordination and he was appointed Saṃgharāja of Sri Lanka.[461] His activities had helped very much to restore the higher ordination and the purity of the Buddhist Saṃgha in Sri Lanka. He inspired the scholars of the literary world of Sri Lanka to study the Pāli language and the Buddha's teachings. Thus his efforts brought about a literary revival in the island. He himself compiled several religious works such as the Muniguṇālaṅkāra, a sinhalese poem in praise of Buddha, the Sārārtha Sangraha, a work on various doctrinal teachings in Buddhism, the Abhisambodhi-alaṇkāra, a Pāli poem on the life of the Buddha from the time of Dipaṅkara up to his enlightenment, the Madhurārtha Prakāsamī and the Rūpamālā, a work on Pāli grammar.[462] He died in 1778 A.D. at the age of 81. The successors of Śrī Saraṇankara Thera belonged to the Syāmopāli Nikāya, now called the Siyam (Syāma) Nikāya.[463] Those who belonged to the highest caste they had the right to receive higher ordination in that nikāya. In the year 1799 a samaṇera named Ambagahapitiya Ñāṇavimalatissa went to Amarapura in Burma (Myanmar) to obtain higher ordination and on his return he established the Amarapura Nikāya in 1803.[464] In 1863 Ambagahawatte Śrī Saraṇankara Thera established the Rāmañña Nikāya.[465] These three nikāyas exist up to this day in Srī Lanka's religious world. There were no doctrinal differences between them.

The next ruler was Rājādhi Rājasiṇha. He was Kirti Śrī Rājasinha's brother.[466] The former was a scholar of Pāli, Sanskrit and Sinhalese. He himself composed the Sinhalese poem Asadisadā-kava.[467] He worked hard for the religion and he took necessary steps to preserve the purity of the Buddhist Saṃgha. He played a great role for the progress of Buddhism in Sri Lanka. His nephew Śrī Vikrama Rājasinha became king of Sri Lanka after him. He was the last king of Sri Lanka.[468] This ruler was always afraid of the intrigues of his Adigar Pilima Talawe and his allies, and in order to forget his sorrows he used to take two much drinks and he was very much cruel towards his enemies. He tortured all his enemies with appalling cruelty.[469] During his reign there was no peaceful atmosphere in the kingdom and these condition did not help Buddhism for its development in the island. In 1796 A.D. during the reign of Rājādhi Rājasinha the Dutch were defeated in battle and than they surrendered their territories to the British and left Sri Lanka.[470] In A.D. 1802 these territories became a British Colony and Sir Fredrick North became the first British Governor.[471] Pilima Talawe, the Adigar of king Sri Vikrama Rājasinha of Kandy, disclosed his plans to ruin the king, to the British governor himself. The king came to know of it and he beheaded the Adigar in 1812 A.D.[472] The next Adigar was Ehelepola. He organized a general rebellion against the king but it was found out. For this reason the king tortured his wife and children cruelly. The king punished all people whom he suspected and there were unrest and disorder in the country.[473] Ehelepola then for help appealed to the British. In January 1815 A.D. the British army invaded the capital city of Senkaḍagala (Kandy) and captured the Sinhalese king. On 2 March, 1815, at an assembly of the Kandyan Chiefs and the Buddhist monks the king was deposed and his dominions were vested in the hands of the British.[474] "Thus ended the glamour of the kingdom of Kandy which had withstood the invasions and attacks of the Portuguese and the Dutch and for some time the English, and thus ended the line of the Buddhist kings of Laṅkā who for 2301 years from the accession of Vijaya in 486 B.C. brought the glory and fame to their country and religion."[475]

In 1796 A.D. the British captured the low country of Sri Lanka and in 1815 A.D. they occupied the Kingdom of Kandy and its territories.[476] Sri Lanka was under the control of the British up to 1947 A.D. and in 1948 A.D. Sri Lanka regained her independence.[477] On 2nd March, 1815 an assembly was held in Kandy and a treaty between the British rulers and the Kandyan chiefs was signed at this assembly. But this treaty the Kandyan chiefs handed over the country to the British and the British promised to protect Buddhism, "declaring its rites and ceremonies sacred and inviolate".[478] In course of time the Sinhalese chiefs and people understood that the British had no respect for Buddhism. The Sinhalese chiefs and the Buddhist monks felt frustrated and unhappy to see their attitude towards Buddhism. They knew that the British had no intention to respect the clause of the treaty relating to Buddhism and they showed their interest to convert the people of Sri Lanka to their own faith. During the early years after the treaty was signed the British governor used to take part in the annual ceremonies of the Tooth Relic and like the Sinhalese things in former times he used to appoint the Chief theras.[479] The Christian missionaries in Sri Lanka and the Christian authorities in England took these ideas badly. They did not like it and soon both practices were dropped and broke their connection with Buddhism and they stayed away from its activities. From A.D. 1847 the Buddhist monks used to elect and to appoint their own chiefs and in A.D. 1853 the Diyawadana Nilame and the chief monks of the Malwatte and the Aṅgiriya monasteries received the custody of the Tooth Relic from the British government.[480] The British government violated the treaty of A.D.1815 and they did not allow the Buddhist to enjoy some of the privileges that were given to the followers of the Christian faith.[481] Even as late as 1850 A.D. no child could be registered legally without previous baptism by a minister of the Christian faith and the clergy was unable to solemnize the marriage of unbaptized individuals.[482] Only those who accepted the Christian faith as their own religion were allowed to receive the government job. This policy of the British had helped them to convert many Buddhists to the Christian faith. Even some of the British governors tried to disrupt the Buddhist organization. They brought about disunity between the monks and the laity and they also won over to their side some of the leading Buddhist monks.[483] The British governors and the British government understood that the conversions were disturbed very badly by the Buddhist monks and as long as the Buddhist monks and the laity remained united they would not be able to meet with great success. So they wanted to bring division in the Buddhist organization. The Christian missionaries received all possible support from the British rulers to do their educational and missionary activities.

Several Christian missionary groups were actively busy in missionary activities in Srī Lanka. In 1792 A.D. the Baptists started their activities in the island.[484] Then the Wesleyan Methodists in A.D.1814, the Americans in A.D. 1816 and the Church of England in A.D. 1818 started the missionary activity in Srī Lanka.[485] They got assistance, encouragement and support to do their works in Sri Lanka from the government. These missionary groups established many missionary schools in different parts of the island. The missionary societies used to manage these schools with the help of the British government and they were partly financed by public funds.[486] Many Buddhist children took their admissions in these schools. They studied there because those were the places where young people got their training for high government offices. During the rule of the British government the temple education became useless. Because it did not give any opportunity to young people to receive necessary qualification for government employment. For this reason, the Buddhist parents sent their children to the missionary schools to get proper training for government job. Each student in these schools used to learn the Christian religion and took part in the morning and evening religious services in the schools. These students were unable to participate in their own religious observances.[487] Every school had its own church. The Christian missionaries criticized the Buddha and the Buddhist practices. They told that Buddhism was a religion of a vulgar people and Christianity was the religion of the civilized people.[488] Gradually the people turned their attention towards the new faith and they began to ignore their own religion. They began to adopt the Chrištion faith and the Christian customs and they took Christian names.[489] The missionaries also opened schools for girls.

Here is given the number of assisted schools in 1886 A.D. in Sri Lanka:[490]

	English	Bi-lingual	Vernacular	Total
Wesley Mission	18	18	170	206
Roman Catholic	25	5	175	205
C.M.S.	28	18	178	224
American Mission	8	9	116	133
Baptist	1	5	32	38
Private	7	5	13	25
Hindu	0	0	5	5
Buddhist	0	1	11	12

The missionaries opened up schools in Sri Lanka to popularize the Christian religion in the country. They also distributed books and pamphlets and they criticized the Buddhist religion and spoke highly in praise of Christianity. They tried to convert the Buddhists to their own religion. They studied Buddhism, the Buddhist literature and the Sinhalese language and they began to write in the Sinhalese language and they criticized the Buddhist religion and praised Christianity. The Christian missionaries went from village to village and met people there. They distributed books and pamphlets and denounced Buddhism and praised their own religion.[491] When the Christian missionaries took active and aggressive roles to propagate their religion in villages and towns and to convert the Buddhists to their faith, the Buddhist monks at that time tried but they failed to give much resistance. On poya (uposatha) days when the villagers came to the temple to offer prayers the Buddhist monks refuted the arguments of the Christian preachers in the course of their sermons, but this attempt was not very helpful. It did not bring any result. In 1860 A.D. a young Buddhist Sāmaṇera (novice) named Mohoṭṭiwatte Gunānanda because very active and challenged the Christian missionaries to come and to talk to him in public debate.[492] This young sāmaṇera got his early education in Christian schools and he knew the Buddha's teachings very well. He visited many villages and made public speeches. In several Christian areas he organized meetings and gave speeches relating to the religion of the Buddha and he challenged the Christian missionaries to face him and to talk to him in open debate. For this reason he became very popular among the people. The people of the island at that time used to like him for his speeches. The Christian clergy accepted the challenge and the two parties met in public debate at Udanvita in A.D. 1866, another at Gompola in A.D. 1871 and last at Pañadura in A.D.1873.[493] The Panadura meeting lasted for a week and it brought a Buddhist re-awakening.[494] The Sinhalese Christians and the Buddhists were present in this meeting. The Ceylon Times sent a special representation to report the proceedings. A complete report was published in English day by day.[495] When this meeting came to an end, it went in favour of the Buddhists. The Buddhist speaker spoke very nicely and gave speeches on the principles and tenets of the Buddhist doctrine. The Christians were defeated by the Buddhists in this meeting. To mark their triumph festivities were held in every temple and in procession in every village the Buddhists carried the effigy of Gunānuda thera.[496] The triumph of the Buddhists at the Panadura Controversy over their Christian adversaries brought a new life in the activities of the Buddhists and it inspired them very much and they then with zeal and enthusiasm worked for the progress of Buddhism in Sri Lanka.[497]

Dr. Peebles, an American scholar, was in Sri Lanka about the time of this Panadura controversy, and on his return to America he published its proceedings in book form.[498] Colonel Henry Steel Olcott, an American, found this report in a public library in America and began to take interest in Buddhism by this report of controversy.[499] After studying the report of the Panadura controversy he understood the importance of the teachings of the Buddha. In A.D. 1880 he arrived in Sri Lanka along with Madame Blavatsky to know a first hand knowledge of Buddhism.[500] He then studied the teachings of the Buddha, accepted Buddhism as his religion and played a great role for the progress of Buddhism and for the improvement of the condition of the Buddhists in Sri Lanka.[501] He inspired and guided the Buddhists to do work for the development of Buddhism in Srī Lanka. Under his instruction the Buddhist leaders in Sri Lanka established the Buddhist Theosophical Society on 17th June, 1880 A.D.[502] The Buddhist monks whole-heartedly supported its foundation. The society's main aim was to establish Buddhist schools in the island and to bring together Buddhist workers in a comparative body without distinction of caste or position. In order to promote the welfare of the Buddhists in Sri Lanka it wanted to do works.[503] There were only three Buddhist schools in Sri Lanka—one at Dodanduwa, another at Panadura, and the third at Bandaragama when Olcott arrived in the island.[504] These schools used to obtain government grants. In 1897 A.D. there were 25 boys' schools, 11 girls' schools and 10 mixed schools and these schools were founded by the Buddhist Theosophical Society.[505] In A.D. 1903 under the management of the society there were 174 schools and about 30,000 children used to attend these schools. In A.D. 1904 there were about 429 schools in the island.[506] For the maintenance of these schools Olcott and his supporters used to visit village after village and requested the people to donate subscriptions. Several leading educationists of his time gave support to make his educational plans a great success. They were C.W. Leadbeater, Bowler

Daly, F.L. Woodward, A.E. Bultjous and Mrs. M.M. Higgins.[507] Ananda and Naluda colleges in Colombo, Dharmaraja in Kandy, Mahinda in Galle, Dharmasoka in Ambalangoda, Visakha in Basantalapitiya and Museus in Colombo are the leading Buddhist schools of the present day.[508] Under the guidance of Olcott and the Sinhalese Buddhist leaders, the Buddhist Theosophical Society bagan to publish newspaper in the Sinhalese language "Sarasavi-Sandarasa in December 1880 and later in English supplement, "The Buddhist."[509] Olcott was a great leader of the Buddhist people. It was because of him the Buddhists of Sri Lanka got right to hold their Buddhist processions and the full-moon day of Vesak was announced as a public holiday.[510] Olcott has created the design of the present Buddhist flag and he requested the Buddhists to hoist it on all important Buddhist occasions in Sri Lanka.[511] The Buddhist registrars of marriages were appointed at the time of marriages by his efforts. The Panadura Controversy and Colonel Olcott's arrival in Sri Lanka had brought a great effect upon the Buddhist world of Sri Lanka. These two events had helped to close down a dark period in Sri Lanka's Buddhism and in its place they brought a new bright era.[512] Olcott died in 1907 A.D. in India.[513] The Sinhalese Buddhists in 1862 A.D. established the first press under the name Lankopakāra Press. Thailand's King donated it.[514] In the same year Mohoṭṭivatte Gunānanda Thera at Koṭahena established the Sarvajña-Sāsanābhivurddhi-dāyakā Press.[515] It was near Colombo. Then the Lakri-Vikirana Press in 1863 A.D. and the Lankābhinavavisruta Press in 1864 were established.[516] Mohoṭṭivatte Gunānanda Thera and Sri Lanka's Buddhists established the printing press to publish books for the study of Buddhism or to give reply to the criticisms of the Christian people. Sri Lanka's learned monks with the help of lay people brought a great revival of Buddhist learning. The Venerable Hikkadure Srī Sumangala founded the Vidyodaya Parivena of Maligakanda in Colombo in A.D.1874 and the Venerable Ratmalāne Sri Dhammāloka founded the Vidyālankāra Parivena of Peliyagoda in Colombo in A.D.1875.[517] Many monks and lay people received education from these two great centres of learning. Many Buddhist scholars for the spread of education established other parivenas in different parts of the country and they also compiled and edited numerous books and in this way they contributed very much to Buddhistic studies. Many foreign scholars visited Sri Lanka to study Buddhism, its culture and its literature and they played a great role to create an interest in these kinsman in the west through their valuable works. Turnour, Tenneut, Childers, Rhys Davids and Geiger contributed very much to Sri Lanka's Buddhist world.[518]

Anagārika Dharmapāla worked hard for the reformation of the Buddhist Saṃgha in Sri Lanka which had fallen into a very low moral state and he also took initiative to revive Buddhism in India. His main aim was to win back the Buddhist sacred places of India for their rightful owners, the Buddhists.[519] Colonel Olcott's speeches and activities had greatly influenced Dharmapāla. In 1883 A.D. a Catholic mob had attacked a Buddhist procession at Kotahena. On seeing this incident Dharmapāla felt frustrated. He was very much disturbed. He then left his Catholic school and in the following year he became a member of the Buddhist Theosophical Society in Colombo.[520] At that time its president was his grandfather. At the age of 20 Dharmapāla got permission from his father to leave home and to lead a brahmacāri life and he wanted to engage himself to do work for the welfare of the Sāsana. From that time he used to stay at the headquarters of the Buddhist Theosophical Society.[521] Colonel Olcott returned to Sri Lanka in 1886 A.D. after a short stay abroad and went from one place to another and collected money for the Buddhist Educational Fund and addressed public gatherings.[522] Anagārika Dharmapāla as his interpreter want with him. At that time he used to work in the Education Department as a junior clerk. But soon he left his job. Because he wanted to spend all his life for the progress of the religion of the Buddha. Gradually Dharmapāla became a good speaker. Sometimes he used to travel throughout the country with or without Olcott. Many times he moved alone and he gave good speeches and the people of Sri Lanka used to like his talk very much. Those were the days when the Buddhists did not like to declare themselves as Buddhists. Because Buddhism at that time was considered as the religion of the uncivilized people. It was the faith of the unurbanised masses.[523] "It was the fashion at that time to become a Christian, to study English and other allied subjects, to adopt a foreign name and to imitate the dress of the foreigners and their customs and manners. Buddhism and Buddhist culture were subjected to ridicule and were the heritage of villagers in the interior."[524] Anagārika Dharmapāla did not like the mentality of the Buddhists. He protected it and criticized the behaviour of the Sinhalese Buddhists. In his public speeches he referred to the mentality of the Buddhists. In newspapers and journals he wrote several articles on this subject and he strongly criticized "the habit of imitating foreigners in religion, names and customs".[525] He mentioned that "this tendency to imitate was a clear manifestation of a lack of the primary element of self-esteam".[526] He also changed his name from David to Dharmapāla. After having his speeches and after reading his articles in newspaper and in Journals the Sinhalese people began to realize that this was not good for the country and for the people to imitate foreigners in names, customs, fashions and in religion. They understood the truth of his philosophy. The people then began to feel for their country, for their religion, for their language and for their customs. Dharmapāla inspired his countrymen so much by his talk and articles in newspapers and journals that there was a great cultural revival in Sri Lanka. In order to guide the destinies of future generations of Buddhists in Sri Lanka many younger men of his time took part in the Buddhist forward movement.[527] Dharmapāla gave helpful services for the revival of Buddhism in Sri Lanka. India and in other parts of the world. He died in India in 1933 A.D. In his last days he entered the Sārana as the venerable Devamitta Dhammapāla Thera.[528]

In the beginning of the twentieth century A.D. the leading men in the Buddhist Community were very much inspired by the activities of Anagārika Dharmapāla and in order to promote Buddhist revivalistic movement an organized body was formed by them. The great personalities were Sir D.B. Jayatillaka, F.R. Senanayaka, Valisinha Harischandra and W.A. de Sīlva etc.[529] They were active members of the Buddhist Theosophical Society of 1880, the Colombo Young Men's Buddhist Association of 1898, the Mahābodhi Society of 1891 and the Ceylon Buddhist Congress of 1918.[530] These Buddhist leaders through these organizations not only united but brought together all Buddhists in Sri Lanka. They inspired them to remain active and requested them to collect funds for educational and other religious purposes and told them to give sound religious and secular education to the Buddhist children and asked them to do social work for the welfare of the country and to uplift the spiritual and moral standard of the people.[531] During this period several literary works were produced. The Vidyodaya and the Vidyālaṅkāra pariveṇas and their affiliated institutions which numbered about 200 had patronized many scholars who in the beginning of the twentieth century edited several canonical and commentarial works.[532] Simon Hewavitarava, the youngest brother of Anagārika Dharmapāla, played an important part during this period.[533] From about 1930 A.D. many monks and laymen have edited and published many texts of Palī Buddhism and on the different aspects of Buddhism they have also compiled many secondary works.[534] Many ancient Buddhist shrines were renovated in Anurādhapura. The Ruwanveli Dāgaba was renovated at this time. The other shrines were also rebuilt. The old city of Anurādhapura has become a sacred city today. The Catholic church and the Commercial sites were shifted from the sacred city and were established in others places.[535] In 1950 A.D. the World Fellowship of Buddhists was formed in order to bring all Buddhist countries together and in the subsequent years several conferences were held.[536] Sri Lanka after a period of British rule of 133 years won independence in 1948 A.D.[537] The Sinhalese leaders worked hard to liberate the country from foreign rule. They led the struggle for liberation from foreign rule and they won it. The Buddhist leaders gave helpful services for the cause of Buddhism and it was because of their activities Buddhism was able to reach the zenith of its glory. The Sinhalese national leaders of the country gained national freedom and from the British rulers they received the charge of the government of Sri Lanka and they were very active to establish Buddhism once more in its right place.[538] Sri Lanka gained its independence in 1948. After that in the island there has been revival of the religion of the Buddha and its Buddhist culture. The western powers occupied Sri Lanka for a very long time.

Sri Lanka was under the control of the Portuguese (1505-1658 A.D.), the Dutch (1658-1796 A.D.) and the British (1796-1947 A.D.) and for this reason Buddhism had suffered very much. It fell on evil days. "They knew little of the past Buddhist tradition of Ceylon (Sri Lanka), but were interested witnesses to the prevalence of that religion on the island. Each power determined its attitude towards it according to its own tradition of dealing with the 'pagan' religion of an oriental people come under its subjection."[539] On seeing the miserable state of Buddhism and the Buddhist Saṃgha in Sri Lanka, several rulers of the island brought Buddhist monks from Myanmar and Thailand for the restoration of the Buddhist Saṃgha in Sri Lanka. With the revival of the Buddhist Saṃgha it has become prominent again and even today it still maintains its position and strength. Once more it has received its rightful place. On the Vesak Full-moon day of 1956, the Buddhists in Sri Lanka and other parts of the world celebrated the Buddha Jayanti.[540] That was the 2500th anniversary of the Buddha's Parinibbāna, "a day specially significant to the Buddhists the world over on account of the tradition that it constitutes half the life span of the Sāsana and that from that year the Dhamma would flourish and spread far and wide."[541] The government of Sri Lanka took active part to commemorate the Buddha Jayanti celebrations. For this reason a committee of leading Buddhist monks and laymen was formed to give advices and instructions to the government on all matters relating to the Buddha Jayanti Celebration.[542] This committee also took interest to translate the Tripiṭaka into Sinhalese and also compile an Encyclopedia of Buddhism in English and one in Sinhalese as well.[543] It also took steps to compile other books dealing with the biography of the Buddha, his teachings and the history of Buddhism. Before the Buddha Jayanti it also completed the renovation of the Daladā Māligawa (the temple of the Tooth Relic) in Kandy and it also planned to reconstruct the Mahiyangana Thūpa.[544] It also gave a substantial grant to the organization which was busy to build a Saṅghārāmaya for the Buddhist monks at the university of Sri Lanka, Pardeniya.[545] A World Buddhist Conference was held in Colombo in 1957.[546] In January 1959 the Vidyodaya and the Vidyālaṅkāra Parivenas became well-known as two Universities.[547] In December 1960, the government of Sri Lanka took over the Private and the Christian schools and now they are managed by the government.[548] In 1966, the four poya days of the month (i.e. Full and New Moon and the two quarter moon days) were made the weak-end holidays, instead of Sundays as in previous times.[549] The government also made a plan to start a new Bhikkhu University in Anurādhapura.[550] Sri Lanka has about seven million Buddhists. About seventy per cent of its present population follow the religion of the Buddha. There are about 6000 Buddhist monasteries in the island and more than 15,000 Buddhist monks live there. Thus it is a Buddhist country. But other religions also exist there side by side. There are Dhamma schools in all the monasteries in the island and Buddhist children get religious lessons there. The Colombo Young Men's Buddhist Association for the students of these Dhamma schools conducts an island-wide examination annually.[551] The children receive free books from the Ministry of Cultural Affairs of the government of Sri Lanka and those who pass these examinations including one on the Dhammapada receive prizes. The Colombo Young Men's Buddhist Association annually spends money for the religious education of children.[552]

NOTES

1. BCPP, 2.
2. *Ibid.*, 3.
3. *Ibid.*, 4.
4. *Ibid.*, 4.
5. *Ibid.*, 4.
6. *Ibid.*, 5.
7. *Ibid.*, 5.
8. *Ibid.*, 5.
9. *Ibid.*, 5.
10. *Ibid.*, 6; HBC, 44.
11. *Ibid.*, 6.
12. *Ibid.*, 6.
13. Mhv. X. 102.
14. HBC, 43.
15. *Ibid.*, 45; Mhv. X. 101-102.
16. *Ibid.*, 45; *Ibid.*, x. 98.
17. HBC, 46.
18. *Ibid.*, 46.
19. *Ibid.*, 49; Dpv. xii, 34-35; Mhv. xiii, 4, 16, 18; BIA, 183.
20. *Ibid.*, 50; *Ibid.*, xii, 40; *Ibid.*, xiii, 18-20.
21. *Ibid.*, 50; *Ibid.*, xii, 53; *Ibid.*, xiv, 22; MN, I, 185.
22. *Ibid.*, 50; BIA, 184.
23. BCPP, 11; HBC, 51; BIA, 184.
24. HBC, 51.
25. *Ibid.*, 52; Dpv, xiii, 7-8.
26. *Ibid.*, 52.
27. *Ibid.*, 52-53; BIA, 185.
28. *Ibid.*, 53; Mhv, xv, 176-AN, 695.
29. HBC, 53.
30. BIA, 185.
31. *Ibid.*, 185; Mhv, xvii, 50.
32. HBC, 57; Mhv, xix, 65.
33. BCPP, 13; BIA, 185.
34. HBC, 58; Mhv, xix, 60-64; BIA, 185-186.
35. HBC, 58.
36. *Ibid.*, 58.
37. *Ibid.*, 58.
38. BCPP, 13.
39. *Ibid.*, 14.

40. HBC, 59-60; BIA, 186.
41. BCPP, 14-15.
42. *Ibid*., 16; BIA, 186.
43. BCPP, 16.
44. *Ibid*., 16; BIA, 186.
45. *Ibid*., 17; *Ibid*., 186.
46. *Ibid*., 17; *Ibid*., 187; HBC, 79.
47. HBC, 79; Mhv, xxv, 2.
48. *Ibid*., 79; *Ibid*., xxv, 17.
49. *Ibid*., 79.
50. *Ibid*., 79.
51. *Ibid*., 79; Mhv, xxv, 103-111.
52. *Ibid*., 80.
53. *Ibid*., 80; Mhv, xxv, 2-4.
54. *Ibid*., 80; Rsv. II, 93.
55. *Ibid*., 80; Mhv, xxv, 1.
56. *Ibid*., 80.
57. *Ibid*., 80; Mhv, xxix, 29.
58. *Ibid*., 80; *Ibid*., xxxii, 35.
59. BCPP, 19-21.
60. HBC, 80; Mhv, xxxiii, 7.
61. BCPP, 22.
62. *Ibid*., 22; HBC, 81.
63. *Ibid*., 22; *Ibid*., 81; Mhv, xxxiii, 37-42.
64. *Ibid*., 22; *Ibid*., 81;
65. *Ibid*., 22; *Ibid*., 81; VbhA, 314-318; AA, 52.
66. HBC, 81-82; Mhv, xxxiii, 100-101; Dpv, xx 45; NKs, 9.
67. BCPP, 22-23.
68. *Ibid*., 23; HBC, 82; Mhv, xxxiii, 78-81; NKs, 10.
69. *Ibid*., 23; *Ibid*., 82.
70. *Ibid*., 23; *Ibid*., 83-84; Mhv, xxxiii, 96; NKs, 10.
71. HBC, 83; Mhv, xxxiii, 95; NKs, 10.
72. HBC, 84.
73. *Ibid*., 84; NKs, 10.
74. *Ibid*., 84; NKs, 10.
75. *Ibid*., 85; Hiuen Tsiang, II, 247.
76. BCPP, 25; BIA, 187-188.
77. HBC, 85.
78. *Ibid*., 85; Mhv, xxxiv, 14.
79. *Ibid*., 86.
80. *Ibid*., 86; Mhv, xxxiv, 59, 66.
81. *Ibid*., 86; *Ibid*., xxxiv, 81.
82. *Ibid*., 86; *Ibid*., xxxv, 6.
83. *Ibid*., 86; *Ibid*., xxxv, 10-11; MT, 640.

84. *Ibid*., 87; *Ibid*., xxxv, 80.
85. *Ibid*., 87; EZ, iv, 287.
86. *Ibid*., 87; Mhv, xxxvi, 31-33, 41.
87. *Ibid*.,90; *Ibid*., xxxvi, 39.
88. *Ibid*., 91; *Ibid*., xxxvi, 38.
89. *Ibid*., 91.
90. *Ibid*., 91; Mhv, xxxv, 40.
91. *Ibid*., 92; *Ibid*., xxxvi, 99-109.
92. *Ibid*., 92-93; *Ibid*., xxxvi, 110-112; Nks, 11.
93. *Ibid*., 93; HIL, II, 352, 354, 355, n.6.
94. *Ibid*., 93.
95. BCPP, 26.
96. HBC, 93.
97. *Ibid*., 94.
98. *Ibid*., 94.
99. *Ibid*., 95; Mhv, xxxvii, 26-30; Nks, 13.
100. *Ibid*., 95; BCPP, 26.
101. *Ibid*., 95; *Ibid*., 26; Mhv, xxxvii, 38.
102. *Ibid*., 95; *Ibid*., 26; *Ibid*., xxxvii, 38-39.
103. HBC, 96.
104. *Ibid*., 96; Dāthā, 301, 302.
105. *Ibid*., 96; Mhv, xxxvii, 102.
106. *Ibid*., 96; *Ibid*., xxxvii, 53-90.
107. *Ibid*., 97; *Ibid*., xxxvii, 92; Dāthā, 340.
108. *Ibid*., 97; *Ibid*., xxxvii, 95-97; *Ibid*., 405-406; Fa-Hian, 106-107.
109. *Ibid*., 97; Dāṭhā, vv. 346, 348, 352.
110. *Ibid*., 97, Geiger, Mhv, tr. Intro. xxxix.
111. *Ibid*., 98; BIA, 189; Fa-Hien, 102, 107.
112. *Ibid*., 98; Mhv, xxxvii, 150.
113. *Ibid*., 98;
114. *Ibid*., 98; Mhv, xxxvii, 203.
115. *Ibid*., 98; *Ibid*., xxxvii, 212-213.
116. *Ibid*., 98; *Ibid*., xxxvii, 243-244.
117. *Ibid*.,98; *Ibid*., xxxviii, 12, 38.
118. *Ibid*., 99; *Ibid*., xxxviii, 14, 17, 42.
119. *Ibid*., 99; *Ibid*., xxxviii, 44-51.
120. *Ibid*., 99; *Ibid*., xxxviii, 61.
121. *Ibid*., 99; *Ibid*., xxxviii, 75-76.
122. *Ibid*., 99; ibid., xxxviii, 61-62; 65-66, 78.
123. *Ibid*., 99; *Ibid*., xxxviii, 58-59.
124. *Ibid*., 100; *Ibid*., xxxix, 1-2.
125. *Ibid*., 100; *Ibid*., xxxix, 10-13.
126. *Ibid*., 100; *Ibid*., xxxix, 15.
127. *Ibid*., 100; *Ibid*., xxxix, 33.

128. *Ibid.*, 100; *Ibid.*, xxxix, 41-43.
129. *Ibid.*, 101; *Ibid.*, xxxix, 44-56.
130. *Ibid.*, 101; *Ibid.*, xxxix, 57.
131. *Ibid.*, 101; *Ibid.*, xli, 1-2.
132. *Ibid.*, 101; *Ibid.*, xli, 28, 30.
133. *Ibid.*, 102; BCPP, 27.
134. *Ibid.*, 102; Mhv, xli, 37-40; Nks, 14-15.
135. *Ibid.*, 102.
136. *Ibid.*, 102; Mhv, xli, 58-60, 62.
137. *Ibid.*, 102; *Ibid.*, xlii, 13; Nks, 15.
138. *Ibid.*, 103; *Ibid.*, xlii, 14.
139. *Ibid.*, 103; *Ibid.*, xlii, 35-37; Nks, 15.
140. *Ibid.*, 103; Nks, 15; HTBSEA, 53.
141. *Ibid.*, 103; Mhv, xlii, 63-66.
142. *Ibid.*, 103; *Ibid.*, xlii, 51-56.
143. *Ibid.*, 104; *Ibid.*, xlii, 43.
144. *Ibid.*, 104; *Ibid.*, xlii, 44-50.
145. *Ibid.*, 104-105; *Ibid.*, xliv, 47.
146. *Ibid.*, 105.
147. *Ibid.*, 105; Mhv, xliv, 75-80.
148. *Ibid.*, 105; *Ibid.*, xliv, 130-140.
149. BCPP, 39.
150. *Ibid.*, 39.
151. *Ibid.*, 39.
152. HBC, 105.
153. *Ibid.*, 105; Mhv, xliv, 146, 148.
154. *Ibid.*, 105; *Ibid.*, xlv, 3.
155. *Ibid.*, 106; *Ibid.*, xliv, 150.
156. *Ibid.*, 106.
157. *Ibid.*, 106; Mhv, xliv, 109.
158. *Ibid.*, 106; *Ibid.*, xlviii, 141.
159. *Ibid.*, 106; *Ibid.*, xlv, 29-31.
160. *Ibid.*, 107; *Ibid.*, xlvi, 6-16.
161. *Ibid.*, 107; *Ibid.*, xlvi, 19-27.
162. *Ibid.*, 107; *Ibid.*, xlvi, 5.
163. *Ibid.*, 107; *Ibid.*, xlvi, 3.
164. *Ibid.*, 107; *Ibid.*, xlvii, 24.
165. *Ibid.*, 107; *Ibid.*, xlviii, 97; xlix, 36; 13.
166. *Ibid.*, 108; ibid., xlvii, 66.
167. *Ibid.*, 108; ibid., xlviii, 16.
168. *Ibid.*, 108; ibid., xlvi, 34-37.
169. *Ibid.*, 108.
170. *Ibid.*, 108; Mhv, xlviii, 71, 72.
171. *Ibid.*, 108; ibid., xlviii, 74.

172. *Ibid.*, 109; ibid., xlviii, 143, 144.
173. *Ibid.*, 109; ibid., 1, 68: Nks, 16.
174. HTBSEA, 55: Nks. 18.
175. HBC., 109; Nks, 16.
176. *Ibid.*, 109.
177. *Ibid.*, 109-110; Mhv, 1, 33-36.
178. *Ibid.*, 110; ibid., li, 50.
179. *Ibid.*, 110; ibid., li, 73-85.
180. *Ibid.*, 110; ibid., li, 52.
181. *Ibid.*, 110; ibid., li, 64.
182. *Ibid.*, 110; ibid., li, 64
183. *Ibid.*, 110; ibid., li, 65-67.
184. *Ibid.*, 111; ibid., li, 69-70.
185. CV, lii, 10; HTBSEA, 55.
186. HTBSEA, 55.
187. HBC, 195.
188. HTBSEA. 56.
189. *Ibid.*, 56.
190. CV, lii, 17; HTBSEA, 56.
191. *Ibid.*, lii, 44; ibid., 56.
192. *Ibid.*, liv, 36; ibid., 56.
193. HTBSEA, 56.
194. *Ibid.*, 56; CV, LIV, 68.
195. BCPP, 39.
196. HTBSEA, 83.
197. CV, lx, 4; HTBSEA, 86: BIA, 190; BCPP, 40.
198. *Ibid.*, lx, 5-6; ibid., 86; ibid., 190; ibid., 40.
199. Sas, 27: GPC, 88; HTBSEA, 86.
200. EZ, II, 242-5; El, xviii, 1925-26, 333; HTBSEA, 87.
201. El, xviii, 331, fn. 3; HTBSEA, 87.
202. Nks (Eng. Tr.), xxxii, 19; HTBSEA, 87.
203. PV, 33-3h; HTBSEA, 87.
204. CV, LX, 8; HTBSEA, 87.
205. GPC, 88; HTBSEA, 87.
206. Sās, 64; HTBSEA, 89.
207. BCPP, 40; BIA, 190.
208. *Ibid.*, 41; ibid., 190; HTBSEA, 89.
209. *Ibid.*, 41.
210. *Ibid.*, 41.
211. *Ibid.*, 41.
212. HTBSEA, 90; CV, lxxviii, 27.
213. BCPP, 41.
214. *Ibid.*, 42.
215. *Ibid.*, 42.

216. *Ibid.*, 42.
217. *Ibid.*, 42.
218. HTBSEA, 90-91.
219. HTBSEA, 92; IA, xxii, 1893, 151.
220. HTBSEA, 93.
221. BCPP, 47.
222. HTBSEA, 96; CV, lxxx, 8.
223. *Ibid.*, 96; Sās, 44.
224. DPRD, 45.
225. *Ibid.*, 46; BCPP, 47; HTBSEA, 96.
226. BCPP, 47; CV., lxxx, 19; CV. Tr., II, 127, II, 2.
227. *Ibid.*, 47.
228. *Ibid.*, 47.
229. DPRD., 46.
230. *Ibid.*, 46; CV. Tr. II, 127, II, 2.
231. DPRD., 46: CV., lxxx, 22-23.
232. *Ibid.*, 46; Ep. Zeyl., I, 9, 132, 24-25; II, 29, 173, 29-31.
233. *Ibid.*, 46; CV., lxxx, 24; *Ibid.*, II, 29, 173, 29-33.
234. *Ibid.*, 46; Ep. Zeyl., I, 9, 131, 21; Ktk. Sng, 31.
235. *Ibid.*, 46.
236. *Ibid.*, 47.
237. *Ibid.*, 47.
238. *Ibid.*, 51; CV., lxxx, 27.
239. *Ibid.*, 51.
240. *Ibid.*, 51; CV., lxxx, 28-29.
241. *Ibid.*, 51.
242. *Ibid*, 56; CV., lxxx, 29; PV, 107.
243. *Ibid.*, 56.
244. *Ibid.*, 56.
245. *Ibid.*, 57; CV., lxxx, 30-31.
246. *Ibid.*, 57; Ep. Zeyl.., I, 14, 180, 6-7.
247. *Ibid.*, 57.
248. *Ibid.*, 58; UCHC; I, II, 846.
249. *Ibid.*, 62; CV., lxxx, 33-34; PV.
250. *Ibid.*, 62; *Ibid*, 107-108, lxxx, 34.
251. PV, 108 RJV: Tr. 52.
252. DPRD, 63; PJV., 108: RJV: 43.
253. *Ibid.*, 63; Ey., lxxx, 42; RJV., 43.
254. *Ibid.*, 63; CV., lxxx, 43-44.
255. *Ibid.*, 64; ibid., lxxx, 45-46.
256. *Ibid.*, 65; ibid., 45-46, 49-50, 51-55.
257. *Ibid.*, 65; ibid., lxxx, 49-50.
258. BCPP, 47.
259. *Ibid.*, 47.

260. DPRD., 90.
261. *Ibid*., 90.
262. *Ibid*., 90; CV., lxxxl, 17-29; PV., 109.
263. *Ibid*., 90; Dal.S., 43-44: RJV., 44-45.
264. *Ibid*., 91; cult.cey.Med.Times, 213-214.
265. *Ibid*., 91; CV., lx, 16; lxxiv, 198; lxxx, 19; CCMT, 213-215.
266. *Ibid*., 91; CV., lxxiv, 100-103.
267. *Ibid*., 91; ibid., lxxiv, 198.
268. *Ibid*., 91.
269. *Ibid*., 91; CV., lxxxi, 31-39; PJV., 109-110.
270. *Ibid*., 91; CV. Tr. 138; JRAS; Cey.Br., NS, VI, 124.
271. *Ibid*., 92; CV., lxxxi, 17, 76-78; Ktk.Sng, 8.
272. *Ibid*., 92; Ktk.Sng., 8.
273. *Ibid*., 92: Nks., 87-88.
274. *Ibid*., 92.
275. *Ibid*., 93; Cv., lxxxi, 17; PJV, 109-112.
276. *Ibid*., 94; RJV., 44; RJV.Tr. 54.
277. CHC, 279.
278. *Ibid*, 279.
279. DPRD., 94; CV., lxxxi, 79; PJV., 112.
280. RJV., 45.
281. DPRD., 94.
282. CHC. 279.
283. DPRD., 103.
284. *Ibid*., 103.
285. BCPP., 48.
286. DPRD., 102; PJV., 111-112: CV., lxxxi, 75.
287. Dmb. A., 30; DPRD., 102.
288. DPRD., 102; Dmb. A., 30.
289. *Ibid*., 102; ibid., 30.
290. DPRD., 103.
291. *Ibid*., 103; CV. Lxxxi.
292. *Ibid*., 103; Sinh. Lit., 148-151: UCR, 1, 86-93.
293. *Ibid*., 103; Sinh. Lit., 148-151.
294. *Ibid*., 103; CV. Lxxxii, 6-7; PJV., 112; Dal. S., 44.
295. *Ibid*., 105; ibid., lxxxii, 8-9: ibid., 112; ibid., 44.
296. *Ibid*., 105.
297. *Ibid*., 105; CV., lxxxii.
298. *Ibid*., 105; ibid., lxxxii, 37-40; PJV., 112-114.
299. *Ibid*., 105; ibid., lxxxii, 28-40; ibid., 114; HVV. 31.
300. *Ibid*., 105; ibid, lxxxii, 41-43; ibid., 115; ibid., 31.
301. DPRD., 105.
302. BCPP., 48.
303. DPRD., 106; CV., lxxxix, 57-59; PJV., 139-40.

304. *Ibid.*, 106; ibid., lxxxix, 51-53; ibid., 139.
305. *Ibid.*, 106-107; ibid., lxxxix, 64-65; ibid., 140.
306. *Ibid.*, 107; ibid., lxxxix, 63, 67-68; ibid., 140.
307. *Ibid.*, 107; ibid., lxxxix, 11: ibid., 138.
308. BCPP., 48.
309. *Ibid.*, 48.
310. *Ibid.*, 48.
311. CHC., 287.
312. *Ibid.*, 287.
313. *Ibid.*, 287.
314. DPRD., 167: PJV; 138, 140.
315. *Ibid.*, 167; CV., lxxxix, 71; RJV., 46.
316. *Ibid.*, 177; Bell, 77-78.
317. *Ibid.*, 177; ibid., 77-78.
318. *Ibid.*, 171.
319. *Ibid.*, 171; Bell, 77.
320. *Ibid.*, 171; Cv., lxxxv, 57-58.
321. *Ibid.*, 175; CV., lxxxiv, 29-31; PJV., 119; Nks., 89.
322. *Ibid.*, 175; ibid., lxxxiv, 26-27; ibid., 119.
323. *Ibid.*, 175; ibid., lxxxiv, 9-10.
324. *Ibid.*, 175.
325. *Ibid.*, 175.
326. *Ibid.*, 176.
327. *Ibid.*, 176.
328. *Ibid.*, 176.
329. *Ibid.*, 177.
330. CHC., 287.
331. *Ibid.*, 287.
332. BCPP., 48.
333. CHC, 288.
334. *Ibid.*, 288.
335. *Ibid.*, 288-289.
336. BCPP., 48.
337. CHC., 289-290.
338. *Ibid.*, 290.
339. *Ibid.*, 290.
340. *Ibid.*, 290.
341. *Ibid.*, 290.
342. *Ibid.*, 290.
343. *Ibid.*, 291.
344. *Ibid.*, 291.
345. *Ibid.*, 291.
346. *Ibid.*, 291.
347. *Ibid.*, 291.

348. *Ibid.*, 291.
349. *Ibid.*, 294.
350. *Ibid.*, 294.
351. *Ibid.*, 297.
352. *Ibid.*, 297.
353. *Ibid.*, 298.
354. *Ibid.*, 299.
355. *Ibid.*, 301.
356. *Ibid.*, 299.
357. *Ibid.*, 301.
358. *Ibid.*, 301.
359. *Ibid.*, 301-302.
360. *Ibid.*, 302.
361. *Ibid.*, 302.
362. *Ibid.*, 303.
363. *Ibid.*, 305.
364. *Ibid.*, 307.
365. *Ibid.*, 307.
366. *Ibid.*, 313.
367. *Ibid.*, 313.
368. *Ibid.*, 313.
369. BIA., 191.
370. CHC., 312.
371. *Ibid.*, 313.
372. *Ibid.*, 313.
373. *Ibid.*, 313-314.
374. *Ibid.*, 314.
375. *Ibid.*, 314.
376. BCPP., 50.
377. CHC, 314.
378. *Ibid.*, 314.
379. *Ibid.*, 314.
380. *Ibid.*, 314.
381. BCPP, 50.
382. HTBSEA., 112.
383. *Ibid.*, 104: CV., xci, 24.
384. *Ibid.*, 104: ibid., xci, 28.
385. *Ibid.*, 104.
386. *Ibid.*, 104.
387. *Ibid.*, 114: PRC., 8.
388. *Ibid.*, 114: ibid., 12, fn. 3.
389. CHC., 316.
390. *Ibid.*, 316.
391. *Ibid.*, 316.

392. *Ibid.*, 316-317: HTBSEA., 114.
393. HTBSEA., 114: PRC., 9.
394. *Ibid.*, 114-115.
395. *Ibid.*, 115.
396. *Ibid.*, 115: CPR., 84-85.
397. *Ibid.*, 115: PRC., 11.
398. BCPP., 52.
399. CHC., 317.
400. BCPP., 52.
401. *Ibid.*, 53.
402. *Ibid.*, 53.
403. *Ibid.*, 53.
404. *Ibid.*, 53.
405. *Ibid.*, 53.
406. HTBSEA., 116.
407. *Ibid.*, 116: JCBRAS, xx, 244-245.
408. *Ibid.*, 116: ibid., 249-250.
409. HTBSEA., 116-117.
410. *Ibid.*, 117: JCBRAS., xx, 251-252.
411. HTBSEA., 117.
412. *Ibid.*, 118: CV., xciv, 11: tr. 228, 1: PRC, 16.
413. *Ibid.*, 118: ibid., xciv, 11-14.
414. BCPP., 54.
415. *Ibid.*, 54.
416. *Ibid.*, 54.
417. *Ibid.*, 54.
418. *Ibid.*, 54: CV., xciii, 10.
419. HTBSEA., 122: CV., xciii, 6-8.
420. HCPP., 55.
421. HTBSEA., 122.
422. *Ibid.*, 122-123: CV., xciv: 15-16: Sas., 27.
423. BCPP., 55.
424. CV., xciv, 15-16: HTBSEA., 123.
425. *Ibid.*, xciv, 17: ibid., 123: BCPP., 55.
426. BCPP., 56.
427. HTBSEA., 123: JCBRAS II, New series, 154.
428. *Ibid.*, 123-124: ibid., II, New series, 154: JCBRAS, III, New series, 74.
429. HTBSEA., 124: BCPP., 56.
430. BCPP., 56.
431. *Ibid.*, 56: HTBSEA., 124.
432. *Ibid.*, 56: ibid., 124.
433. HTBSEA., 124.
434. BCPP., 56.

435. *Ibid.*, 56.
436. *Ibid.*, 56.
437. *Ibid.*, 57.
438. *Ibid.*, 57-58.
439. *Ibid.*, 58: HTBSEA., 124.
440. HTBSEA., 124: CV, xcvii, 10-13.
441. *Ibid.*, 124-125: ibid., xcvii, 10-13: SK., 91: BCPP., 58.
442. BCPP., 58.
443. HTBSEA.,125.
444. *Ibid.*, 125: BCPP., 58-59.
445. BCPP., 59.
446. *Ibid.*, 59: HTBSEA., 125.
447. BCPP., 59.
448. *Ibid.*, 59: HTBSEA., 125: CV., 100, 59-60.
449. HTBSEA., 168: f.n.1: About A.D. 1479 or 1750.
450. *Ibid.*, 168: CV, II, CH. C, 4.
451. *Ibid.*, 168: ibid., I, xxxvii, 180, 17, Sn. 3.
452. *Ibid.*, 169: ibid., C, 71.
453. *Ibid.*, 169.
454. *Ibid.*, 169-170: CV., C., 79-90.
455. *Ibid.*, 171: ibid., C., 128.
456. *Ibid.*, 171: ibid., C., 137-140.
457. BCPP., 60.
458. *Ibid.*, 60.
459. *Ibid.*, 60.
460. *Ibid.*, 61.
461. *Ibid.*, 61.
462. *Ibid.*, 61.
463. *Ibid.*, 61-62.
464. *Ibid.*, 62.
465. *Ibid.*, 62.
466. *Ibid.*, 62.
467. *Ibid.*, 62.
468. *Ibid.*, 62.
469. *Ibid.*, 62.
470. *Ibid.*, 62.
471. *Ibid.*, 62.
472. *Ibid.*, 63.
473. *Ibid.*, 63.
474. *Ibid.*, 63.
475. *Ibid.*, 63.
476. *Ibid.*, 63.
477. *Ibid.*, 63.
478. *Ibid.*, 64.

479. *Ibid.*, 64.
480. *Ibid.*, 64.
481. *Ibid.*, 65.
482. *Ibid.*, 65.
483. *Ibid.*, 65.
484. *Ibid.*, 66.
485. *Ibid.*, 66.
486. *Ibid.*, 66.
487. *Ibid.*, 66.
488. *Ibid.*, 66-67.
489. *Ibid.*, 67.
490. *Ibid.*, 67.
491. *Ibid.*, 68.
492. *Ibid.*, 68.
493. *Ibid.*, 69.
494. *Ibid.*, 69.
495. *Ibid.*, 69.
496. *Ibid.*, 69.
497. *Ibid.*, 69.
498. *Ibid.*, 70.
499. *Ibid.*, 70.
500. *Ibid.*, 70.
501. *Ibid.*, 70.
502. *Ibid.*, 70.
503. *Ibid.*, 70.
504. *Ibid.*, 70.
505. *Ibid.*, 71.
506. *Ibid.*, 71.
507. *Ibid.*, 71.
508. *Ibid.*, 71.
509. *Ibid.*, 71.
510. *Ibid.*, 72.
511. *Ibid.*, 72.
512. *Ibid.*, 72.
513. *Ibid.*, 72.
514. *Ibid.*, 72.
515. *Ibid.*, 72.
516. *Ibid.*, 72.
517. *Ibid.*, 73.
518. *Ibid.*, 73.
519. *Ibid.*, 73-74.
520. *Ibid.*, 74.
521. *Ibid.*, 74.
522. *Ibid.*, 74-75.

523. *Ibid.*, 75.
524. *Ibid.*, 75.
525. *Ibid.*, 75.
526. *Ibid.*, 75.
527. *Ibid.*, 75-76.
528. *Ibid.*, 76.
529. *Ibid.*, 76.
530. *Ibid.*, 76.
531. *Ibid.*, 76.
532. *Ibid.*, 77.
533. *Ibid.*, 77.
534. *Ibid.*, 77.
535. *Ibid.*, 77.
536. *Ibid.*, 77.
537. *Ibid.*, 77-78.
538. *Ibid.*, 78.
539. BIA., 191: BEA., 40.
540. BCPP., 78.
541. *Ibid.*, 78.
542. *Ibid.*, 78.
543. *Ibid.*, 78-79.
544. *Ibid.*, 79.
545. *Ibid.*, 79.
546. *Ibid.*, 79.
547. *Ibid.*, 79.
548. *Ibid.*, 79.
549. *Ibid.*, 79.
550. *Ibid.*, 79.
551. *Ibid.*, 80.
552. *Ibid.*, 80.

2

Mahāyānism in Sri Lanka

In the religious history of South-East Asia, Sri Lanka has occupied a very unique place as a prominent Theravāda country. Here under the patronage of the Srī Lankan rulers Theravāda Buddhism has prospered and progressed to a great extent. From the Chronicles of Sri Lanka we learn that the first traces of Mahāyānism in this country can be found in the third century A.D. during the reign of Vohārika Tissa (214-236 A.D.).[1] In his time a new school of thought known as the Vetulyavāda (Vetullavāda) (Skt. Vaitulyavāda) appeared.[2] The chronicles of Sri Lanka refer to it. This was not long after Mahāyānist doctrines were mentioning by Nagarjuna. Kern and Mironov have stated that the Vaitulya-sūtra is the same as the Vaipulya-sūtra which "is one of the commonest names of the Mahāyānist scriptures."[3] Mironov has given evidence from the Chinese sources to say that the term Vaitulya is older than Vaipulya.[4] From Buddhaghosa's commentary to the Kathāvatthu the Vaitulyas maintain the views that Sakyamuni was not really born in the world of men, that he remained in the Tusita heaven, and only sent a phantom of himself to the world, and the Buddha did not himself preach the law, that Ānaada preached it.[5] According to scholars, the term Vetulyavāda is used to refer to the Mahāyāna.[6] The doctrines of the Vaitulyas mentioned above find their parallel in Mahāyāna works such as the Saddharma-pundarika.[7] The Vaitulyas were possibly known in Sri Lanka earlier, but probably in the time of Vohārika Tissa they became very prominent and made a great influence in the religious history of Vohārika Tissa. In his reign we hear for the first time of a sect called the Vaitulya-vādins or Vitaṇḍavādins. They were followers of the Mahāyāna school of Buddhism. The Mahāvihāra monks in religious doctrine and practice did not like their appearance. They were not welcomed by them. At their request the king ordered a minister named Kapila to inquire into the doctrines of the Vitaṇḍa or Vaitulyavādins. He pronounced that their doctrines do not agree together with the words of the Buddha. The king thereupon "consigned their scriptures to the flames and thus 'illuminated the religion of the Buddha'."[8] In this way the king purified the religion. The Vaitulyas were banished in the reign of Vohārika Tissa. But, again they appeared on the scene and they gained followers at the Abhayagiri monastery. In the reign of king Goṭhābhaya (Meghavaṇṇa Abhaya) (253-266 A.D.) the Dhammaruci monks of the Abhayagiri monastery again accepted the Vaitulyavāda.[9] The king took the side of the Mahāvihāra monks and adopted strict measures against the Vaitulyas. He suppressed the Vetulyavāda or the Vaitulyavada which again asserted itself in Sri Lanka. He burnt their books and banished their teachers from the island. But they again gave troubles to the Mahāvihāra monks. This time they were led by Sanghamitta or Saṃghamitra, an Indian monk and he won the favour of the king. He was king Mahāsena (276-303 A.D.) under his influence the king even destroyed some of the Mahāvihāra buildings. A minister and a queen of the king came forward and suppressed the Vaitulyavāda and saved the Mahāvihāra. Meghavaṇṇābhaya, the minister, persuaded the king to rebuild the Mahāvihāra and the queen requested the king to bring the death sentence of Samghamitta and burnt the Vaitulya books.[10] According to Buddhaghosa, the Vetullakas were called Mahāsuññavādi (Mahāsuññavādi saṅkhātānaṃ Vetullakānaṃ).[11] This view mentions that "the Buddha as such does not take anything (na Bhagavā Kiñci paribhuñjati), but pretends to accept offerings in order to be in conformity with the world (lokānuvattanatthaṃ). Therefore, what is given to him bears no fruit because it is of no help (nirupakārattā)."[12] In the same manner, "they held that the Saṃgha, in the ultimate sense of the term, meant only the path-fruitions (paramatthato maggaphalāneva saṅgho), that there was no Saṃgha apart from the path-fruitions; but "path-fruitions" do not accept anything. Therefore, it is wrong to say that the Saṃgha accepts gifts (dakkhiṇaṃ paṭigaṇhāti) or purifies gifts (dakkhiṇaṃ visodhati) or that the Saṃgha enjoys food or drink. So that nothing can be given to the Saṃgha and nothing whatever given to the Order bears fruit."[13] They also held that "sex relations may be entered upon by any human pair by mutual consent."[14] The Dīpavaṃsa refers to the term Vitaṇḍavāda in place of Vetullavāda.[15] The Mahāvaṃsa mentions the Vetullas who came to Sri Lanka in the third century A.D.[16] The Pāli commentaries [17] mention the Vitaṇḍa-vādins, "evidently dissenting Buddhists, holding unorthodox views with regard to the subtle points in the Dhamma, particularly the Abhidhamma. The Vitaṇḍavādin and the Theravādin both quote the same authorities and name the sūtras of the Tripiṭṭaka, in order to support their positious, the difference being only in the mode of their interpretation." The Nikāyasaṅgrahaya describes that the monks of the Abhayagiri Vihāra were well-known as the Dhammarucikas and they not only accepted but also proclaimed the Vaitulya-piṭaka as the teaching of the Buddha.[18] The heretic Brāhmaṇs called the Vaitulyas composed this piṭaka. In order to ruin Buddhism during the time of Aśoka they wore the dress of Buddhist monks. The monks of the Theriya-nikāya compared their doctrine with the dharma and the Vinaya and they told it as false teaching.[19] They totally rejected it as false doctrine. Because they knew that their doctrine does not agree with the dharma and the Vinaya. The Vaitulya-piṭaka which was brought to Sri Lanka was written in Sanskrit. All Mahāyāna sūtras are in Sanskrit. H. Kern in his Manual of Indian Buddhism stated that the term Vaipulya was commonly used as a designation for the

Mahāyāna systems.[20] Sometimes they are also known as the Vaitulya systems.[21] Asanga's Abhidharma-samuccaya[22] describe that the three terms Vaipulya, Vaidalya and Vaitulya refer to the same thing. Vaipulya is explained by him as Buddhisattva-piṭaka.[23] Both H. Kern and S. Paranavitana have identified the Vaitulyavādins with the Mahāyānists.[24] It may be noted here that "the periods in which the Vaitulyakas were active in Sri Lanka synchronized with the dates of some of the important developments in Mahāyānism in India. Thus the appearance of the Vaitulyakas, for the first time in Sri Lanka during the days of Vohārika-Tissa, took place after the tremendous activities of Nāgārjuna, the great Mahāyāna master, who flourished in India somewhere about the latter half of the second century A.D.[25] Although the Vaitulyakas or the Mahāyānists as an organized body were suppressed by political authorities, under the instructions of the Mahāvihāra, whenever these new elements were active in Sri Lanka, their influence over the ideas and teachings of the theravāda was persistent and irrepressible. As time went on Mahāyāna ideas and practices crept slowly into the theravāda system and were accepted and incorporated into the orthobox teachings without question of their validity".[26] Most probably, the author of the Mahāvaṃsa, when he referred to the word Vetulla, did not think of anything about a particular Buddhist school in view, but he used it to indicate any sect of Mahāyānism that "represented dissenting views and new interpretation not acceptable to the Mahāvihāra."[27] Even today in Sri Lanka any Buddhist who opines new ideas against the accepted beliefs and practices becomes known as a Vaitulya. The term Vetulla or Vaitulya indicates "dissenting" or "different", (secondary derivative form from Vittulya).[28] From a fragmentary inscription found at the Jetavanārāma, belonging to the reign of Mahāsena, we learn that he caused to be deposited in " the five great āvāsas" of the Mahāvihāra, books which evidently contained the doctrines of the Vetullavāda to be read by the inmates of these residences of the orthodox church.

In the time of Silakāla (518-531 A.D.) (522-535 A.D.) (524-537 A.D.) other doctrines were introduced. The Mahāvaṃsa has stated thus: "In the twelfth year (of his reign) a young merchant who had betaken himself from here to Kesipura brought hither from there the (book) Dharmadhātu. The king was incapable of distinguishing truth from falṣehood as the moth which flies to the lamp it takes for gold, when he saw it, believing it to be the true doctrine of the Buddha received it with ceremony. He showed it reverence and honour and placed it in a house not far from the royal palace. Every year he was wont to talk it over the Jetavana-vihāra and there to arrange a festival which he made into a permanent institution, regarding this as a blessing for all beings."[29] In the reign of Silakāla a Vaitulyan book called the Dharmadhātu was brought to Sri Lanka from India and it was kept at the Jetavana-vihāra and venerated. Thus from this time the monks of the Jetavana-vihāra became followers of the Vaitulyavāda.[30] Silakāla most probably had contact with the Mahāyānist in India during the days of his early exile in that country and with great honour he received the Dharmadhātu and he kept it in a house near the palace. He used to take it to the Jetavana-vihāra once a year for a festival which was an annual event.[31] S. Paranavitana describes: "There is hardly any doubt that the Vaitulya sūtra introduced to Ceylon from Benares in Silakāla's reign was a treatise dealing with the doctrine of the three bodies of the Buddha."[32] The 13th Century Sinhalese work the Nikāya Saṃgraha gave Purṇa as the merchants' name and mentioned that the Dharmadhātu was a Vaitulya-sūtra. In also refers to the monks of the Abhayagiri-vihāra with the honours paid to the book.[33] Silakāla in his young days had been a sāmaṇera in Bodh Gaya and probably had some respect and sympathy towards doctrines which reached from the land of his early exile. "Although the title Dharmadhātu as such may not be found elsewhere identically in this form, the word itself is synonymous with the Dharmakāya, the first of the three bodies of the Buddha according to the Mahāyānist Trikāya doctrine. This doctrine was not unknown in mediaeval Ceylon, there is evidence that, in the 10th century, a book named Dharmadhātu was known and held in high esteem."[34] Most probably, the Vaitulya doctrines flourished in the reign of Aggabodhi I (571-604 A.D.) (568-601 A.D.) (575-608 A.D.).[35] A great thera named Jotipāla, who arrived in Sri Lanka from India, defeated the Vaitulyas in a public controversy in the island.[36] The dissenters were led by the fraternities of the Abhayagiri vihāra and the Jetavana vihāra. The Nikāyasaṅgraha narrates that "after this public defeat there were no more converts to the Vaitulya doctrine, and the monks of the two Vikāyas, namely the Abhayagiri and the Jetavana, dismissed pride and lived in submission to the Mahāvihāra."[37] It is known from the records that the heretical teachings "had a following among the ignorant people."[38] From this it may be concluded that "they were considerably in vogue among the masses."[39] Hiuen-tsang, the Chinese traveller, states that the monks of the Mahāvihāra were opposed to the great vehicle while those of the Abhayagiri-vihāra studied both the vehicles and widely diffused the Tripitakas.[40] I-tsing, another Chinese traveller, mentions that in Sri Lanka all belong to the Ārya-Sthaviranikāya and the Ārya-Mahāsaṃghika is rejected.[41]

The reign of Sena I (833-853 A.D.) (831-851 A.D.) witnessed the introduction of the Vajiriyavāda or Vajrayāna in Sri Lanka.[42] for nearly three centuries after the reign of Aggabodhi I the chronicles do not refer to the Vaitulyavāda or any other heretical teaching until in the reign of king Sena I a monk of the Vajraparvata Nikāya arrived in Sri Lanka from India and introduced the Vajiriyavāda in the island. He converted the king to his doctrines.[43] He resided at the Virāṅkura-ārāma in the Abhyagiri-vihāra.[44] The Nikāya Saṃgraha[45] mentions: "During his reign (Sena I) as ascetic of the Vajraparvata Nikāya, clad in the robes of a priest, came to his country from Dambadiva and lived in the dwelling called Viraṅkura. Having presented fifteen Kalandas of gold which he had brought to the cook of the royal household, Girivase Sen by name, he got him to sound his praises to the king, who, hearing of his virtues, just as the grasshopper leaps into the fire taking it for gold, went to the ascetic and being impressed with his secret discourse, which he called a confidential teaching, accepted the false Vajiriya doctrines, and abandoning the true doctrines, such as the Ratnasūtra, which shine forth in power extending over a 100,000 crores of worlds, he by reason of his embracing these false doctrines fled from the place he lived in, and giving up the city to the Tamils went to Polonnaruva, and died there." The Nikāya-saṅgraha called Sena I as Matvala-Sen. It states that king Matvala-Sen rejected such powerful sūtras as the Ratana-sutta and accepted the secret teachings of the Vajiriyavāda.[46] From the time of Matuala-Sen the Vajiriyavāda was "prevalent among the foolish and ignorant people of this country because it was protected and practised secretly as a mystic teaching."[47] Charles Eliot has identified the Vajiriyas with the Vajrayānists who then "flourished in Eastern India and were exponents of the worst phases of Tantrism."[48] The Vajiriyavādins composed the Gudhavinaya (Secret Vinaya) and they have described their writings as Secret Teachings.[49] The Vajrayānists very often used enigmatic language in their writings and some of their principal scriptures became known by such titles as the Tathāgathaguhyaka.[50] Sena I was converted to the Vajiriya-vāda doctrine. About this time the Ratanakūṭa sūtras and other writings of the Mahāyānists were introduced in Sri Lanka.[51] The Ratanakūṭa is regarded as the second of the seven classes into which the Mahāyāna sūtras of the Chinese canon are subdivided.[52] About this time the Nilapaṭadarsana appeared in Sri Lanka.[53] Its followers used to wear blue robes and they practised extreme forms of Tantrism.

From the middle of the 9th Century A.D. until the early 11th century A.D. the chronicles of Sri Lanka do not refer to the Vaitulyas or any other heretical sects. But a study of the religious monuments of this period shows that they existed. No new schools of Buddhism reached Sri Lanka from India "where the religion was now pursuing a downward course and what was introduced from India hereafter was mainly confined to the Puranic forms of Hindu belief, which was reflected on the faith of the masses; the process is still going on. On the other hand, the traces of Mahāyānistic beliefs and practices in Sri Lanka in the later centuries were local developments of the cults which had already been introduced."[54] In the 11th Century A.D. Buddhism fell on evil days in Sri Lanka. It did not flourish. For this reason the Buddhist monks from Myanmar were invited to purify the Buddhist Saṃgha in Sri Lanka. Most probably, a certain section of the Buddhist monks still followed the principles of the Mahāyānist doctrines. In the 12th Century A.D. an ecclesiastical council was held under the patronage of king Parākramabāhu I to purify Buddhism and its Buddhist Saṃgha in Sri Lanka. Then the heretical elements were thrown out from the Buddhist Saṃgha and its unification took place in the island.[55] "One consequence of this was the disappearance, as a separate sect, of the monks of the Abhayagiri vihāra who had been notorious for their readiness to accept unorthodox teachings; for over a millennium this sect had an important part in Sri Lanka's Buddhist history. But some of the principal colleges of this institution flourished till the advent of the Portuguese in the 16th Century A.D."[56] Sri Lanka has produced several Mahāyānist writers. According to S. Beal, Deva or Aryadeva, a Mahāyāna teacher of great reputation, was either born or lived in Sri Lanka. But Nanjio did not agree with him.[57] The latter said that a monk of Sri Lanka (Sh.Trz-Kuro or the Country of the Lion) named Samghavarman (San-Kie-poh-mi), who translated into Chinese an extract from the Vinaya of the Mahisāsakas professed doctrines closer to the Mahāyānists than those of the Theravādins.[58] The Mahisāsakas were not Mahayānists. Their doctrines are kept in Mahāyānist countries. Some scholars believed that Amogha (Pu-Kung), the famous Tantric teacher, belonged to Sri Lanka. In 719 A.D. he visited China and twenty-two years later he revisited India and Sri Lanka. In Sri Lanka he worked out in detail his doctrines.[59]

The earliest inscription connected with Mahāyānism in Sri Lanka was found on a rock a few feet below Mihintale hill. It is a fragmentary one.[60] The characters are of the 8th century A.D. and they resemble closely Grantha. It has a Sanskrit hymn in praise of the Buddha and it mentions the Nirmānakāya.[61] In another verse it refers to Sambho............ (Sambhogakāya).[62] "Thus we have two of the three bodies of the Buddha, according to the Mahāyānist Trikāya doctrine ...."[63] The Dharmadhātu (Body of the law) or the Dharmakāya, the essence of all the Buddhas, is the third one. It may be noted here that "the former word is not unknown in Pāli literature in the sense of "the eternal truth", but the other two are totally unknown in the sense in which they are used by the Mahāyānists."[64] The author of the hymn was the Bhikṣu who was "a mine of Bodhisatva virtues" as well as in the use of the Sanskrit language.[65] Copper votive tablets with Sanskrit inscriptions of the 9th Century A.D. was unearthed at Mihintale.[66] According to Dr. Luders, the Mahāyāna character of the sentiments expressed in them need not be doubted.[67] Sri Lanka's scholars have failed to identify these fragments with any of the published Mahāyāna texts. Similar plaques of the period were discovered at Vijayavama in Anurādhapura. In them there are references to Tārā, the Bodhisatvas Avalokitervara (Mahakaruna) and Akasagarbha, the Boddhas Sikhin and Gaganabuddha and mystic syllables like Om, Kili Kili, Huru, Huru, Svaha.[68] They indicate that in the 9th Century A.D. the Mahāyāna gods and goddesses were worshipped by the people in Sri Lanka. These plagues inform that Sri Lanka's Buddhists, especially those with Mahāyāna learnings, used to deposit metal plates with short extracts from Sanskrit Buddhist writings in chaityas. Two inscribed weathered slabs were found at Puliyankulam (ancient Pubbarama) monastery near Anurādhapura.[69] One of the slabs says a benefaction made for the daily supply of rice to a person who performed daily something which had connection with the Dharmadhātu.[70] The record of the other also refers to the same word. Probably, it signifies a Vaipulya sūtra (Mahāyāna text) and the two records speak of this Mahāyāna text.[71] A third slab inscription describes that the monastery was connected with the Abhayagivi-vihāra which became famous for heterodox learnings.[72] A 10th Century bronze label from Anurādhapura mentions the book Dharmadhātu.[73] There is a Nāgarī script in a part of it. Probably, due to the Vajiriyavādins, (Vajrayānists) this system was introduced in the 9th Century A.D. Another copper plate from Anurādhapura of the same period was found.[74] It has an inscription "Om vajrati (or-ni) Ksa(?) ram" which is no doubt a mantra addressed to a Tantric deity. The word 'vajra' indicates the Tantric character, "although information is not known in regard to a Mahāyāna deity with the name Vajraniksa or Vajratiksa."[75] Several votive tablets with Nāgari legends were found in different regions and three of them refer to Namo Bhagavate (in the first line) and Hapaya para, Para Svaha (in the last two lines) .. evidently a Tantric charm.[76] The Nāgarī character and the mystic syllable 'Svaha' show that the followers of the Mahāyana system used them.

Several Mahāyānist images of the 8th and the 9th Centuries A.D. were found in Sri Lanka. They were the representations of Avalokiteśvara (one with Amitabha in the headdress), Vajrapāṇi and Kuvera (Jambhala). Some of these are kept in Sri Lanka and others are in Boston (USA) and the British Museum.[77] Avalokiteśvara-Tārā relief was found at Vijayarama in Anurādhapura.[78] A Colossal Avalokiteśvara sculpture exists at Weligana on the south coast.[79] There is the Dhyānī Buddha Amitabha in the headdress. It holds a lotus in one hand and is like a king. According to local traditions, it is a foreign king who got leprosy and was cured by a physician who was Simhanada Lokeśvara.[80] Another tradition mentions that it was the god Natha.[81] At Budhuruvagala near Wellawaya in Uva province the Mahāyāna sculptures were discovered in high relief.[82] On each side of a central Buddha which is nearly 50 ft. high they are a group of three. The trio on the Buddha's proper right informs Avalokita in the middle. In the headdress there is the Dhyani Buddha Amitabha.[83] In the attitude of Katakahasta the hands are arranged. Gopinatha Rao's 'Elements of Hindu Iconography' refer to it.[84] On the right he is attended by a female with an unblown lotus or a fruit in her hand. She may represent Tārā. The other figure is a male one. In the Buddhist iconography on one side of Avalokita is Tārā and on the other side there is Hayagriva or Sudhana Kumara. Most probably, the figure in Sudhana Kumāra. The figure is not that of Hayagriva because the horse's neck is not found.[85] On the Buddha's left there are three figures and in the middle there is a Bodhisatva. Most probably, it is Maitreya. A male figure is there on either side of him. One of them has a double vajra in the right hand.[86] According to the art critics, the 9th Century would not be too early a date for these sculptures.[87] In the Journal of the Bengal Asiatic Society[88] Dr. J.Ph. Vogel published a paper on a Mahāyānistic sculpture which was found by a British soldier when Kandy was occupied by the British in 1815 A.D. It is a small slab and in its centre there is the Buddha and Avalokitesvara and Maitreya are these and there are seven other scenes from the Buddha's life.[89] Dr. J.Ph. Vogel thinks that it belongs to the Magadha school of art and it dates from about the 11th century A.D.[90] It shows that there was a religious intercourse between the Mahāyāna Buddhists of North Eastern India and the Buddhists of Sri Lanka. A manuscript from Nepal written in Bengali 11th Century script was found.[91] In it there are miniature paintings of Mahāyānist deities with inscriptions mentioning the names and titles. The following from Sri Lanka are included among them: "Simahaladvipe Dipaṁkara arisasthana" the Buddha Dipankara of Ceylon (Sri Lanka); what makes this icon a Mahāyānistic one is that the Buddha is attended on the right by Avalokitesvara and on the left by Vajrapani; another Buddha is named "Simhaladvipe Dipaṁikara Abhayahasta" (the Buddha Dipaṃkara of Ceylon (Sri Lanka) with hand in the abhaya mudrā); "Simhaladvipe Jambalah" (the god Jambhala i.e., Kuvera of

Ceylon (Sri Lanka)."[92] The manuscript is now in Cambridge, England. All these facts show that Mahāyānism existed in Sri Lanka.

The Natha or Avalokitesvara cult became very popular in the 15th Century in Srī Lanka during the reign of Parākramabāhu VI of Koṭṭe (1412-1467 A.D.).[93] Totagamuwa was the principal centre of the cult. Sri Rāhula, the priestly poet and grammarian, was a worshipper of the Mahāyāna Bodhisattvas. At Pepiliyana the deity received daily worship and for this reason royal endowments were given. An inscription of King Bhuvanaikabāhu or Bhuvanakabāhu V of the 14th Century A.D. was found at Sagama in Central Province. It mention the god.[94] The Vegiriya inscription (early fifteenth century A.D.) discusses the dedication of certain fields for daily offerings to Lokesvara Nātha.[95] A frequentecy record at Gadaladeniya in the Central province (mid-14th century) refers to Natha and Matteyya (Maitreya) together whilst the eighty-seventh and the one-hundredth chapters of the Mahāvaṃsa also describe Natha.[96] During the time of the Kandyan kings the Natha Devale occupied an important place in Kandy. In the annual festival "now conducted in connection with the Temple of the Tooth Relic it takes procedure next to the Tooth Relic."[97] An important ceremony in connection with the inauguration of the Sinhalese kings used to hold at the Natha Devale. "This was the rite of choosing a name and the putting on the regal sword. As most Kandyan institutions keep old traditions and it was an erticle of faith the Abhayagiri monks (10th century) that every king of Ceylon (Sri Lanka) was a Bodhisattva and as the epithel "Bodhisattvavatara" (incarnation of Bodhisattva) was applied to the late kings, it is probably that the ceremony mentioned above at the heads of the Bodhisattva Avalokitesvara was an ancient custom".[98] During the new year celebrations another important ceremony was held in Sri Lanka. On this occasion "the royal physician had to superintend the preparation of a thousand small posts of the juices of wild medicinal plants at the Natha Devale, from whence, carefully covered and sealed they were sent to the palace and distributed with much ceremony to the other temples" (Paridham:Ceylon and its Dependencies, Vol.X, p.32). This practice indicates the idea that Natha like one form of Avalokiteśvara, was a god of healing.[99] The image of Avalokita named "Lokavātha' of the hospitals in Ceylon" (Sri Lanka) informs that the god for his healing activities was advised and worshipped.[100] The Sāriputra is a Sanskrit work on iconometry and the local imagemakes use it. It has a chapter which discusses dhyanas of the different deitics. From this it is known that at the time of the dhyana of Natha was composed the general characteristics of Avalokitesvara had been attributed to Natha e.g., one hand holds the lotus and there is the Dhyana Buddha on forehead.[101] The same work refers to eight different forms of this deity "which are interesting as showing the fusion which took place, in later times, of Hindu and Buddhist beliefs."[102] They are Śivanātha, Brahma Nātha, Viṣṇu Nātha, Gauri Nātha, Matsyendra Nātha, Badra Nātha, Bauddha Nātha and Gana Nātha.[103] From these descriptions one concludes that "Nātha or Lokeśvara" was believed to be identical with all the members of the Hindu Trinity."[104] According to certain Buddhists, Nātha is but another name for Śiva.[105] A Nepalese verse inscription of 1672 A.D. refers to Matsyendra Nātha as a form of Nātha and says that in Nepal he is considered a form of Avalokiteśvara.[106] The cult of Matsyendra Nātha is very popular in Nepal. But his worship does not exist in any other Buddhist country. It was due to the Vajrayānists, the Vajiriyavādins of the writings he was known in Sri Lanka.

Among the four guardian deities in Sri Lanka, Saman or Sumana of Adam's Peak was included and he may be identified with Samantabhadra, one of the eight principal Mahāyānist Bodhisattvas.[107] This god of Sri Lanka takes his seat on an elephant and the colour is nil, which is used for blue as well as green. The copy of the (non-extant) Saman Davale inscription at Ratanapura mentions the god's name as Lakṣamana.[108]

The god Upulvan is now considered to be the same as Viṣṇu but, at the same, the people of Sri Lanka have accepted him as one of the future Bodhisattvas.[109] The merging of local god Upulvan with Viṣṇu seems to have taken place not more than three or four countries ago.[110] Devundera in the southern provice of Sri Lanka was the principal seat of the deity.[111] The Chinese pilgrims visited this place to worship it and in an inscription their benefactions were mentioned by them. This inscription belongs to A.D. 1409.[112] "When the Buddha was about to enter Nirvana, He (according to the Mahāvaṃsa) summoned Sakka and requested him to ward off any evil which might overwhelm Vijaya who had just landed in Ceylon (Sri Lanka), where the Buddha foresaw that this religion would be glorified in the future years. Sakka entrusted his task to Upulvan who, with holy water, protected the prince from the machinations of the she-demons."[113] In the Karandavyuha version of Simhala, Avalokiteśvara performs Upulvan's part. This signifies that Upulvan is a local name for the other.[114] The epithet "Kihirali" (for Kirali) is very often applied to Upulvan. It is corrupted from the two words "Kihiri-li", and means Khadira word and out of this word several images of the god were made. The word was also known as Kaira and it was sacred to Avalokita and Tārā.[115]

The Dasa-Bodhisattupatti-Kathā, an almost unknown Pāli work, mentions the antecedents and the future of the ten particular Bodhisattvas and the manner in which they met Gautama Buddha.[116] Perhaps the work has Mahāyāna influence and it was composed when the people who were well-known with the Mahāyāna doctrines "were hankering after more Bodhisattvas than allowed in the Theravāda."[117] Except Maitreya, the Ten Bodhisattvas have nothing in common with their Mahāyāna types. The another of the Nikāya Saṃgraha knew a large number of historical works, almost all in Sanskrit and Mahāyānist or Tantric.[118] The names of these books are: The Varṇṇapiṭaka of the Hemavatas, the Aṅgulimālapiṭaka of the Rājagirikas, the Gudha Vessantara of the Siddharthakas, the Rāstrapālagarjjita of the Purvvasailiyas, the Alavakagarjjita of the Aparasailiyas, the

Gudhavinaya, the Mayajalatantra, the Samajattanta Mahasamayatattra Tantra, the Tattvasamgraha Tantra, The Bhutacamara Tantra, The Vajramṛta Tantra, the Cakrasmvara Tantra, the Dvadasacakra Tantra, the Bharukadbhuta Tantra, the Mahamaya Tantra, the Padanihksepa Tantra, the Catuspista Tantra, the Paramardda Tantra, the Maruyudbhava Tantra, the Sarvvaluddha Tantra, the Sarvvaguhya Tantra, the Samuccaya Tantra, the Maricikalpa, the Herambha Kalpa, the Trisamaya Kalpa, the Rajakalpa, the Vajragandhara Kalpa, the Maricigulya Kalpa, the Suddhesamuccaya Kalpa, the Mayamarici Kalpa (nos. 6-13 all composed by the Vajraparvatavasins, i.e., the Vajrayānists), the Vaitulyapiṭaka of the Vaitulyavādins, the Ratnakūṭa Sūtras of the Andhrakas and the Aksariyasutra of the Mahāsaṃghikas.[119] Besides the Tantras, the Mahāyāna charms called the Dharamis were known in Sri Lanka.[120] Parakramabāhu I in the second half of the twelfth century A.D. built the palace at Polonnaruva. In it a special chamber called Dharanighara was constructed for the recital of mantras.[121] During the mediaeval period in Sri Lanka the grammatical and other works of candragomin were studied and the Jātakamālā of Āryasūra was quite well-known in the island. The Jātakamālā is not a Mahāyāna work, but the Mahāyānists held it in high esteem.[122] The author of the Pūjāvaliya of the 13th century came under the influence of the Mahāyāna teachings. In the introductory chapter of the work, he has said that "it is only the state of a Bodhisattva that is worth striving for and the attainment of Nirvāṇa by being an arhat or a pratyekabuddha should not be one's aim."[123]

NOTES

1. Paramvitana, 225; BIA., 188; BCPP., 25; CHC., 82.
2. *Ibid.*, 225; ibid., 188; ibid., 25; ibid., 82: Mhv., xxxvi, 31-32: Geiger tr. 258, n. 4.
3. Paramavitana, 225.
4. *Ibid.*, 225.
5. Paramavitana, 225.
6. Gunawardana, 55; f.h.1.

7. Paramavitana, 225.
8. CHC., 82; BIA., 188; BCPP., 25.
9. *Ibid.*, 85; ibid., 188-189; ibid., 25.
10. BCPP., 26.
11. Pañca A., 109; HBC., 88.
12. *Ibid.*, 192; ibid., 88.
13. *Ibid.*, 190-192; ibid., 88.
14. *Ibid.*, 209; ibid., 88.
15. Dpv., xxii., 41, 42; HBC., 88.
16. HBC., 88.
17. *Ibid.*, 89; VbhA, 7, 36, 223; MA., I, 520, 549.
18. Nks., 11; ibid., 89.
19. *Ibid.*, 11; ibid., 89.
20. *Ibid.*, 89; MIB., 4.
21. *Ibid.*, 89.
22. *Ibid.*, 89.
23. *Ibid.*, 89; Pradhan, 79.
24. *Ibid.*, 89; CjSC. G., II, 35-36.
25. HIL., II, 342; ibid., 89.
26. HBC., 90.
27. *Ibid.*, 89-90.
28. *Ibid.*, 90, f.n.1.
29. Paramavitana., 225.
30. BCPP., 27.
31. HBC., 102.
32. *Ibid.*, 102: CjSC., G., II, 38.
33. Paramavitana., 225.
34. *Ibid.*, 225-226.
35. *Ibid.*, 226; HBC., 102; BCPP., 27.
36. *Ibid.*, 226; ibid., 103; ibid., 27.
37. HBC., 103: Nks., 15; Paramavitana, 226.
38. Paramavitana, 226.
39. *Ibid.*, 226.
40. *Ibid.*, 226.
41. *Ibid.*, 226.
42. *Ibid.*, 226; HBC., 109; BCPP., 27.
43. BCPP., 27.
44. HBC., 109; Mhv., I, 68; NKS., 16.
45. Paramavitana., 225., Nks., 16.
46. NKS., 16; HBC., 109.
47. *Ibid.*, 16; ibid., 109.
48. Paramavitana, 226; HBC., III.
49. *Ibid.*, 226.
50. *Ibid.*, 226.

51. *Ibid.*, 226.
52. *Ibid.*, 226.
53. *Ibid.*, 226; BCPP., 27.
54. *Ibid.*, 227.
55. *Ibid.*, 227.
56. *Ibid.*, 227.
57. *Ibid.*, 227.
58. *Ibid.*, 227.
59. *Ibid.*, 227.
60. *Ibid.*, 227.
61. *Ibid.*, 227.
62. *Ibid.*, 227.
63. *Ibid.*, 228.
64. *Ibid.*, 228.
65. *Ibid.*, 228.
66. *Ibid.*, 228.
67. *Ibid.*, 228.
68. *Ibid.*, 228.
69. *Ibid.*, 228.
70. *Ibid.*, 228.
71. *Ibid.*, 228.
72. *Ibid.*, 228.
73. *Ibid.*, 228.
74. *Ibid.*, 228.
75. *Ibid.*, 228.
76. *Ibid.*, 228.
77. *Ibid.*, 229.
78. *Ibid.*, 229.
79. *Ibid.*, 229.
80. *Ibid.*, 229.
81. *Ibid.*, 229.
82. *Ibid.*, 229.
83. *Ibid.*, 229.
84. *Ibid.*, 229.
85. *Ibid.*, 229.
86. *Ibid.*, 229.
87. *Ibid.*, 229.
88. *Ibid.*, 229; JBAS., 1915, Plate XX, 298.
89. *Ibid.*, 229; ibid., 298.
90. *Ibid.*, 229.
91. *Ibid.*, 229.
92. *Ibid.*, 229.
93. *Ibid.*, 230.
94. *Ibid.*, 230.

95. *Ibid.*, 230.
96. *Ibid.*, 230.
97. *Ibid.*, 230.
98. *Ibid.*, 231.
99. *Ibid.*, 231.
100. *Ibid.*, 231.
101. *Ibid.*, 231.
102. *Ibid.*, 231.
103. *Ibid.*, 231.
104. *Ibid.*, 231.
105. *Ibid.*, 231.
106. *Ibid.*, 231.
107. *Ibid.*, 231.
108. *Ibid.*, 231.
109. *Ibid.*, 231-232.
110. *Ibid.*, 232.
111. *Ibid.*, 232.
112. *Ibid.*, 232.
113. *Ibid.*, 232.
114. *Ibid.*, 232.
115. *Ibid.*, 232.
116. *Ibid.*, 232.
117. *Ibid.*, 232.
118. *Ibid.*, 232.
119. *Ibid.*, 232-233.
120. *Ibid.*, 233.
121. *Ibid.*, 233.
122. *Ibid.*, 233.
123. *Ibid.*, 233.

3

Buddhist Education of Sri Lanka

Like Vedic culture centred round the sacrifice, Buddhist education and learning centred round monasteries. We can say that the history of the Buddhist system of education was history of the Buddhist Saṁgha. Apart from monasteries, the Buddhist world never gave any opportunity to the people to go for this education. Monasteries were the only places where the people got their education. The Buddhist monks were the custodians, guardians and bearers of the Buddhist culture and education. All education sacred as well as secular were kept in the hands of the Buddhist monks.[1] In Srì Lanka the Buddhist saṃgha conducted the whole system of education, both religious and lay.[2] The Buddhist monks played their prominent roles in educational and cultural activities of the island. From the Sigāla Sutta of the Dīhga Nikāya we learn that the duty of the monks was to guide the laity and to give them proper education.[3] It may be noted here that the Buddhist monks of Sri Lanka were very active in performing their duties as they took the charge of the education of the whole nation.[4] They educated the rulers, leaders and commoners of the country. They also trained them in a proper way. We can easily understand how efficient they were to perform their duties. For this reason they occupied the prominent place in the country. The kings like Siri Saṅgha Bodhi (307-309 A.D.), two brothers Jeṭṭha-Tissa and Mahasena (4th century A.D.), Dhātusena (406-478 A.D.), Aggabodhi VIII

(801-812 A.D) and many other things in later times received their education on training from the Buddhist monks.[5] In the ancient system of education memory played a very great role than today. Learned masters for their strong memory became well known in the world of education. They gained fame for it. Majjhima-Bhānaka Deva Thera, the specialist of the Majjhima Nikāya, who for intensive meditation did not go well with his studies for 19 years, but at the end of this long period, used to recite by memory and teach the whole of the Nikāya without a single mistake or omission.[6] Naga Thera of Kiraliyagiri, who had left his studies for 18 years, taught the Dhātau katha without a single mistake.[7] Dharmarakkhita of Tulādhara-pabhata in Rohaṇa had no connection with certain texts for 30 years, but without hesitation he used to teach the whole of the Tripiṭaka. These people had great reputation for good memory.[8] Whatever they used to learn, they used to put it in their memory and without hesitation, and without a single mistake or omission they used to recite the whole thing. For this reason in ancient days a learned person was mentioned as bahussuta "one who has heard much." But in modern days a learned person is known as "well-read." Because now-a-days, through reading knowledge is acquired. The Digha Nikāya commentary says that two thesis — Mahā-gatimta-Abhaya and Dīgha-bhānka-Abhaya were able to remember certain incidents in their life which took place when they were five days and nine days old respectively.[9] Tipiṭaka Cūlābhaya Thera remembered the names of all the citizens of Anurādhapura and he recognized them again if only once they were presented to him.[10] Many Buddhist monks used to recite the whole of a Nikāya by heart and this indicates that memorizing in these days as a common thing.[11] The Samantapāsādika informs that books were read even in the night by the light of oil lamps (dīpāloka).[12] The Mahāvaṃsa says that young Dhātusena in the fifth century A.D. under a tree studied a book (potthaka).[13] The Vibhanga commentary mention a student monk who took a long distance journey, i.e., a distance of a hundred yojanas, "just to have a point made clear by his teachers."[14] This monk was Tissa, the son of Punabhasu, the households. After his education in Sri Lanka, the former went to India for further study and he studied under Yonaka Dhammarakkhita Thera. After completing his education in India he wanted to return to Sri Lanka. When he was about to embark on a ship, then relating to a certain point a doubt appeared in his mind. He at once cancelled his trip and then travelled a distance of a hundred yojanas to meet his teacher Dhammarakkhita and after his talk with him, he was able to clear his doubt.[15] This shows that how sincere and curious these students were in their studies in ancient days in Sri Lanka. Although memory played a great role to carry on education, yet books were also used, but infrequently. Every student was unable to possess his text. Most probably, manuscripts were kept at the principal Monasteries for references.

Education always helped to develop moral and spriritual character of a person. If a person in order to gain material profits studied religion but he did not study to improve his moral and spiritual character, then his study was useless. There was no need to spend his time in study. It was better for him to sleep.[16] The duty of a teacher was not only to teach, but also to improve the moral and spiritual welfare of his students. The head of the Kāladīgha Vāpidvāra-vihāra did not allow a certain pupil to come to his class until the latter promised not go about in the village. The teacher though that if he was allowed freedom of movement, then the young student had a chance to fall from his right path. He might not then move in a right way.[17] When Kāla-Buddharakkhita after finishing his education returned to his monastery, then his preceptor spoke to him that he should devote his time to meditate and should do something to gain some spiritual realization. Then Kāla-Buddharakkhita eagaged himself in meditation at became an arahant.[18] Everyone wanted to learn from a teacher who had moral character and who was quite well-known as a good person. Mahā-Rakkhita Thera did not like to learn the Mahāniddesa from a Buddhist monks whose character was not pure and who used to lead an impure life. Even then, he went to learn the Mahāniddesa from this monk who was the only monk in Sri Lanka, who knew the Mahāniddesa.[19] This text would have been lost with the death of the bad monk, had Mahā-Rakkhita Thera not go there to learn this text.[20] When education was kept in the hands of Buddhist monks, then it was connected with the religion. "It should primarily be religious." No one was accepted as a cultured person if he did not know the religion well. When he was well versed in religion, then he was recognised as a cultured person in the society. A bhikkhu or a layman who had a sound knowledge of Buddhism, including the Vinaya or the Abhidhamma, became known as a cultured person in Sri Lanka. The government's high officials knew Buddhism well. Abhidhammika Godatta Thera knew the Bhddhist philosophy and the Vinaya very well and for this qualification he was able to occupy the position of Chief Justice of Sri Lanka.[21] "The accomplishment of monks in the sphere of learning, including a knowledge of the law of the land, seems to have been so complete that a Thera named Abhidhammika Godatta of the Mahāvihāra was raised by king Bhatiya (38-66 A.D.) to a position virtually equal to the office of the Chief Justice of ceylon (Sri Lanka). Godatta was an acknowledged specialist both in the Vinaya and the Abhidhamma. The king who was greatly blessed with the judgement given by the Thera in an ecclesiastical case, issued an edict by beating of drum declaring. "As long as I live, judgements given by Abhidhammika Godatta Thera, in cases either of monks, nuns or laymen, are final. I will punish him who does not abide by his judgement."[22] It is not certain whether Godatta even acted as a judge in secular matters. The king's declaration may be regarded as an expression of his recognition of the Thera's wisdom and knowledge of the law and his high qualities. This also is an indication of the high esteem in which the Thera was held by the public. Even if the Thera had provided over any secular cases, there is no doubt that he would not have passed any judgement involving capital punishment or physical torture. There were even kings who prohibited physical torture at capital punishment."[23] "Not only literature, but also the fine arts were included in the sphere of interest of bhikkhus engaged in ganthadura. Ananda K. Coomaraswamy says, "Buddhism became indeed the chief patron rather than the opponent of fine arts, which spread with it from India to Ceylon, Burma, Siam and Java in the south and to the China and Japan in the north. It thus came to pass that it was important for even the priests to have some knowledge of the theoretical side of craftsmanship at least, at this was often the case; they were rather expected to explain such works as Sariputta to the less learned craftsman than to learn from him. In the eighteenth century there were even craftsmen amongst the priesthood."[24] Originally ganthadhura indicated only the learning and teaching of the Tipiṭaka. But, after some time it referred to languages, grammar, history, logic, medicine and other branches of study as well. Buddhist monasteries became well-known as centres of learning and culture and the Buddhist monks knew all subjects and they used to teach to everyone from prince down to peasant.[25]

The Abhidhamma was an important subject in Buddhism. Everyone wants to study it and wishes to learn something from it. Proficiency in it had helped a person to establish him to the reversed position of a philosopher. All persons desired it but it was a very difficult achivement no doubt. This Jettha-Tissa III requested his queen to become a nun and to study the Abhidhmma.[26] Kings like Kassapa II (640-650 A.D) and Mahinda II (772-792 A.D.) played great roles to spread a knowledge of the Abhidhamma.[27] "The Abhidhamma was considered so sublime and profound that it is said that at the expiration of the sāsana (sāsanantaradhāna), the Abhidhamma Piṭaka will die out before the other two Piṭakas. The teachers of the Abhidhamma were honoured more than teachers of the other two Piṭakas."[28] Even in the study of the Tipiṭaka (Tripiṭaka) the Vinaya Piṭaka which deals with paṭipatti or practice was mentioned as less important than the Abhidhamma Piṭaka which discusses metaphysical and psychological problems but" the latter was a Piṭaka of comparatively late development."[29] The Mihintāle Inscription of Mahinda IV describes that five shares (Vasag) should be allotted to the teacher of the Vinaya Piṭaka and seven shares to the teacher of the Sutta Piṭaka, while twelve shares should be offered to the teacher of the Abhidhamma Pitaka.[30] All these shares inform that the teacher of the Vinaya was kept into the third grade, while the teacher of the Abhidhamma was placed in the first grade. This shows that intellectual discipline got a higher place than moral discipline.[31] Sri Lanka's people appreciated very much the value of learning. They knew the valuable contribution of the learned to the society. The society needed it very much. For this reason, attention was given to the learned people. All able monks showed their keen interest to become learned persons and they wanted to do work for the development of the country. The commentaries on the Dīgha and Majjhima Nikāyas narrate: "... learning is enough for the perpetuation of the Sāsana .... The Sāsana (religion) is stabilized when learning endures."[32] The vibhaṅga commentary also describes that "it is a great mistake to belittle the value of learning."[33] A citizen was recognized as a good citizen when he had a general knowledge of Buddhism. Many learned monks were honoured by good kings of Sri Lanka and they arranged facilities for both adults and children to learn the dhamma. King Moggallāna II (537-556 A.D.) gave sweetmeats to children to learn the Dhamma.[34] Apart from religion, cultural and vocational subjects like grammar, prosody, rhetoric, literature, history, logic, arithmetic, medicine and astrology were taught in monasteries in ancient Sri Lanka. Possibly, the law of the land was also a subject and students used to study it. They also used to get training in fine arts like painting and sculpture in monasteries. The Cullavagga mentions that the Chabbaggiya monks painted male and female figures in their Vihāra. But the Buddha prohibited it. He allowed only such designs as creepers and flowers for the purpose of painting.[35] The Buddhist monks were encourged to decorate their vihāras with various Jataka stories and events of the life of the Buddha with the idea of creating "Severe joy" and "emotion" into the minds of the pious persons. In about the 5th century A.D., the Sinhalese monk was unequalled in the art of sculpture."[36] From a Chinese account we learn that a certain Sinhalere monk called nan-te' (Nanda) went to the court of the emperor of China in the year 456 A.D. and Thera on this occasion took with him three statues as gifts to the Chinese emperor. He himself made these three statues.[37] The historian of the Wei Tartar dynasty, 386-556 A.D. records that people from the countries of central Asia at the kings of these countries sent artisans to procure copies of the statues but none could reach the same level of the productions of Nan-te'. "On standing about ten paces distant they appeared truly brilliant, but the lineaments gradually disappeared on a nearer approach."[38] A Sinhalere monk named Devaragampola Silvatenne (Silvat Tana) Unnause, "The most famous painter of the late 18th century A.D." did paintings at Degaldoruva at Ridīvihāra. These paintings were executed under the supervision of Moratoṭa Mahānāyaka Thera of Malvatta Vihāra. Many critics of art praised these paintings. Ratnatāne Srī Dharmāloka Mahāthera (1828-1887 A.D.), the founder of the Vidyālainkāra Pirivena, painted several vihāras in Sat-korale.[39] King Jeṭṭha-Tissa II had a great reputation for ivory carving. Many people received training from him.[40] Military arts such as archery and swordmanship were handed down from father to son. Phussadeva was one of Duṭṭha-Gamani's ten generals. This father gave him training in archery. In their family this art was handed down.[41]

In ancient Sri Lanka every monastery was a great centre of learning. It served the purpose of a free school. There were also centres of learning and they held the position of universities for higher studies and specialized knowledge. Among them the chief centre was the Mahāvihāra at Anurādhapura. A few other centres were in ancient Sri Lanka and they were even more famous than the Mahāvihāra, for certain specialized knowledge. Rohaṇa became well-known for it. Because if had several such centres.[42] Many highly educated monks from the Mahāvihāra for specialised studies visited these places. Tipiṭaka cūlabheya of the Mahāvihāra knew the Tipiṭaka very well but he did not studied the commentaries. In order to get a good knowledge of the commentaries, he went to Tulādhāra Pabbata in Rohaṇa to study under the guidance of a professor named Dhammarakkhita, who was well-versed in all the teaching (sabba-periyattika).[43] The Tissamahāvihara at Mahāgama was an important centre of learning in Rohaṇa Thera of this monastery used to teach "eighteen great groups" (atthīrasa-mahā-gaṇe) both texts and commentaries (aṭṭhavasena ca pālivasena ca) day at night without much rest. Even the commentators to clear their doubts used to come to him.[44] A young monk from Koraṇ-daka-vihāra went to Rohana for studies.[45] Kāla-dīghavāpidvāra-vihāra at the Maṇḍalārāma in Killigīma were other famous centres of learning.[46] The celebrated Maliyadeva Thera at Mahī-Tissabhūti Thera got their education and the latter place.[47]

In Sri Lanka there were centres of learning and the centres became famous for specialized knowledge. There were also certain groups who specialized in a particular branch of the doctrine.[48] The Suttantika-gana was a group of monks who got special training in the Sutta Piṭaka. The Abhidhammika-gaṇa was a group of monks who specialized in the Abhidhamma.[49] There were certain teachers and pupils who specialized in the Nikāyas. There were certain Theras who became well known as Dīgha-bhāṇakas, Majjhima-bhāṇakas, Aṇguttara-bhāṇakas and Saṃyutta-bhāṇakas. There Thesas were mentioned as Masters of these Nikāyas or Collections.[50] A Bhaṇaka means a reciter. Hence Dīgha-bhāṇaka means "reciter of the Dīgha Nikāya". So are the Majjhima and other bhaṇakas. There were several monks who became famous for their proficiency in all the four Nikāyas, such as Cātunikāya Tissa Thera of Kolita Vihāra.[51]

Mahā Padmma Thera of Tulādhāsa was a specialist in the Jātakas.[52] This Thera used to live during Ilanāga's time (93-102 A.D.).

The Sāmantapāsādikā refers to three grades of the learned (bahussuto nāma tividho).[53] The three grades were the preliminary, intermediate and the final and for each grade there were the syllabuses. The monk who belonged to the lowest grade became known as Nissayamnccauaka (independent); counting five years after his upasampadā he should learn by heart (vācggata) at least two Mātikasof the Bhikku-Bhikkhum Patimonnha.[54] He should also know from the Suttanta four Bhāṇavāras, i.e. the four Bhāṇavāras of the Paritta. In order to preach on Uporatha days he should learn the four Bhāṇavāras.[55] He should know some important suttas like the Andhakavinda, the Mahā-Rahulovāda and the Ambattha for the purpose of talking to these persons who visited him.[56] In order to give benedictory talks on special occasions he should know by heart the three annmodanā which were saṇgha-bhatta (alms-giving), maṅgala (an auspicions occasion like occupying a new house or a wedding) and aramṅgala (a funeral of a mataka-dāna, alms giving for the dead).[57] He should know by heart certain fundamental Vinaya kamnas such as uposatha at parāranā and also a topic of meditation (kammaṭṭhāna) leading up to arahantship.[58] He should learn all these things mentioned above and then he was allowed to go about freely (catuddiso) and to live in independent manner (attano issariyena vasituṃ).[59]

The monk of the second grade became known as Parisupaṭṭhāpaka (Attendent of the Assembly).[60] Counting ten years after his upasampadā he should learn by heart at least the two vibhaṅgas of the Vinaya, i.e. the two Vinaya texts known as Pārājika and Pācittiya.[61] When he failed to do it, he then recited these texts with three others. He should also know the Vinaya-Kamnas and the Khandhakavatta. If he was a Majjhima-bhāṇaka, he should know the M̄lapaṇṇāsaka (the first 50 suttas) of the Majjhima-Nikāya. If he was a D̄igha-bhaṇaka, he should know the Mahāvagga (10 suttas of the second Vagga) of the Dīgha Nikāya. If he was a Saṃyutta-bhānaka, he should know the first three sections of the Mahāvagga of the Saṃyutta Nikāya. If he was an Aṅguttara-bhāṇaka, he should know the first or the second half of the Aṅgattara Nikāya If he failed to do it, he should learn from the beginning to the Third Section (Tika-Nipāta).[62] But the Mahā-paccariya commentary mentions that if a bhāṇaka knows only one section (wipāta), he should choose the Fourth or the Fifth Nipāta.[63] A Jātaka-bhāṇaka should know the whole of the Jātaka text with its commentary—not less then that.[64] The Mahā-Paccariya says that is addition he should also know the Dhammapada with the stories. Sometimes the Dhmmapada-bhāṇakas are also refused to as a separate class.[65] When a monk was well-versed in these texts, he was then accepted as well-read or well-educated (bahussuta), he was then able to serve the assemblies. He was a leader (disāpāmokkho), wherever he expressed his desire to go, he went there.[66]

The monks of the highest grade became known as Bhikkhunorādaka (Adviser to Bhikkhunis).[67] He should know the three Piṭakas with their commentaries. When he failed, he should master the commentry of one of the Four collections (Nikāyas).[68] That would help him to explain the other Nikāyas. Among the seven Abhidhamma texts, he would master the commentaries of four, because that would help him to explain the rest.[69] But the whole of the Vinaya Piṭaka should be learnt with its commentary. When a Monk knew all this, then he would be able to become an "Adviser to Bhikkhus." It may be pointed out that a master of the Tripiṭaka "was considered competent to function as an adviser to nuns". Because he should then be able to answer any questions that were asked. He was then a competent person for this position. A bhikkhuṇī's movements were very restricted. A Bhikkumorādaka was the only person who would be able to satisfy her curosity whenever she wanted to learn something from him.[70]

Generally, classes were held three times a day in a monastery: in the morning before the start of the mid-day meal, all again in the afternoon. The third lesson was taken place in the evening. Most probably, it was held after the evening religious routine.[71] Sometimes, these classes were like public lectures. Tipiṭaka Chūlābhaya Thera of the Mahā Vihāra studied under Dhammarakkhita there of Tulādhāra Pabhata in Rohaṇa. A large number of monks went with him. At night the student recited the texts before the teacher and the teacher explained them by day. A big pavilion was built by the villagers before the pariveṇa (residence) and they used to attend these lectures daily.[72]

In ancient Sri Lanka two great convocations were held twice a year before and after the vassa (rainy) season. One was the Mahāvihāra at Anurīdhapura and the other was the Tissamahāvihara at Mahāgāma in Rohana.[73] The monks who belonged to the north of the Mahāvali-gaṅga assembled at the Mahāvihara and the monks who belonged to the south of the Mahavali-gaṅga assembled at the Tissamahāvihāra.[74] Before the vassa season they were present there to clean and to whitewash the catiya, and in order to obtain topics of meditation from the celebrated Mahātheras they came there to meet them. After the vassa season they met again to say their spiritual attainments during their retreat and also to recite and revise their learning of the dhamma. On these occasions they discussed difficult points with experts and cleared their doubts. During the time of the Buddha himself a great convocation was held twice a year.[75]

In ancient Sri Lanka there was a freedom of discussion. A pupil disagreed with his teacher and he discussed freely a point without offence, and the teacher without any hesitation accepted the pupils view if he knew that his pupil was correct.[76] Tipiṭaka Cūlā-Summa and his pupil Tipiṭaka Culla-Nāga were well versed in the Tripiṭaka. They opined two different views with regard to the term ekāyanamagga in the Satipaṭṭhāna-Sutta. The teacher gave opinion but he found that his pupil's opinion was correct. Tipiṭaka Culla-Summa before a public gathering accepted his pupil's view. Many people assembled there to listen to a sermon by his pupil Tipiṭaka Culla-Nāga.[77]

Dhammarakkhita Thera of Tulādhāra-Pablata in Rohaṇa was a great scholar. He after teaching Tipiṭaka Cūlābhaya Thera from the Mahavihāra took his seat on a mat (taṭṭika) at the feet of his pupil and requested him with folded hands to give him a topic of meditation (Kammaṭṭhān). "Why, Sir," cried the pupil, "haven't I studied under you? What can I say that you don't know?" "But my friend," said the teacher, "the path of realization is quite a different thing".[78] At that time Tipiṭaka Cūlābhaya was a sotapanna. The teacher attained arahantship on the Kammaṭṭhāna given by his pupil.[79] Mahā-Nāga Thera of Uccavālīka sat down upon the heels in the posture of Ukkuṭika at the feet of his pupil Dhammarakkhita of Talasigera to get a topic of meditation.[80] It was better to show your humbleness and don't he proud of one's learning. This was mentioned as a sign of great scholarship. Saketa-Tissa Thera was a great expounder of the dhamma. He was also a teacher of large number of monks. The commentaries refer to him as an example of the virtue of not showing one's learning. Once the Thera left his mastery and his pupils, and stayed as an ordinary monk at a distant monastery called Kaṇikāravālika-samudda-vihāra and helped other bhikkhus during a rainy season.[81]

In ancient Sri Lanka many villages were illiterate. A passage in the Majjhima commentary throws light on the extent of literacy then obtained in the rural areas in Sri Lanka. When a king sent out an edict to a remote province, then some villagers, who could not read, took the help of others to read it for them. "Yathā hi raññā paccantajanapad pahitaṃ lekhaṃ tattha manussā likhaṃ vācetuṃ ajānantā yo vācetum, jānāti tena vācāpetvā taṃ atthaṃ sutrā rañño ānāti ādarena sampādenti."[82] The illiterate villagers in this way used to learn the contents of a royal inscription established in a remote province. The words "remote province" (paccanta-janapada) indicate that in the urban areas no one took the help of other person to know the inner meaning of such a document.[83] Many learned monks used to live in Sri Lanka. Practically, the country's education system was in their hands. Among the laity, there were men and women, who were learned and cultured. Even the monks themselves accepted some of the learned lāity as authority. The Sammtapāsādikā describes that king Bhatiya (38-66 A.D.) appointed a minister name Dīgha-Kārāyana, a brahmin," "to decide on a textual and doctrinal point over which the Mahāvihāra and the Abhayagiri vihāra held conflicting views."[84] This Brahmin minister was a great scholar and was well-versed in various languages (pandita bhāsantara-kusalo).[85] Kapila was a minister during the time of king Vohārika Tissa (269-291 A.D.). The king asked this minister to hold an inquiry and purge the dhamma of the Vaitulya doctrines.[86] When king Mahāsena (334-362 A.D) reigned, the Minister of Justice helped the expulsion of Tissa Thera from the Order of monks after an inquiry according to the Vinaya into certain charges against him.[87] All these matters mentioned above inform that the Ministers of State were learned and cultured persons. They interfered and took active part in academic and ecclesiastical matters and they were highly qualified persons. For this reason they used to deal with such situations. In Aggalodhi I's (568-601 A.D) resign twelve celebrated poets wrote poetical works in Sinhalese.[88] The Nikāyasangraha[89] mentions the names of the twelve poets and they were: (1) Sakdamala, (2) Asakdāmala, (3) Damī, (4) Bābiri, (5) Dalabiso, (6) Anurutkumaru, (7) Dalagot-kumāru, (8) Dalasala-Kumaru, (9) Kitsiri-kumaru, (10) Puravaḍu-Kumaru, (11) Sūriyabāhu and (12) Kasupkoṭa-Āpā. All the names reveal that they were lay people. Not a single work of these poets was found so far. There were learned Buddhist nuns in Sri Lanka and they were busy in educational work. So the education of women was not far behind that of men. Generally, women used to do work for the intellectual and moral welfare of the members of their own sex. King Jettha-Tissa III's queen became a member of the order of Nuns. She joined the Bhikkhuṇī-samgha and devoted her time to study the Abhidhamma with its commentary.[90] Generally advanced intellectual people used to study this subject.

It may be noted here that among the 12 poets referred to above there was one called Dalabiso. Most probably, this was the name of a woman.[91]

Most probably, the Mirror-wall (Kadapat-pavura) at Sigiriya was built in the fifth century A.D. by Kassapa I (478-496 A.D) himself. It has a large number of small writings on its glass-like surface. Palaeographically, they range in date from the sixth centry A.D. to some time after the Polonnaruva period.[92] Many visitors during this period visited Sīgiriya. Because it was a place of historical importance. Various visitors recorded their presence on its glass-like surface. So this mirror-wall at Sgiriya gives us information about the standard of general education in ancient Sri-Lanka.[93] These records are written in verse but a few records are in prose. Most of them refer to the beauty of the famous Sīgiriya paintings while others mention the colossal lion figure at the entrance to the summit of the rock or some other matters of Sīgiriya. There are names and addresses of the authors on the records. There are kings, princes, ministers, monks, government officials and ordinary men and women. They belonged to different parts of the island.[94] In ancient Sri-Lanka writing was very popular. "Each individual has used the hand he was used to, and the idiosyncracies noticeable in the various graffiti are infinite. While some of the graffiti are among the best examples of ancient Sinhalese calligraphy, others are incised in a most careless manner."[95] These records were written by ordinary visitors. Even women composed several stanzas and they inform that in ancient Sri Lanka female education was not far behind that of males.

Sri Lanka's fame as a land of learning had spread far and wide. Hiuen-Tsang or Tsiang had "heard that in the middle of the ocean there was a country called Sinhala; it was distinguished for its learned doctors belonging to the Sthavira school, and also for those able to explain the yoga-sāstra."[96] Later the Chinese monk met at Kāñchipura in South India about 300 Sinhalese monks headed by Bodhimegheśvara and Abhayadanistra.[97] Hiuen

Tsiang[98] asked them: "It is reported that the chief priests of your kingdom are able to explain the Tripiṭaka according to the Sthavira school and also the Yoga-sāstra. I am anxious to go there and study these books. May I ask you why you have come to this place?" They then replied that "they had come there because there was a famine in Cylon (Sri Lanka) at the time, and also because Jamdvipa was the place of the Buddha's birth." Further they told: "Among the members of our school who know the law there are none who excel ourselves as to age and position, if you have any doubts therefore, let us, according to your will, speak together about these things."[99]

The Sīgāla sutta of the Dīgha Nikāya (D.III, 117) mentions the mutual responsibilities between the Buddhist Saṁgha and the laity. The Buddhist Saṁgha's great responsibility towards the lay person was his education. The Buddhist monk or the Buddhist nun was primarily responsible for guiding and teaching the laity. "This education was in the form of Dhamma preaching, especially at the four lumar quarters of the month (Uposatha), and also in the education of youth both in Dharma and in more secular subjects, such as writing."[100] In most monasteries in Sri Lanka there were schools for young people of the district and this traditions has continued up to the present day. In many Theravāda countries the Buddhist Saṁgha gives opportunities and facilities to the lay people to train themselves in medicine, agriculture, literacy and other topics connected with local development schemes as well as in traditional Dhamma. The Buddhist monks also contributed very much to the development of traditional irrigation projects in Sri Lanka. The duty of the Buddhist Samgha was to provide secular as well as religious education from classical to contemporary times. The Buddha refers to the teaching situation as one wherein the teacher grows spiritually. According to Buddhism, teaching is a natural expression of one whose mind is freed, be he an arahant or a Buddha, as both by compassion are moved.[101]

NOTES

1. HBC., 287; AIE., 394.
2. HBC., 287.
3. DN., III., 117; *ibid.*, 287
4. HBC., 287.
5. *Ibid.*, 288; f.n. 1.
6. *Ibid.*, 288-289.
7. *Ibid.*, 289.
8. *Ibid.*, 289; Vsm., 71-72.
9. *Ibid.*, 289; DA., 365.
10. *Ibid.*, 289; *ibid.*, 365.
11. *Ibid.*, 289.
12. *Ibid.*, 290; Smp. 501.
13. *Ibid.*, 290; Mhv., xxxviii, 16-18.
14. *Ibid.*, 290; VbhA., 273.
15. *Ibid.*, 290.
16. *Ibid.*, 290; MA., 325.
17. *Ibid.*, 291; *ibid.*, 353.
18. *Ibid.*, 291; *ibid.*, 469.
19. *Ibid.*, 291; Smp., 503.
20. *Ibid.*, 291.
21. *Ibid.*, 291.
22. *Ibid.*, 163; Smp (SHB), 220-221.
23. *Ibid.*, 163, f.n. 4.
24. *Ibid.*, 163-164., MSA., 47.
25. *Ibid.*, 161.
26. *Ibid.*, 292; Mhv., xliv, 107 ft.
27. *Ibid.*, 292; *ibid.*, xliv, 150; xlviii, 141-142.
28. *Ibid.*, 292; MA., 881, "Pathamàṃ abhidhammapitakaṃ massati."
29. *Ibid.*, 161.
30. *Ibid.*, 161; EZ., I, 85.
31. *Ibid.*, 161.
32. *Ibid.*, 159; DA., 654; MA., 881.
33. *Ibid.*, 159; VbhA., 336; Smp. III, 92.
34. *Ibid.*, 292; Mhv., xli, 58-60; xliv, 47; xlv, 2; xlix, 33.
35. *Ibid.*, 165; Clvg., 247.
36. *Ibid.*, 164.
37. *Ibid.*, 164-165.
38. *Ibid.*, 165; Tennent, I, 615, 620.
39. *Ibid.*, 165; MSA., 47, 59, 168; Koṭahena, 8.
40. *Ibid.*, 292; Mhv, xxxvii, 100-101.
41. *Ibid.*, 293; *ibid.*, xxiii, 85.
42. *Ibid.*, 293.

43. *Ibid.*, 293; Vsm. 71.
44. *Ibid.*, 293; AA., 24; DA., 521-522.
45. *Ibid.*, 293; Vsm., 68.
46. *Ibid.*, 293; MA., 353.
47. *Ibid.*, 293; *ibid.*, 55., AA., 23.
48. *Ibid.*, 294.
49. *Ibid.*, 294; Vsm, 69.
50. *Ibid.*, 294; Smp., 297; AA., 363; Vsm, 211.
51. *Ibid.*, 294; AA., 343.
52. *Ibid.*, 294; Mhv., xxxv, 30.
53. Smp. (SHB), 577-578; *ibid.*, 294.
54. *Ibid.*, 295. The Bhikkhu-Bhikkhunī-Mātikā generally known as the Pātimokkha.
55. *Ibid.*, 295.
56. *Ibid.*, 295.
57. *Ibid.*, 295.
58. *Ibid.*, 295.
59. *Ibid.*, 295.
60. *Ibid.*, 295.
61. *Ibid.*, 295.
62. *Ibid.*, 295.
63. *Ibid.*, 295, f.n. 5.
64. *Ibid.*, 295.
65. *Ibid.*, 295; DhpA., II (SHB), 600.
66. *Ibid.*, 296.
67. *Ibid.*, 296.
68. *Ibid.*, 296.
69. *Ibid.*, 296.
70. *Ibid.*, 296; f.n. 1.
71. *Ibid.*, 296; AA., 23, 24.
72. *Ibid.*, 296; Vsm., 72.
73. *Ibid.*, 172, 296.
74. *Ibid.*, 172.
75. *Ibid.*, 172; DA., 406.
76. *Ibid.*, 297.
77. *Ibid.*, 297; DA., 535; MA., 186-187.
78. *Ibid.*, 297.
79. *Ibid.*, 297; Vsm. 71-72.
80. *Ibid.*, 297; *ibid.*, 476-477.
81. *Ibid.*, 298; AA., 44; MA., 350.
82. *Ibid.*, 298; MA., 157.
83. *Ibid.*, 298.
84. *Ibid.*, 298; Smp. (SHB), 418.
85. *Ibid.*, 298.

86. *Ibid.*, 299; Mhv. xxxvi, 41.
87. *Ibid.*, 299; *ibid.*, xxxvii, 39.
88. *Ibid.*, 299; *ibid.*, xlii, 13., Nks, 15.
89. *Ibid.*, 299; Nks., 15.
90. *Ibid.*, 299; Mhv, xliv, 108-117.
91. *Ibid.*, 299; f.n. 5.
92. *Ibid.*, 299-300.
93. *Ibid.*, 300.
94. *Ibid.*, 300.
95. Paramavitana, 311, 312; *ibid.*, 301.
96. HBC., 302; Beal, 133.
97. *Ibid.*, 302.
98. *Ibid.*, 302; Beal, 139.
99. *Ibid.*, 302; *ibid.*, 139.
100. BPE., 331.
101. *Ibid.*, 331.

4

Buddhist Art, Architecture and Sculpture of Sri Lanka

The architecture, sculpture and monumental history of Sri Lanka began with the introduction of Buddhism in the island. The Andhra tradition played a great role to influence the sculpture art of Sri Lanka.[1] Most of the monuments of Sri Lanka were found in the Rajarata region particularly in Anurādhapura and Polonnaruva. Giant stūpas, monasteries, remains of palaces, the celebrated Lohapāsāda and stone sculptures were discovered and they were of the indigenous character. They were of wooden construction. Because of this, they were unable to remain for a very long time. On the sites new buildings were raised. The first stūpa or dāgaba (dhātugarbha), the Mahāuihāra, and the Thupārāma were established besides the first Abhayagiri vihāra at the Jetavanārāma in Anurādhapura. The most famous dāgaba of Sri Lanka in the Mahāhathempa or the Ruvanvelisaya with 295 ft diameter. The Mahayagiri dāgaba is still bigger at the Jetavana dāgaba is the largest of all, 393 ft high with a diameter at the base 377 ft.

The origin of the stupa was pre-Buddhist. But at a very early period the Buddhists adopted it. The corporeal relics of the Buddha were enshrined in the stūpa. During the reign of Aśoka, numerous stupas were constructed at different places in India. Devānamipiya Tissa built the famous Thūpārāma Dāgaba or stūpa at Anurādhapura.[2] At first it was constructed in the form of a heap of paddy. But it was restored several times and today it has a diameter of 59 feet 6 inches at the base.[3] Architecturally, a dāgaba has a terrace (maluva) with a screen or gateway (vahalkada) at each cardinal point, surmounted by a dome (dāgaba proper) on the summit of which stands a square platform where rises a conical spire (kotha) of which the finial may be of gold and or of rock crystal. There are four traditional shapes for the dome in Sri Lanka: the bubble, the paddy heap, the bell and the water-pot. Some authorities say that the dāgaba (also called thupa-tope, stope, stupa seya, chatiya or vihara) in the parasol's logical architectural development in the East, "Whence it came, not a protection from the weather but an honorific symbol. As the parasol grew more magnificent the stem became for architectural reasons, the more manageable feature, while the canopy had to be represented by the more or less highly ornamented kotha." Other authorities see in the shape no more than a tumulus. And others "yet a model of the symmetrical cosmos." The auspicious circumambulation of a dāgaba places the structure on the right. A little more than a century after the introduction and the establishment of Buddhism in Sri Lanka, the stūpa was built in a very colossal pattern in Sri Lanka. King Dutthagāmanī built to monuments of this type. The earlier was the maricavaṭṭi(Murisavati). It has a diameter of 168 feet at the base.[4] The Mahāthūpa (Ruvanvelisiya or Ruvanvali) has a diameter of 289 at the base. Some say it has a diameter of 295 feet. Its height in 120 cubits, which in equivalent to 300 feet.[5] Archacological evidence shows that when king Dutthagāmanī built it, the dimensions of this monument more the same as they were later.[6] King Dutthagāmanī celebrated The seventh day after his victory over Elāra with a water-festival at the Tissa tank. Near this place he planted his spear (the king's spear, generally containing a relic of the Buddha, was the royal standard in battle) on the shore and laid his clothes. Here he constructed his first dagaba the Mirisavati Dāgaba and he enshrined in it his spear with its relic - "in expiation, as he himself explained, of his impicty in having once eaten a relish (miris)" without a thought of the Brotherhood."[7] "The Vahalkadas are particularly striking. The Ruvanvali Dāgaba has been mentioned as the greatest pious reconstruction undertaken in Anurādhapura - not with any conspicuous success; for modern engineers saw it necessary to flatten the shoulders of the dome, thus sacrificing the perfection of its original "bubble" shape."[8] The present finial is plated in gold. The huge rock crystal that points it was a gift from the Buddhists of Myanmar (Burma). The dāgaba is about 300 feet high. King Duttha gāmaṇī's most munificent gift was the Ruvanvali dāgaba, but he died before its completion. He did not live to see that the dāgaba was completed." His dying wish to see it finished, however, so moved his subjects that they covered the enormous frame of the unfinished structure in white cloth; and so gave it in his failing sight the semblance of its perfect shape".[9] Devanampiya Tissa built the Thupārāma Dāgaba at Anurādhapura. This was the most ancient of Sri Lanka's dagabas and this was built by Devānampiya Tissa to enshrine the Buddha's collarbone relic. Originally, its shape was like the "paddy-heap" shape, but in 1840s its present "bell" shape was reconstructed.[10] "The graceful monolithic pillars surrounding it once upheld a circular roof making the shrine a vata dage (circular relic-house) a characteristically Sinhala architectural feature."[11] The brazan palace was the work of Duttagāmanī and it was burnt down only 15 years after its building. Largely it was a wooden structure. The 1600 pillars (in 40 rows) that now indicate the site are ascribed to king Parakrama Bahu I (1153-1186 A.D.) of Polonnaruwa. The original building had 9 graded storeys and at ground level it was 100 cubits square and its height was also 100 cubits square. The monks who lived here were also graded. The simple folk used to live on the ground floor; doctors of the teaching used to live on the second floor and the saintliest arahants used to stay on the highest of all.[12] The Mahāvaṃsa describes it: "... a white parasol with a coral foot, resting on mountain crystal and having a silver staff. On it, depicted in the seven gems the eight auspicious figures ... and rows of little silver bells hung upon the edge ...."[13] The stūpa of the Abhayagiri monastery was built in the region of Vattagāmanī Abhaya. But it was not very large. In the reign of Gajabahu I subsequent enlargements took place and this helped to make it larger than the Mahāthūpa.[14] The Dakkhina Thūpa was founded in the reign of Vattagāmanī Abhaya at Anurādhapura.[15] At present it is the fifth largest shrine at Anurādhapura. During kaviṭṭha Tissa's time it was enlarged to its present dimensions. King Mahāsena was the originator of the Minneriya Tank. He constructed the largest stūpa of Sri Lanka—the Jetavanaramaya[16], visible, to the east, from the neighbourhood of the Ruvavaliseya, the Jetavana arameya (monastery) built by king Mahasena for one of his Mahāyānist proteges on ground confiscated from the Mahāvihiāra which Devānampiya Tissa had founded, has its site marked by the mightiest of Sri Lanka's dāgabas."[17] It has a diameter of 367 feet at its base and in its ruined condition it still stands to a height of 232 feet. Its original height was 160 cubits. Originally it was 350 feet tall. The door-posts of the attached Image House still stand and each one was 36 foot, counting 9' buried in the foundations.[18] It may be noted here that Sri Lanka was unable to preserve intact to early stūpa in its original form. From descriptions in literary works as well as from miniature models which served as reliquaries we can say that the ancient stūpas of Sri Lanka in their design closely followed designs of the Indian monuments. "The main feature of the stūpa was the bubble-shaped dome which, in the case of the colossal monuments, rose from a triple-based platform, as against the single medhi or terrace of the Sāñchī stūpas. The dome was surmounted by a square railing of wood or stone which later became a cube of brick masonry; a stone pillar embedded in the dome rose above the railing. The stūpa was crowned by an umbrella (chattra) or a series of umbrellas. The railings at gateways of the early stūpas in Sri Lanka were of wood and have perishad. It is the super-structure of the stupas, i.e., the portion above the dome, that underwent development in later times. The three basal terraces of the Ruvanvali and the Kaṇṭaka-catiya at Mihintale have been faced with blocks of limestone in the and first century B.C.[19] In the second century or thereabouts, the pattern of the colossal stūpas at Anurādhapura, Mihintale at Māgama was altered and frontispieces projecting from the base and facing the cardinal points were added.[20] These frontispieces have moulded bases, a succession of string courses alternating with vertical bands, both of limestone, and a superstructure of brick consisting of a central vimāna and two similar features of smaller size on either side. The architectural designs were elephant-heads, makara-brackets, lotus peterae, gloval designs and friezes of ganas and animals. There were two stelae on either side of each frontispiece. One of them reached in height to the base of the brick superstructure and the other was shorter. The front and the exposed side of the stelae were found with sculptures. Limestone platforms projecting from the base existed before the frontispieces were erected at the Ruvanvali Dagaba and these were introduced in later structure. In ancient times these frontispieces became known as āyakas, and they were like the āyaka-platform of the stūpas in the Andhra Country.[21]

The earliest remains of structural edifices from about the fourth century A.D. were found at the moated site near the Nuvaravava in Anurādhapura and at Madirigiriya.[22] In these edifices stone was used for pillars, free standing or embedded in the brick masonary of the walls and flights of steps flanked by wing-stones terminating at slabs with rounded top. There were semicircular slabs of store at the foot of the flight of steps. Wooden construction was used for the superstructures of these edifices, and roof was built with flat tiles of burnt clay. The walls were done with a coating of lime plaster and there were figures and floral designs of stucco or terracotta and these were used for the decorative scheme.[23] In the architectural monuments for ornamental figures limestone was used. There were huge octagonal pillars of gneiss with accurate angles and smooth surfaces in the colossal stūpas.[24] A colossal granite pillar was found at Tissamahārāva and it has an inscription of the first century.[25]

The stone sculpture found at Anurādhapura has reliefs on stela and pillars besides many gigantic rock-cut statues. The figures in the round are the great standing Buddhas, they belonged to the 3rd or 4th century A.D. The height of some of the statues is 8 feet. The attitude of these figures in very rigid.[26] The Colossal Buddha was found at Avukana. It belonged to the 8th century A.D.[27] The Anurādhapura and Midirigiriya Buddhas of the 3rd and 4th centuries A.D. indicate Gupta influence.[28] The stelac at the Abhayagiri and the Jetavana dāgabas are figure sculptures and they represent divine beings or the Chakravarti monarch.[29] The bas-reliefs ornamenting the stelae of the frontispieces are the earliest specimens of sculpture in Sri Lanka. The stelae of the eastern frontispiece of the Kaṇṭaka Cetiya has reliefs and in style and subject they "belong to a class distinct from the others."[30] Some of the motives among the sculptures has a great resemblance to those ornamenting the gateways of the stupas at Sāñcī.[31] The sculptures found at the eastern frontispieces of the Kantaka Cetiya and the sculptures found at the southern one of the Abhayagiri are flat and not deep. They appear like shadow outlines filled in with black or other colours. The attitudes of these figures are very rigid. They look like the early work at Bhārhut, Bodhgayā and Sāñcī.[32] The figure sculptures found at the frontispieces of the Abhayagiri and those of the Jetavana Dāgaba in their modelling, graceful attitudes and the vivacious expressions in their faces remind the bas-reliefs of Amarāvatī.[33] There are representations of Nāgas in the animal and also representation in the human form on the shorter stelae.[34] Most probably, Sri Lanka's art-world was greatly influenced by the artists from the Central Indian School. Sri Lanka's artists and sculptors had established close contact with the artists and sculptors of the Vengī country. Because Sri Lanka must have imported some pieces of bas-reliefs in marble from that country.[35]

The earliest standing Buddha images were found in Sri Lanka and they show the influence of the style of Amarāvatī.[36] A Buddha image of marble, six feet in height, was carved in the Vengī country and in ancient times it was brought to Sri Lanka. It was found in the Anurādhapura District.[37] The earliest seated Buddhas of Sri Lanka show that Mathura has made a great influence upon them.[38] The Gupta sculpture of India played a great role for the development of sculpture in Sri Lanka. Its influence was found in several Buddha images and the bas-relief at Isurumuniya in Anurādhapura.[39] It is difficult to give any date to any of these works of art. Copper images under the feet of the Buddhas in a shrine at Madirigiriya may belong to the 4th century A.D.[40] The figurine of a nude female, about three inches in height in ivory found at the Ruvanvali Dāgaba may belong to the second centuryA.D.[41] Relic caskets of earthenware were found in the stūpas.[42] Polished black-ware, red and black-ware, polished red ware and rouletted ware were found at the ancient sites in Sri Lanka.[43] Several small bronze images of Bodhisattvas, the seated Buddha from Badulla, the Pattini Devi (Tārā) from Sri Lanka's eastern region, the seated Tārā from Kurunagala were found and they were bronze images.[44] The Buddhist monasteries have cells and image houses "as part of the enclosure wall facing the central court where a large stūpa stands like the Mahāvihāra, Abhayagiri Vihāra at Anurādhapura."[45] Some image houses of the stūpas have seated Buddhas in four directions. Smaller monosteries known as Pabhat Vihāras constructed in the later Anurādhapura period were discovered with beautiful architecture.[46]

In the late Anurādhapura period the stūpa occupied an important place in Buddhist worship and many new stūpas were built. But none was like the earlier colossal stūpas in size. Near Sigiriya a stūpa was built. It belongs to the fifth century A.D.

and it measures 92 feet in diameter at the base.[47] Another stūpa was constructed on an easterly spur of Mihintate in the seventh or eighth century A.D. It has a base diameter of 88 feet.[48] These later stūpas or dāgabas in the form and shape of the base and dome tried to follow the lines of the earlier ones. Their superstructures above the solid cubical feature (hatavas-koṭura) had a conical spire (kot-karalla) established on a cylindrical neck which became known as the devatā-kotura because there were figures of deitsies on it.[49] In the seventh century A.D. there were no circular platforms from which the colossal stūpas were built and in their place a square shape appeared and their areas were enlarged greatly. In the ninth or tenth century A.D. there were the introduction of the stone paving of the great stūpas of Anurādhapura, the broad flights of stone steps together with their accessories, the processional paths bordered by enclosing walls outside the platforms, the monumental gateways which at the cardinal points crossed the enclosing walls and the flights of stone steps which helped to give access to the processional paths.[50] In the eighth or ninth century A.D. several stūpas of small size were built. In them important architectural developments took place. Stone for paving, platform, retaining walls of the platform etc. was used.[51] This type was found at the Indikatusāya at Mihintale. This was Mahāyana monument.[52] The wooden pillars of the circular shrines (Cetiyaghra or Vata-dā-ge) which enclosed stūpas of smaller size were replaced by covered stone pillars surrounded by ornamental capitals.[53] The shrines of this type are the vata-dā-ges at Thūpārāma and Laṅkārāma at Anurādhapura and at Mihintale, Medirigiriya and Tiriyāy.[54] The pillars are palced "in four to two concentric circles, diminishing in size outwards: the shafts are of slender and graceful porportions and the capitals which surmount them are a conventionalised lotus in basic form carved with figures of dwarfs, geese, lions and other motifs."[55] The Boddhighara at Nillakgana in the Kurnnagala district in the 'Bodhi-tree-house', a double platformed building and the Bodhi-tree stood on the upper platform of the building.[56]

The vast majority of the architectural remains of the later Anurādhapura period "consist of stylobates with moulded retaining walls of brick or stone, flights of steps leading up to them, and stone pillars, dressed or plain, rising from them: partial remains of the superstructure have survived in a few cases."[57] The first category of stylobates has a square sanctum, "divided internally into two inter-communicating rooms, from which projects a person of smaller size, with a flight of steps giving access to the shrine."[58] The other type "is oblong on plan, and the flight of access steps is in front of a projecting porch: a larger edifice in the centre is surrounded by a four smaller edifices of similar plan placed at the four corners of an enclosing, walled quadrangle, a 'five of cards' arrangement as Bell called it. The pillars rising from these stylobates are monoliths generally about 12 feet high, squared and usually smoothly dressed: their carved capitals are sometimes monolithic with the pillars. The superstructures of these edifices were of wood . . . . .."[59]

The flights of steps which gave access to the shrines were decorated in a lavish manner. The risers of the steps were plain or decorated with carved dwarfs or other designs between pilasters. There were wingstones or balustrades consisting of a volute coming from the mouth of the makara animal whose feet are kept on pilasters on the sides of the balustrades.[60] The moonstone, a semi-circular slab of stone, sculptured in unequally divided scrolls, is at the foot of the flight of steps.[61] The Padhānaghara or 'meditation house' and the 'western monasteries' of Anurādhapura were constructed on rocky sites and had stone-lined ponds and moats, stone porches, raised walls and outhouses.[62] Other monastic buildings of a special nature were the sannipātasāla, where the monks used to assemble on pubic occasions, the mahāpali, where the monks during meal times met together and hospitals, where their sick were looked after.[63] Small cells were built for the rasidences of the monks. For the construction of pillars, gneiss or granite was used. But in the early period, for steps, balustrades and moulded bases the softer limestone was used.[64] From about the sixth century A.D. limestone was replaced by granite and in the eighth century A.D. the Sinhalese stone-masons had done very well in carving elegant and intricate desings on the harder medium.[65] There were buildings of brick, with massive walls, rvaulted roofs and arched openings, and these buildings were found at Anurādhapura.

Many Sinhalese sculptors after the fourth century A.D. worked in gneiss for both bas-relief and figures in the round.[66] The well known relief of an amatory couple, representing the prine Sāliya and his life Aśokamālā, and other sculptures were found at the Isurumumiya rock-temple at Anurādhapura and they belonged to the fourth and fifth centuries A.D.[67] These works show the influence of the style of the Gupta age of India. They remind that the Gupta characterstics of refinement of features and serenity of expression are very prominent.[68] The sunken relief of the 'Man and Horse' of the seventh century A.D. was found at Isurumuniya and it belonged to the Pallava era.[69] A Bodhisattna figure in the round at Situlpavura and a similar figure at Kurukkalmadam in the Batticaloa district were found and they belonged to the same age.[70] In the design decorating a moonstone the general characteristics are[71]:—"a constructionalised half-lotus in the centre enclosed by concentric bands which, proceeding outwards, are decorated respectively with a procession of geese, an intricate foliage design, a procession of the fourt beasts—elephant, lion, horse and bull, racing each other and an outer most band of stylised flames.

The various elements of the design are skilfully integrated into a very effective whole. The motifs which constitute the design are symbolic." Sri Lanka's sculptors took interest to make standing Buddha images. They slightly modified the attitude of the hands, the details of the drapery, the expression in the face and the general proportion of the body.[72] The image at Māligavela, near Buttala in height was over 34 feet and 10 feet acrosss the shoulder. It was carved in the round. The sculptor placed it on a pedestal of appropriate proportion.[73] The standing colossus at Sasserura, not far from Avukana and the seated and recumbant ones at Tantrimalai and Alahere belonged to the later part of the Amurādhapura period.[74] Among the rock-cut Buddhas of Sri Lanka, the tallest one was over 50 feet in height and it was found at Buduruvegala neer Vallavāya.[75] There were images of Bodhisattvas on its either sides. They were smaller than the Buddha.[76] The well-known Kusta-rājā (leper king) of Valigama, which from the figures of Dhyāni Buddhas on the head-dress, can be mentioned as a representation of Avalokitesvara.[77] The seated Buddha image was found at Pankuliya in Anurādhapura and it beloged to the seventh or eighth century A.D.[78] The group of four seated Buddha image in the Vat-dā-ge at Madirigiriya belonged to the reign of Aggabodhi IV (667-683 A.D.).[79] In the treatment of the robe the seated Buddha images of the later Anurādhapura period differ from the standing Buddha images. In the former the robe was shown clinging to the body, while in the latter schematic folds were shown.[80] The seated Buddha image on the outer circular road at Anurādhapura may belong to the fifth or sixth century A.D. According to some authorities, it may belong to the earlier period.[81] In style it was more archaic than that of Pankuliya. When Sri Lanka's sculptors created the images of the Buddha, they always wanted to impress the superhuman might and power of the Buddha on the minds of the devotees.[82]

Many bronze images of the later Anurādhapura period we found in different parts of the island. Some of these show that they are of Mahāyānisitc character. They were the Buddha, Bodhisattvas, Lokapālas and Brahmanical gods.[83] Terracotta and stucco figures found at Sigiriya belonged to the fifth century A.D. while those found at Kantaka-cetiya at Mihintale may belong to a century later. Wall paintings of Sigiriya fortress-cum-palace constructed by Kassapa in the fifth century A.D. present the figures of Apsaras in Ajanta style.[84] A great part of the western rock-face of Sigiriya was used with line plaster and on this part hundred of figures of divine damsels were painted by the painters.[85] Of these, twenty one figures have survived this day.[86] The female figures were found with jewellery and head-dress. The golden coloured female figures have no dresses and they are nude above the waist while other figures of dark complexion have used a breast-band. Most of the female figures in their hands hold flowers, while the darker ladies hold tray with flowers.[87] These figures show that they are coming out from clouds and this informs that they are not earthly creatures. The colours used in the paintings of Sigīrīya are yellow, brick-red and green. The outline of the figures was drawn first in red and afterwards the pigments were used. When the plaster was dry the paintings was done at the colours were taken from minerals.[88] The fragmentary remains of paintings were found in a cave at Hindagala near Peradeniya and they belonged to the same period as Sigiriya.[89] In the relic-chamber of a stūpa at Mihinitale, outline sketches of divine beings rising from clouds were found and they belonged to the eighth century A.D.[90] A figure of a dwarf with flute, floral designs and the outline of a lion were found on the Vāhalkadas at Anurādhapura and Mihintale.[91] Jewellery of the tenth century was found in several places of the island and the art of the lapidery flourished also in the island.[92] Large storage jars decorated with incised lines and pots used for drainage purposes of the late Anurādhapura period were found.[93] Vessels of foreign manufacture were found at Mihintale. Glazed roof tiles of various colours of local manufacture were found.[94]

The Colas after their conquest of Sri Lanka destroyed the palace and many buildings at Anurādhapura. Many religious edifices at that ancient city and elsewhere were destroyed by them also. But at Polonnaruvna, which was the seat of their government they constructed many temples for Saivism, which was their own faith.[95] The Śiva temples (now known as Śiva Devale Nos. 1 and 2) at Polonnaruva were built by the colas for the glorification of Śiva.[96] When they settled at this place, they built those temples there. Śiva Devale No. 1 displays superlative stone work. The upper portions have vanished.[97] Śiva Devale No. 2 is the oldest building in Polonnaruva. It is the city's one all-stone shrine.[98] Its ancient name was Vāṇavan-mādevī-iśvasam. It got its name after a queen of Rājarāja I. It is a stone building and it is well-proportioned and in outline it is harmonious.[99] An image house of brick, now called Natanār-Kovil was known anciently as Velgam-vehera.[100] The only monumnet dating from the reign of Vijayabahu I is his Temple of the Tooth at Polonnruva, now known as the Aṭadāge.[101]

In the eighth to tenth centuries A.D. the type of stūpa which existed was "one with an elongated dome, with mouldings in place of the basal terraces and placed on a square platform".[102] But Parsākramabāhu's architects did not follow this design. They accepted the style of the colossal stūpas of the ancient period. The Kiri-vehera can be mentioned as the best preserved stūpa at Polonnarura.[103] The Rankot-vera built by heissankamalla is the largest one.[104] The architects of these stūpas followed the design of the colossal stūpas at Anurādhapura. The Damila-thūpa was constructed by the labour of Tamil prisoners of war and it had a new design.[105] The dome has take its rise from the huge, terraced and moulded base and is left unfinished at a height of about fifty feet above the ground so as to make an extensive, circular plateau: in the middle of this plateau there is a small stūpa on a square platform.[106] There were two other large stūpas of the same design Parākramabāhu I built these two stūpas. One was at Dadigama, the king's birth place and the other one was at Yudanganāra, near Buttala, the place of his mother's cremation.[107] The Sat-mahal-prāsada, a square pyramidal tower of seven diminishing stages, was also a stūpa. It was built on the Tooth Relic Terrace a Polonnaruva. It was originally octagonal: each side of each stage of its present altered shape is ornamented by the figure of a deity within an arched niche.[108]

Among other significant works of art are the Lanka Tilaka and Tiranka brick temples with huge standing Buddha of brick finished in stucco.[109] The Atadage and Vatadage complex is a group of several temples and each temple has a different architecture.[110] The Thūpārāma, the Lankātilake and the Tiranka Image-House or Northern temple are three large image-houses at Polonnnarura.[111] All three shrines followed the designs of image-houses in the later Anurādhapura period. There was a seated Buddha image in the inner sanctum of the Thūpārāma. But the other two shrines had standing images all of brick and stucco.[112] The Thūpārāma, this finely preserved image house, formed past of the establishment of the Temple of the Tooth. Through its walls, of extravagant thickness, there was a stairway which went to the roof.[113] The Lankatilaka Vihāra is the vest image house (170'×69') and its walls stand still 55' high although the resulted roof—a characteristic, corbelled arch has perished.[114] The Triranka Image House has received its name from the "thrice-curved" pose of the Buddha image within, a pose normally assigned to sculptures of the female form. There are frescoes and they decorate the interior. The building was part of the Jetavana monastery of Polonnaruva.[115] In the Gal Vihāra there are three splendid statues of the Buddha in upright, sedent and recumbent postures. From a scarp of rock it was cut in the round. The largest figures measures 44'. Hewn out of the rock is a small cave shrine which was protected by the customary "drip-bedge".[116] The Hatadage or the Tooth-Relic Temple of Nissankamalla has its own distinctive characteristics.[117] "It is entered by a porch which admits to a square vestibule projecting from a larger square cella. The base is effectively moulded and from this the walls of stone rise to a height of nine feet, the plain ashlar surface being relieved most artistically by a double border, vertical as well as horizontal of faintly incised carving."[118] The Baddhasīmā-pāsāda is an uposatha-ghara. There was a large hall with 108 stone pillars inside the building. The walls of this splendid edifice were once coated with the red, polished plaster.[119] The Potgul-Vehera or the Poth-gul Vehera is an uncommon circular shrine with a domed roof.[120] "It is a rotunda with an oblong vestibule attached on the east, and it was roofed by means of a corbelled vault."[121]

In the four Buddha images in the Vata-dā-gī at Polonnaruva the hair on the head is not shown as ringlets, but the Buddha is shown as wearing a close-fitting, small cap. The robe without folds is close-fitting.[122] The balustrades at Lankātilaka, the guardstones at the eastern entrance to the upper terrace of the Vata-dā-gī, and the balustrades at both the Rajavesyā-bhujanga-maṇḍapa and the Tivaṇka Image-house belong to the ninth or tenth century A.D.[123] The two chauri-bearers attending on the Buddha in the excavated cave at the Galvihāra inform that the Polonnaruva sculptors had the ability to do works of considerable merit.[124] There was not a single moonstone at Polonnaruva which was equal to those of Anurādhapura.[125] The best moonstone at Polonnaruva can be found at the northern entrance to the upper terrace of the Vata-dā-gī. Its execution was very fine. But it lacks that indefinable something which helps to make the Anurādhapura speciments great works of art.[126] At Anurādhapura we do not see decorated stone pillars. But there are many decorated stone pillars at Polonnaruva. The most striking ornamentation of pillars can be found in the Temple of the Tooth constructed by Vijayabahu I. The carving of dwarfs, mithunas, floral and foliage designs has been done with greater skill.[127] Effective decoration can be found on the pillars of the Rājaveś yā-bhujanga-maṇḍapa and the mandapa opposite Lankātilaka, as well as on the walls of the Hatadāgī, the screen of the Vata-dā-gī, and the background toraṇa to the seated Buddha at Galvihāra.[128] "All this decorative work was carried out with unerring good taste and restraint and fulfilled its object of emphasising the lines of the architectural design."[129] The stucco and terracotta figurines of deities on the walls of Image-houses and the friezes of dwarfs throw flood of light on a high standard of art in modelling.[130] Bronze Śaiva images were found at the śiva Devales. Among then are Natarājas, śiva and Pārvati, and several śaiva saints.[131] According to scholars, these bronzes were imported from South India. A remarkable local example of the bronze-caster's art was the elephant-lamp discovered in Parākramabāhu's stūpa at Dadigama.[132]

The earliest paintings of the Polonnaruva period are the fragments discovered from a Relic-chamber of the Mahi-Yaṅgaṇa-thūpa.[133] The subject-matter of the paintings is the victory of the Buddha over the Evil one. Several paintings were found in the caves at 'Dimbulāgala and at Pulligod-galage near Dimbulagala.[134] In the latter, the line drawing is very good but "the poses are formal and the colouring rather flat."[135] In the cave at the Galvihāra at Polonnaruva fragments of several divine figures were found. They indicate that a crowd of painted Devas and Brahmas attended the rock-cut figure of the Buddha.[136] At Lankātilaka on an arch another fragment was found. "It is little more than a decorative floral design."[137] The largest cycle of paintings was found in the Tiraṅka shrine or the Northern Temple at Polonnaruva.[138] They may belong to the late twelfth or early thirteenth century A.D. There were paintings from top to bottom on the walls. The paintings give religious subjects, Jātaka stories and scenes from the life of the Buddha. The colours are brick red, yellow and green. At first in outline the figures were drawn in red and then to produce varied tonal effects repeated layers of paint were applied. The painters gave much attention to produce in a beautiful way the costumes and ornaments of the kings, princes, nobles and divinities of the paintings.[139] These paintings at Polonnaruva inform us that "the ideals and canons of that art were still creative in Sri Lanka at a time when they had lost their vitality in India itself. Sri Lanka was the last refuge of that art which produced the masterpieces of Ajanta."[140]

During the rule of Vijayabāhu V and his successors, the neighbouring Tamil country of South India came under the rule of the Muslim rulers. As a result, many artisans left their homes and took shelter in Sri Lanka. For this reason, in the Sinhalese kingdom several Buddhist shrīnes in Dravaidian style were built. One of the earliest temples of this category was constructed at

Alaratura, now known as Gaṇegoda in the Kāgalla District by Dharmakīrti the first.[141] The edifice is now in ruins. But the shrine was constructed some years later and the same hierarch completed it in 1344 A.D. at Gaḍalādeniya in the Kandy district and its presentation is still in good condition.[142] There is a sedent Buddha image in the Gaḍalādeniya shrine. It is 78 ft in length, 37 ft in maximum breadth and 40 ft in height.[143] The building is of stone construction for the śikhara (the crowning dome). After some modifications the shrime was built in the Dravidian style.[144] The Laṅkātilaka shrine was about two miles away from Gaḍaladeniya and it was completed in 1344 A.D. The great minister Senā-Laṅkādhikāra built it.[145] The shrine is 96 ft in length and 78 ft in breadth and its original height is 32 cubits i.e., 80 ft.[146] Originally, it had four storeys. Now the ground floor is utilised. The second storey still remaining. The building was constructed with brick. But stone was used for the moulded base. According to scholars, the design indicates the Myanmarese influence. But it follows the traditions of Polonnaruva.[147] When the shrines of Gaḍalādeniya and Laṅkātilaka were built, Gaṁpala was the seat of royalty. At Niyamgampāya the only architectural remains of note were found. Brick was used for the construction of this shrine and its roof was timber and it was supported by stone pillars which rose from a platform faced with moulded and carved stonework.[148] In its architectural style it followed a continuation of the Anurādhapura tradition.[149] There are two edifices in Kandy and they are Nātha Devāle and the Geḍigī in Adāhanamalura.[150] The first one belongs to the second half of the fourteenth century A.D. and the second one in date is about a century later.[151] At Yāpavuva, Gaḍalādeniya and Niyamgampāya the moulded bases of buildings on their facias have dados of dancing figures and musicians in various lively attitudes.[152] The pillars on the porch of the Gaḍalādeniya temple have figures of Hindu deitics such as Natarāja in bas-relief.[153] The stone door-frames of many of the buildings had the decoration of floral designs of great intricacy.[154] A Buddha image was found at Gaṇīgoḍa.[155] The two colossal seated images at Gaḍalādeniya and the Laṅkātilaka temples were found.[156] It is very difficult to say whether they are of stone or of brick and stucco. There are figures of deitics which adorn the makara-toraṇas behind these Buddha images.[157] In the niches on the exterior of the inner shrine at Laṅkātilaka they are also found. Several Buddha images of gilt bronze of this period are kept in the temples of the Kandy district.[158] A seated bronze image of the Buddha was found at the Kandy Palace and it belongs to this period. It is now kept in a Museum at Edinburgh.[159] A bronze statue of a king of about a foot in height was kept at the Laṅkātilaka temple. It was a representation of Bhuvanakabāhu IV.[160]

NOTES

1. Pachori, 211.
2. CHC., 116.
3. *Ibid.*, 116.
4. *Ibid.*, 116-117.
5. *Ibid.*, 117.
6. *Ibid.*, 117.
7. Ceylon, 10.
8. *Ibid.*, 8.
9. *Ibid.*, 5.
10. *Ibid.*, 7.
11. *Ibid.*, 9.
12. *Ibid.*, 7.
13. *Ibid.*, 7.
14. CHC, 117.
15. *Ibid.*, 117.
16. *Ibid.*, 117.
17. Ceylon, 9.
18. *Ibid.*, 9.
19. CHC., 117.
20. *Ibid.*, 118.
21. *Ibid.*, 118.
22. *Ibid.*, 118.
23. *Ibid.*, 118.

24. *Ibid.*, 118.
25. *Ibid.*, 118.
26. Pachori, 212.
27. *Ibid.*, 212.
28. *Ibid.*, 212.
29. CHC., 119.
30. *Ibid.*, 119.
31. *Ibid.*, 119.
32. *Ibid.*, 119.
33. *Ibid.*, 119.
34. *Ibid.*, 119.
35. *Ibid.*, 119-120.
36. *Ibid.*, 120.
37. *Ibid.*, 120.
38. *Ibid.*, 120.
39. *Ibid.*, 120.
40. *Ibid.*, 120.
41. *Ibid.*, 120.
42. *Ibid.*, 120.
43. *Ibid.*, 120.
44. Pachori, 212.
45. *Ibid.*, 212.
46. *Ibid.*, 212.
47. CHC., 176.
48. *Ibid.*, 176.
49. *Ibid.*, 176.
50. *Ibid.*, 176-177.
51. *Ibid.*, 177.
52. *Ibid.*, 177.
53. *Ibid.*, 177.
54. *Ibid.*, 177.
55. *Ibid.*, 177.
56. *Ibid.*, 177.
57. *Ibid.*, 177.
58. *Ibid.*, 177-178.
59. *Ibid.*, 178.
60. *Ibid.*, 178.
61. *Ibid.*, 178.
62. *Ibid.*, 179.
63. *Ibid.*, 179.
64. *Ibid.*, 179.
65. *Ibid.*, 179.

66. *Ibid.*, 180.
67. *Ibid.*, 180.
68. *Ibid.*, 180.
69. *Ibid.*, 180.
70. *Ibid.*, 180.
71. *Ibid.*, 181.
72. *Ibid.*, 181.
73. *Ibid.*, 181.
74. *Ibid.*, 181.
75. *Ibid.*, 181.
76. *Ibid.*, 181.
77. *Ibid.*, 181.
78. *Ibid.*, 182.
79. *Ibid.*, 182.
80. *Ibid.*, 182.
81. *Ibid.*, 182.
82. *Ibid.*, 182.
83. *Ibid.*, 182.
84. Pachori, 212.
85. CHC, 182.
86. *Ibid.*, 182.
87. *Ibid.*, 182.
88. *Ibid.*, 183.
89. *Ibid.*, 183.
90. *Ibid.*, 183.
91. *Ibid.*, 183.
92. *Ibid.*, 183.
93. *Ibid.*, 183.
94. *Ibid.*, 183.
95. *Ibid.*, 268.
96. *Ibid.*, 268-269.
97. Ceylon, 16.
98. *Ibid.*, 16.
99. CHC, 269.
100. *Ibid.*, 269.
101. *Ibid.*, 269.
102. *Ibid.*, 270.
103. *Ibid.*, 270.
104. *Ibid.*, 270.
105. *Ibid.*, 270
106. *Ibid.*, 270.
107. *Ibid.*, 270.

108. *Ibid.*, 270.
109. Pachori, 212.
110. *Ibid.*, 212.
111. *Ibid.*, 212.
112. *Ibid.*, 271.
113. Ceylon, 14.
114. *Ibid.*, 16.
115. *Ibid.*, 20.
116. *Ibid.*, 20.
117. CHC., 271.
118. *Ibid.*, 271.
119. *Ibid.*, 271.
120. *Ibid.*, 271., Ceylon, 20.
121. CHC., 272.
122. *Ibid.*, 273-274.
123. *Ibid.*, 274.
124. *Ibid.*, 274.
125. *Ibid.*, 274.
126. *Ibid.*, 274.
127. *Ibid.*, 275.
128. *Ibid.*, 275.
129. *Ibid.*, 275.
130. *Ibid.*, 275.
131. *Ibid.*, 275.
132. *Ibid.*, 275.
133. *Ibid.*, 275.
134. *Ibid.*, 275.
135. *Ibid.*, 275-276.
136. *Ibid.*, 276.
137. *Ibid.*, 276.
138. *Ibid.*, 276.
139. *Ibid.*, 276.
140. *Ibid.*, 276.
141. *Ibid.*, 338.
142. *Ibid.*, 338.
143. *Ibid.*, 338.
144. *Ibid.*, 338.
145. *Ibid.*, 338.
146. *Ibid.*, 338.
147. *Ibid.*, 339.
148. *Ibid.*, 339.
149. *Ibid.*, 339.

150. *Ibid.*, 339.
151. *Ibid.*, 339.
152. *Ibid.*, 339.
153. *Ibid.*, 339.
154. *Ibid.*, 339.
155. *Ibid.*, 339.
156. *Ibid.*, 340.
157. *Ibid.*, 340.
158. *Ibid.*, 340.
159. *Ibid.*, 340.
160. *Ibid.*, 340.

5

Buddhist Festivals of Sri Lanka

Rituals, ceremonies and festivals always were not in touch with the spirit of Buddhism but they naturally appeared in the society and played great roles in the minds of the people when Buddhism became the state religion of Sri Lanka. These religious festivals were not always dull but they were colourful. There were music, singing and dancing in them. Sometimes the kings used to supply dancers and musicians for religious festivals.[1] People of the island used to like these festivals very much and for this reason they used to come to see them from long distances.[2] Religious festivals always gave entertainment and satisfaction of religious sentiment. In ancient times there were not much opportunities for public entertainment. That was the reason, why many religious festivals gradually appeared and continued to remain throughout the year in Sri Lanka.

Preaching

In Sri Lanka preaching became very popular in the society and for this reason in later times it took the form of a festival. For this festival people used to construct a great pavilion or hall (mahā-maṇḍapa) in a village and whole-night sermons were organised (sabbarattiṃ dhammasaraṇam) for this purpose.[3] Men, women and children from long distances used to come to the place where the cermony took place and they spent the night at the preaching place and the sermon and other activities continued throughout the night.[4] At monsteries generally preaching began after sunset. The Buddhist monks by beating a gong used to announce it.[5] The preacher had a fan (vījanī) in his hand.[6] When a preaching ceremony continued to spread over both day and night, then three monks at different periods acted as preachers.[7] The first one became known as Dīvā-kathika, "the day-preacher". During the day time he used to do his duty. He recited the text only. Then came the Pada-bhāṇaka, the "word-recite". He in Sinhalese paraphrased the sutta word for word. But he did it without details and explanation. The first one was not a very learned person. But the second one was a learned person no doubt. The third one was the most educated and most important of the three. He during the greater part of the night preached the sermon with details and expositions. This system no doubt produced good results because they not only allowed people to stay there for a very long time but they helped them to spent the day and night to observe the preaching ceremony without monotony and weariness.[8] Till recently in some parts of Sri Lanka day and night preaching for several days was in practice. This type of preaching became known as Sangi-bana "the preaching of the Sanigāti or Nikāyas."[9] At Anurādhapura the preaching halls were constructed at the heads of the four principal streets and four times a month sermons were delivered there.[10]

Ariyavṃsa

From Pāli commentaries and early inscriptions we learn that in ancient Sri Lanka a great festival was held in order to celebrate the preaching of the Ariyavaṃsa-sutta.[11] During several centuries before and after the fifth century A.D. "the Ariyavaṃsa was not only a popular sermon, but also an important institution held in high esteem for the perpetuation of which grants were made by kings and ministers and rich people at the time."[12] The

Mahāvaṃsa records that king Vohārika Tissa (269-291. A.D.) had given order to establish all over the Island a regular giving of alms at every place where the preaching ceremony of the Ariyavaṃsa took place.[13] The Toṇigala Inscription of the fourth century A.D. says that a person named Deva(ya), the son of Siva(ya), a member of the Council of ministers, made a grant in paddy, undur and beans.[14] According to the agreement, the capital should remain unspent and the interest should be used for giving meals to the monks at the Yahisapavata monastery located most probably at the place of the present Toṇigala near Vavuniya for the purpose of guiding the Ariyavaṃsa.[15] Two rock inscriptions from Labnaṭabandigala (about the fifth century A.D.) in the North-Central Province mention that a certain man called Sirinaka deposited 100 Kahavaṇas and another person called Naṭalaviṭiya Siva offered 20 Kahavaṇas to a great monastery known as Devagiri for the purpose of conducting the Ariyavaṃsa once a year.[16] The Aṅguttara commentary refers to a woman who went five yojanas to listen to a sermon on the Ariyavaṃsa by Dighabhāṇaka Mahā-Abhaya Thera.[17] The same commentary states that thirty bhikkus who were in retreat for the rainy season at Gavaravala-aṅigana gave a talk on the Mahā-Ariyavaṃsa fortnightly on poya days.[18] There are references to the Ariyavaṃsa in the Rasavāhinī.[19] A Thera from the Kuḍḍa-rajja province went to the Mahāvāpi-vihāra in Mahāgāma to listen to the preaching of the Ariyavaṃsa "which was an annual occurrence of the place at the time."[20] Many people from long distances came there to listen to this sermon. During the reign of Dubbiṭṭhi Mahārāja the preaching ceremony of the Ariyavaṃsa took place once every six months at Udumbaa-Mahāvihāra (Dimbulāgala) and people from within four yojanas arrived there to listen to the sermons preached by the Buddhist monks. For the festival elaborate arrangements were made (mahantaṃ pūjāvidhānaṃ).[21] Even today, at Dimbulāgala during the Vas or Vassa season the Buddhist monks preach the Ariyavaṃsa "which is significant of the persistence of the old tradition".[22] The preaching of the Ariyavaṃsa as a festival was held (Ariyavaṃsa Disanāmale vattamāne) at a monastery called Ariyākasa-vihāra near Kumbala-Tissapabbata.[23] There were certain theras who became well-known as Ariyavaṃsa-bhāṇakas distinguished for preaching the Ariyavaṃsa-sutta and they were the authorities in the dhamma.[24]

The Ariyavaṃsa is in Uruvala-Vagga of the Catukkanipāta in the Ariguttara-nikāya.[25] It discusses the four Ariyavaṃsā and it is known by several names: Ariyavasṃsa, Mahā-Ariyavaṃsa and also Vaṃsa-sutta.[26] The four sections of the sutta are as follows:—

(i) "A bhikkhu is satisfied with whatever roles he gets, praises the value of contentment in whatever roles he obtains, does not commit any impropriety in order to secure roles, nor does he exalt himself or look down upon others on account of his possession of this quality of contentment. So is he with regard to:

(ii) Whatever food he gets, and

(iii) Whatever lodgings he is provided with

(iv) The bhikkbu takes delight in meditation and abandonment (bhāvanārāmo hoti bhāvanārato, pabānārāmo hoti pahānarato). But on account of this quality he does not exalt himself, nor does he look down upon others."[27]

This is the Ariyavanṃsa-sutta and it gives the essence of the life of a bhikku on whom "the perpetuation of the sutta depends." The preceding of the Ariyavaṃsa was accompanied by a festival and this celebration took place on "the twelfth day of the bright half of the month of Nikini during evry rainy season."[28] "Vanaya Vanaya atorasahi Nikamaniyacada Puṇamasa dolasapaka-divasa."[29] Even today, the Ariyavaṃsa was celebrated regularly during the vassa or vas season. The kings, ministers and rich persons played a great role to contribute generously "towards the performance of the Ariyavaṃsa". This indicates that for the celebration of this festival a considerable amount of money was needed. It was expensive no doubt. Most probably, meals and quarters were given to the bhikkhus who come from long distances and stayed at the place for a few days and temporary sheds were arranged for the people who came to hear the sermon from long distances.[30]

It may be noted here that Aśoka's Bhabrn edict refers to Aliyavasāni. In this edict, addressed to the Buddhist Saṇgha, Aśoka requests the monks and nuns of the Buddhist Saṇgha, and the lay disciples of either sex, frequently to hear and to meditate upon seven selected texts from the Pāli canon, among which Aliyavasāni is mentioned. Aççording to Kosambi, Lanman, Barna and Walpola Rahula, Aliyavasāni is the same as the Ariyavaṃsa-sutta described above.[31] Even today, the Ariyavaṃsa-sutta was preached several days during the Ariyavaṃsa festival at a cave-temple near Gurulabadda in Pasdun Korale in Sri Lanka.[32]

VESAK

The Vesak (Pāli Vesākha) festival is held in the month of Vesak (May) to celebrate the Buddha's birth.[33] "Vesākhamāse puṇṇamayaṃ sambuddho upapajjatha, taṃ māsaṃ pūjanatthāya."[34] Vesak is one of the most ancient Buddhist festivals. Even in India from early days the Buddhists celebrate this festival. Fa Hien, the Chinese pilgrim, says that about the 5th century "every year, on the eighth day of the second month, they celebrate a procession of images. They make a four-wheeled car and on it erect a structure of five stories by means of bamboos tied together .... they make figures of devas with gold, silver and ... on the four sides are niches, with a Buddha seated in each, and a Bodhisattva standing in attendance on him. There may be twenty cars all grand and imposing, but each one different from the other."[35]

It may be noted here that "Aśoka's Rock Edict IV records that the Emperor had organised shows and processions in which were exhibited images of gods in their celestial cars with 'heavenly sights' attractive and fascinating to the masses. What Fa Hien saw in the 5th century in India was perhaps the continuation of the same old festival with certain modifications and improvements after seven centuries. It is also possible that Mahinda, having seen those shows and processions organised by his father and realised their effect on the mass, mind, introduced the same practice into Ceylon. It may be conjectured, with some justification, that the Ceylon Vesak festival was modelled on Aśoka's 'shows and procession' and also on 'the processions of images' seen by Fa Hien. The Chinese monk says that the Indian procession was held in the second month. Now the second month of the year according to the Indian calendar is Vesākha, and it is possible, therefore, what Fa Hien saw in India was a Vesak festival, though he did not mention it by name."[36]

The Mahāvaṁsa in its accounts first refers to the Vesak festival in Sri Lanka during the time of Duṭṭha-Gāmaṇī (101-77 B.C.). The latter celebrated twenty-four Vesak festivals.[37] This gives indication that the festival existed in Sri Lanka much earlier. Most probably, Duṭṭha-Gāmaṇī revived the festival and on a grander scale than before he celebrated it.[38] After him many kings celebrated the festival regularly. Bhātiya (38-67 A.D.) celebrated twenty eight Vesak festivals.[39] while Vasabha (127-171 A.D.) celebrated forty-four Vesak festivals.[40] Regular annual celebrations were organized by these two kings. Vohāra Tissa (269-291 A.D)[41], Goṭhabhaya (309-322 A.D.)[42], Jeṭṭha Tissa (323-333 A.D)[43], Dalla-Moggallava (611-617 A.D.)[44], Sena II (851-885 A.D.)[45] are all referred to as kings who with pomp and grandeur celebrated the Vesak festivals. Sena II used to celebrate the Vesak festival with the poor people and he used to give them food, and drink and clothes as they wanted.[46] In Sri Lanka up to this day the Vesak festival is celebrated by the Buddhists with pomp and grandeur every year and the Buddhist societies and individual constructed free refreshment halls (don-sāl) throughout the island to entertain the pilgrims who on that day come to the holy places.[47]

Giribhaṇḍa-Pūjā

Mahādāthika Mahānāga (67-79 A.D.) took active part to originate the Giribhanda-Pūjā.[48] After completing the construction of the Mahāthūpa at Mihintale the king made an arrangement to celebrate this great festival. "Within the radius of a yojana of Mihintale the whole place was magnificently decorated. A road was constructed running round the mountain and four gateways erected on either side of the streets shops and stores were opened. The roads were adorned with flags, arches and triumphal gates itluminated all with rows of lamps. Dancing, singing and music added to the merriment of the occasion. The road from the Kadambanadī (Malvatu-oya) to Mihintale was covered with carpets so that the devotees might walk with clean feet after their abilutions at the river. At the four gates of the city a great alms-giving was organized. Over the whole Island an unbroken chain of lamps was lighted. Even over the sea lamps were lighted within a distance of a yojana round the Island. To the great multitude of monks assembled at this consecration ceremony of the thūpa, alms and gifts were offered at eight places with the beating of eight golden drums. A remission of the prison penalties (bandhamokkha) was also ordered. Barbers were employed to carry on their work continually at the four gates."[49]

It is not clear why this festival became known as Giribhaṇḍa-Pūjā. Giri means "mountain", Bhanda means "goods", and Pūjā means "offering" or "ceremony".[50] Probably, they could be taken to mean "offering of goods on the mountain" or "offering of a mountain of goods."[51] Sometimes this festival is called Giribhaṇḍa-gahana-Pūjā "the ceremony of taking goods on the mountain"[52] and also Giribhaṇḍa-vāhana-Pūjā "the ceremony of bearing goods on the mountain."[53] The Rasavāhinī II mentions the term Girimaṇḍa-mahā-Pūjā "the great mountain offering."[54] The Pāli commentaries mention this festival in connection with Tissa Thera of Loṇagiri who at this ceremony got the best pair of cloths.[55] This was an important festival no doubt and at this festival great offerings were made. Mahādāṭhika Mahānāga organized it. The Rasavāhini II states that Dubbiṭṭhi Mahārāja organized this festival.[56] But he was the same as Mahādāthika Mahānāga.[57] But there is no reference to the celebration of this festival by other kings. Eight centuries later, Udaya II (885-896 A.D.) restored a vihāra called Giribhaṇḍa.[58] But it is difficult to say whether this was a vihāra at Mihintale which had connection with Mahādāthika's Giribhaṇḍa-Pūjā or a different vihāra.[59]

Gaṅgārohaṇa

Buddhadāsa's son Upatissa I inaugurated a ceremony called Gaṅgārohaṇa in the early fifth century A.D.[60] At that time famine and disease broke out in the Island. The king wanted to know from the Buddhist Sangha that in such a situation what the Buddha did in order to remove the suffering of the people, and the Buddhist monks told him when such a calamity appeared in Vesāli how the Buddha arranged the recitation of the Ratana-sutta.[61] The Mahāvaṁsa mentions it Gaṅgārohaṇa-sutta as well.[62] When Vesāli was afflicted by famine and pestilence, the Buddha was invited by the Licchavis to visit their city. The Buddha went there and recited the Ratana sutta. (The Khuddakapāṭha as well as the Sutta-nipāta include it). The Buddha first taught this sutta to Ānanda and asked him to go round the city with the Licehavi princes. According to the Buddha's advice, they did it, recited the sutta and sprinkled water from the alms-bowl of the Buddha. There was no more calamity and the city was free from it. In order to show honor of the Buddha's visit a great festival was held. Then two boats were joined together on the river and a pavilion was built thereon. The Buddha then along the Ganges returned to Rājagraha from Vesāli. This journey became known as Gaṅgārohaṇa and the festival itself then got its name.[63]

After his talk with the Buddhist monks, the king then made a golden image of the Buddha and placed in its hands the

Buddha's stone alms-bowl filled with water and mounted it on a chariot. He then arranged a great alms-giving and asked the citizens to observe the moral precepts (sīla) and he himself observed them.[64] The city was decorated very beautifully and many monks followed the chariot with the golden Buddha image and they took a walk round the streets and in this way they spent the whole night and they recited the Ratana-sutta and they sprinkled water.[65] According to Geiger, this was a fine example of popular rain magic adopted by the official religion.[66] The king also took a walk with the Buddhist monks. Then rains came and famine and pestilence disappeared. Upatissa them gave order that whenever a similar calamity appeared in the Island, the ceremony was performed.[67] King Sena II (851-885 A.D.) performed a similar ceremony when there was an epidemic in the Island. The king, in place of the Buddha image, took the image of Ānanda and carried it round the streets and the monks followed it and recited the pirit and sprinkled the pirit-pan (paritta water).[68] It may be pointed out here that Ananda recited the Ratana-sutta and sprinkled water from the Buddha's alms-bowl when he went round in Vesāli.[69] But Sena II did not imitate Upatissa's ceremony in all its details. The Ratana-sutta was written on gold plates by him.[70] Kassapa V (913-923 A.D.) removed the dangers of famine and pestilence by asking the monks of the three fraternities to recite the pirit in the city.[71] But there was no reference to the image of the Buddha, or of Ānanda or of the alms-bowl in it. Most probably, in the course of time, there was a great change in the ceremony.[72] Aggabodhi IV (658-674 A.D.) organised pirit ceremonies in his time but neither the reason nor the details were mentioned.[73] About the middle of the 19th century A.D., a Gaṅgārohaṇa festival was organized at Mātasa in South Sri Lanka.[74]

Pirit

Pirit (Pāli Paritta) means "protection". It was a ceremony held for various purposes like driving away evil spirits and diseases as well as blessing an auspicious occasion like occupying a new house.[75] The Book of Paritta (Pirit-pota) known as the Catubhāṇavāa is a compilation and it has suttas from the original Nikāyas.[76] The Milinda-paha says that the Ratana-sutta, the Khudha-paritta, the Mora-paritta, the Ddhajagga-paritta, the Atānātiya-paritta and the Aṅgulimāla-paritta are the most important parittas.[77] The Digha commentary mentions that the Metta-sutta, the Dhajagga-sutta and the Ratana-sutta are important suttas.[78] The present book of Parittas (Pirit-pota) or Catubhāṇavaa, in addition to the suttas described above, comprises the following suttas: the Dasadhamma-sutta, Maṅgala-sutta, Mettānisaṃsa-sutta, Canda-paritta, Suriya-paritta, Mahākassapa-thera-bojjhaṅga, Mahā-moggallāna-Thera-bojjhaṅiga, Mahā-cunda-thera-bojjhaṅga, Girimānanda-sutta, Isigili-sutta, Dhammacak-kappavattana-sutta, Mahā-samaya-suta, Ālavaka-sutta, Kasībhāradvāja-sutta, Parā-bhava-sutta, Vasabha-sutta and Sacca-vibhaṅga-sutta.[79]

In the matter of exorcism the Āṭanātiya-sutta is the most important and powerful.[80] The Dīgha commentary[81] narrated a detailed account of how and when to recite it. The Matta-sutta, the Dhajagga-sutta and the Ratana-sutta should be recited for seven days in the first instance, when the expulsion of an evil spirit is desired. It is well and good if the spirit leaves the patient. But if he does not, then the recitation of the Aṭanāṭiya-sutta takes place. In this case several precautions and observances should be followed The bhikkhu should eat neither meat nor preparations of flour if he recites the sutta. He should not stay in a cemetery, lest the spirits should get a chance to harass him. From the monastery to the sick man's house he should be protected why man who will carry weapons and shields. In the open air the recitation should not be held. In a room with doors and windows closed the bhikkhu should take his seat and then with thoughts of love foremost in his heart he should recite the sutta. At the time of recital he should be protected by men carrying arms.

The paritta should be recited after making the patient accept the precepts (sīlāni).[82] If the spirit does not leave him, then the patient should come to the monastery and should take his palace on the courtyard of the catiya. At first the people should sweep the courtyard, then flowers should be offered and lamps should be made. Then the Maṅgala-gāthā should be recited. A full assembly of deities should be called. If there is an old tree (Jeṭṭhaka-rukkha) in the vicinity of the vihāra, then in the name of the saṁgha a message should be sent the deity residing these asking him to be present. The man possessed should be questioned as to his name. When the name is told, then by that name the spirit should be addressed. He should be stated that the merits of alms-giving and offering of flowers and lamps had been transferred to him, and as a gift to him the vases of blessing had been recited and out of respect for the Buddhist Saṁgha he should leave the patient. If he does not like to leave him, then the devatās should be informed of his obtimacy and the Atānātiya-sutta should be recited, after announcing that "this spirit (amanusso) does not do our word, and we shall obey the order of the Buddha."[83] If a bhikkhu is possessed by a spirit, the altars should be cleaned and flowers should be offered, the merits of offerings should be transferred and after addressing a great assembly of devatās, the paritta should be recited.[84] "This is an equivalent to exorcism and faith-healing which all popular religions are compelled to offer to the believing masses."[85] The full-fledged pirit ceremony was developed only after the Polonnaruva period.[86]

The Tooth Relic Festival

The left eye-tooth of the Buddha (Vāmadāṭha-dhātu)[87] in the ninth year of Mahāsena's son Siri-Meghavaṇṇa was brought to Sri Lanka from Dantapura in Kaliṅga.[88] Of all Buddhist relics ever brought to Sri Lanka this was the most important and precious.[89] The Dhātuvaṁsa mentions that there were two tooth-relics of the Buddha in Sri Lanka.[90] When internal troubles broke out in Sri Lanka, claimants to the throne wanted to possess the Tooth Relic, because the person who brought the Tooth Relic under his control had got public support.[91] The Dāthāvaṁsa describes that before it was brought to Sri Lanka among the ruling princes in India, there was fighting for the possession of the Tooth-Relic.[92] Thus the lefteye-tooth of the Buddha was brought to Sri Lanka from Dantapura in Kalinga in the ninth year of king Sirimegahavanna. It was kept in a special house within the city and annually it was brought to the Abhayagiri for public exhibition.[93] Percy Brown (Indian Architecture) describes that "the holy city of Dantapura, the town of the Tooth, where the priceless possession was at one time deposited, lay in the vicinity of one of the neighbouring towns, either of Bhubanesvar or Puri, although all traces of it are now lost. As a token of the antiquity of these parts, near at hand is Danlia hill, where is inscribed one of the rock edicts of Aśoka."(p.35). "This elevated position suggests that the Jagannāth temple occupies the site of some still more ancient monument, not improbably the shrine of the Buddha's tooth at Dantapura, before that precious relic was transported to Ceylon (Sri Lanka)" (p.123).[94] It may be noted here that the Mahāvihara should have had no part in the worship of the Tooth Relic which became national palladium of the Sinhalese.[95] During the days of Mahāsena the Abhayagiri became known in India as an important centre of Mahāyāna Buddhism in Sri Lanka. Most probably, the prince and the princess who came with the Tooth Relic from India were Mahāyānists and for this reason they probably established their contract with the monks of the Abhayagiri vihāra. The monks of the Abhayagiri vihāra took the possession of the Tooth Relic and the custodianship of it became their business and not of the Mahāvihāra.[96]

From the very beginning the Tooth Relic was closely associated with the Abhayagisi Vihāra. For this reason, in the Abhayagiri vihāra its exposition and its annual festival were held.[97] A special building was built for the Tooth Relic.[98] "By the side of the king's palace in the vihāra of the Buddha's Tooth, several hundred feet high, brilliant with jewels and ornamented with rare gems. Above the vihāra is placed an upright pole on which is fixed a great padmarāga (ruby) jewel ...".[99]

Fa Hien says that the Tooth of the Buddha in the middle of the third month was always brought forth.[100] "Ten days beforehand the king grandly caparisoned a large elephant on which he mounted a man dressed in royal robes who could speak distinctly, and the man went round beating a large drum, describing the life and the virtues of the Buddha and announcing to the public: Behold! Ten days after this, Buddha's Tooth will be brought forth, and taken to the Abhayagiri-vihāra. Let all and each, whether monks and laity, who wish to amass merit for themselves make the road smooth and in good condition, grandly adorn the lanes and by-ways, and provide abundant store of flowers and incense to be used as offerings to it."[101] When this proclamation was over, the king placed for exhibition on both sides of the road, the five hundred different bodily forms in which the Buddha had apperaed in his previous births according to the Jātaka stories. All these figures were brightly coloured and grandly executed "looking as if they were alive."[102] "After this the Tooth of the Buddha was brought forth, and was carried along in the middle of the road. Everywhere on the way offerings were presented to it, and thus it arrived at the hall of the Buddha in the Abhayagiri-vihāra. Three the monks and the laity collected in crowds burned incense, lighted lamps and performed all the prescribed services, day and night, without ceasing till ninety days had been completed, when the Tooth was returned to the vihāra within the city. On poya days the doors of the vihāra were opened, and forms of ceremonial reverence were observed according to the rules."[103]

Hiuen Tsiang describes, "The king three times a day washes the Tooth of the Buddha with perfumed water, sometimes with powdered perfumes. Whether washing or burning the whole ceremony is attending with a service of the most precious jewels."[104]

Up to the present day in Sri Lanka, the festival of the Tooth Relic, accompanied by Kandy Perahara is held annually.[105]

From the Dalada Maligawa the Esala Perahera, are of the world's most dramatic religious festivals, takes place. Held annually for ten nights in July-August and finishing on the day following the night of the full moon, the procession involves five temples which with their own groups of drummers, dancers, torch bearers and elephants join forces to march slowly in procession. By the last night as many as eighty or more elephants, caparisoned in velvet, satin and silk with silver trappings, took part in procession. Chief of them all is the Maligawa tusker carrying a replica of the casket in which is treasured the Sacred Tooth Relic of the Buddha.

Other Peraheras are:- (1) Wesak Perahera: commemorating the birth, enlightenment and death of the Buddha in April or May full moon or poya. (2) Poson Perahera: Commemorating the coming of Buddhism to Sri Lanka on the full moon day in June. (3) Karthika Perahera: commemorating the victory of God Maha Vishnu and his general Kataragama Skanda Kumara over a king of India. Generally, it takes place between November and December.

Mahinda Festival

Mahāsena's son Sri-Meghavaṇṇa inaugurated a new festival in honour of Mahinda.[106] A life-size image of Mahinda was made of gold by him and on the seventh day of the month of Vap (Pubbakattika, October-November) he took it to Ambatthala at Mihintale where Mahinda's meeting took place with Devānampiya Tissa.[107] On this occasion a great alms-giving was organized. From Mihintale to Anurādhapura the road was decorated beautifully. In the ninth day of the month, the Buddhist monks, laymen and the king himself took part in a procession and the image was brought to Sotthiyākasa, a vihāra constructed by Siri-Meghavaṇṇa himself near the eastern gate of the city. The image was kept there for three days. On the twelfth day of the month the image in a procession was brought to the Mahāvihāra and for three months it was exhibited in the courtyard of the Mahā Bodhi. Then the image was kept in a specially built house in the south-east direction, near the royal palace. The kin in that house had also built the images of Iṭṭhiya and other companions of Mahinda. For the maintenance of the place endowments were made and also for the performance of the festivals endowments were made. The king issued a decree that all succeeding kings should arrange this festival annually.[108]

Dhammakitti, the author of the second part of the Mahāvaṁsa (also called the Cūlavaṃsa), states that kings from that day tried to honour this decree and the festival was held in his time in the 13th century —a nine centuries after its inauguration.[109] Dhatusena (460-478 A.D.) celebrated the Mahinda festival. The recital and exposition of the Dīpavaṃsa formed a special feature in this festival.[110] The Mahinda festival has been revived recently and annually it is now held in Sri Lanka.[111]

The Offering of a Vihāra

Fa Hien describes how a monastery was given to the Buddhist Sangha by a king in ancient Sri Lanka. First, a great assembly was convoked by the king. First he gave a meal of rice to the monks and then on the occasion he presented his offerings and afterwards two first-rate oxen were selected by him. Then he decorated the horns of these two oxen with gold, silver and precious substances. A golden plough had been supplied, and the king himself did the trench made by a plough on the four sides of the ground within which the building was to be constructed. He then endowed the community of the monks with the population, fields and houses and on plates of metal he wrote the grant to the effect that from that time onwards, from generation to generation, no one should venture to cancel or alter it.[112]

The Anointing of Images

Some of the Bodhi-trees were known by special names like Vaḍḍhamāna Bodhi, "which is evidence of the affection and vaneration in which the holy tree was held by the Buddhists."[113]

In the same way different Buddha-images had got their own personal names like Upasumbha and Abhiseka.[114] There was a particular kind of ceremony known as abhiseka (anointing) of Buddha-images. Migāsa, the general, was refused permission by Kassapa I to perform the anointing ceremony of Abhiseka Buddha (image) which the general wanted to celebrate it on a grander scale than even that of the Silā-Sambuddha (image). Migāsa did not show his displeasure. But he waited for Moggallāna.[115] When Moggallāna occupied the throne, Migāsa, the general, then celebrated the ceremony in a very nice manner. This he desired and waited for the time of the arrival of Moggallāna. But he did it nearly eighteen year after.[116] This shows that to the people of ancient Sri Lanka the anointing ceremony of Buddha images was of great interest and importance.[117] It was an important festival no doubt.

Lamp Offering

Dīpa-Pūjā or the offering of lamps was an important and popular festival in Sri Lanka.[118] On this occasion many devotes lighted thousands of lamps in regular rows on the grounds of a monastery. They did it with an idea to get good results from it.

In the same way, there was a ceremony known as a āsana-pūjā which was performed by covering the altars and even the terraces of the catiya with flowers.[119]

There are references to an offering known as thalasanthara-pūjā.[120] Most probably, it was celebrated by spreading flowers on the courtyard.

Madhubhaṇḍa-pūjā is another festival celebrated in Sri Lanka.[121]

Worship at a Monastery

A Buddhist had to follow certain customs in his worship when he goes to a monastery. The dāgata (cetiya) had the bodily relics of the Buddha. For this reason he had to worship the dāgaba first. Three times he had to cumambulate the dāgaba and he had to keep the object of worship to his right. When the dāgaba was large in size, he should then stop and worship at four places; if its was small, he should stop and worship at eight places. But certain commentaries say that a devotee should stop and worship at sixteen places.[122] The practice of worshipping a cetiya at sixteen places seems to have come down at least to the 15th century. For, Toṭagannure Śrī Rāhula in his Sālalihini Sandesāya describes: "Maha dāgap himin vandu solasa tan siṭa"— "worship the great and lordly dāgaba (at Kalaniya) stopping at sixteen places" (v. 65). But in the Pāli commentaries the instruction regarding the worship of a cetiya are sometimes different.[123] In ancient days the devotees ascended the Vedikā-bhūmi (terraces) and offered flowers and worshipped while he circumamubulated the cetiya. After worshipping the cetiya, he should worship the Bodhi.[124] Then he should worship the image of the Buddha. But in early literature there is no reference to the worship of the Buddha image.[125] The Buddha should treat the cetiya as a living Buddha. Everybody should pay respect to the Buddha as well as to the cetiya. If a bhikkhu does not like to go to worship at the cetiya, "it is considered as not attending on the Buddha."[126] A bhikkhu should neither cover both shoulders, nor wear sandals, nor hold an umbrella, nor bathe, nor answer calls of nature within the sight of a cetiya.[127]

Vassa of Kathina

The vassa (Sinhalese Vas) seesa generally takes places from July to October. When monks observed the Vas retreat, then they remained in one place. It was a period during which the whole country become religiously conscious.[128] For the maintenance of monks during this period particular arrangements were made.[129] The Kathina ceremony was the culmination of the whole Vas season.[130] At the end of the three months a special robe known as Kathina was given to the monks of every monastery who observed the retreat.[131] Dalla-Moggallāna (Moggallāna III) offered Kathina to all the monasteries in the Island.[132] Even today the Sinhalese Buddhists observed the Kathina ceremony with pomp and grandeur. This was an important festival in Sri Lanka.

Funeral

Fa Hien gives an account of the funeral rites of a monk in the fifth century A.D. in Sri Lanka.[133] He describes, "Four or five li east of the vihāra there was reared a great pile of firewood, which might be more than thirty cubits square, and the same in height. Near the top were laid sandal, aloe and other kinds of fragment wood.

"On the four sides (of the pile) they made steps by which to ascend it. With clean white hair cloth, almost like silk, they wrapped (the body) round and round. They made a large carriage frame, in form like our funeral car, but without the dragons and fishes.

"At the time of the cremation, the king and the people in multitudes from all quarters, collected together, and presented offerings of flowers and incense. When this was finished, the car was lifted on the pile, all over which oil of sweet basil was poured, and then a light was applied. While the fire was blazing, everyone, with reverent heart, pulled off his upper garment, and threw it, with his feather-fan and umbrella, from a distance into the midst of the flames, to assist the burning. When the cremation was over, they collected and preserved the bones, and proceeded to erect a tope. Fa Hien had not arrived in time (to see the distinguished śramana) alive, and only saw his burial."[134]

NOTES

1. Dpv., xxi, 26, 27; xxii, 3; Mhv, xxiv, 60.
2. DA., 128., MA., 205; VbhA., 244.
3. HBC., 267.
4. *Ibid.*, 267; DA., 128; MA., 205; VbhA., 244; AA., 385-386.
5. MA. 1025., RSV., II, 1.
6. DA, 535; MA., 187; HBC, 267.
7. HBC, 267; AA, 23, 386.
8. HBC, 268.
9. *Ibid.*, 268., f.n. 1.
10. *Ibid.*, 268.
11. *Ibid.*, 268.
12. *Ibid.*, 268.
13. *Ibid.*, 268; MHv. xxxvi, 38.
14. *Ibid.*, 268-269; Epigraphic Zeylanica, (E.Z.), III, 177.
15. *Ibid.*, 269.; *ibid.*, III, 177.
16. *Ibid.*, 269; *ibid.*, III, 250, 251.
17. *Ibid.*, 269; AA, 386.
18. *Ibid.*, 269; *ibid.*, 385.
19. *Ibid.*, 269; Rsv. II, 4, 183, 190.
20. *Ibid.*, 269-270; *ibid.*, II 4.
21. *Ibid.*, 270; *ibid.*, II, 183.
22. *Ibid.*, 270, f.n. 2.
23. *Ibid.*, 270; RSV, II, 190.
24. HBC, 270; SA, III, 151.
25. *Ibid.*, 270; A., 204.
26. *Ibid.*, 270.
27. *Ibid.*, 271.
28. *Ibid.*, 272; EZ, III, 178.
29. *Ibid.*, 272; f.n. 3.
30. *Ibid.*, 272.
31. *Ibid.*, 273.
32. *Ibid.*, 273.
33. *Ibid.*, 273; Dpv. xxi, 28.
34. *Ibid.*, 273; f.n. 5.
35. *Ibid.*, 274; Fa Hien, 79.
36. HBC, 274.
37. *Ibid.*, 274; Mhv, xxxii, 35.
38. *Ibid.*, 274.
39. *Ibid.*, 275; Mhv, xxxiv, 59.
40. *Ibid.*, 275; *ibid.*, xxxv, 100.

41. *Ibid.*, 275; *ibid.*, xxxvi, 40.
42. *Ibid.*, 275; *ibid.*, xxxvi, 109., Dpv., xxii, 59.
43. *Ibid.*, 275; Mhv., xxxvi, 130.
44. *Ibid.*, 275; *ibid.*, xliv., 46.
45. *Ibid.*, 275; *ibid.*, li., 84.
46. *Ibid.*, 275.
47. *Ibid.*, 275.
48. *Ibid.*, 275.
49. *Ibid.*, 275-276; Mhv., xxxiv, 68-84.
50. *Ibid.*, 276, f.n. 2.
51. *Ibid.*, 276, f.n. 2.
52. *Ibid.*, 276; Dpv., xxi, 32.
53. *Ibid.*, 276; Vsm., 280; AA., 13. f.n. 2.
54. *Ibid.*, 276; f.n. 2., Rsv, II, 185.'
55. *Ibid.*, 276; f.n. 2., DA., 369; M.A., 545., AA., 654.
56. HBC, 276., f.n. 3 RSV., II, 185.
57. HBC, 276, f.n. 3.
58. *Ibid.*, 276; Mhv., xlix, 29.
59. *Ibid.*, 276.
60. *Ibid.*, 276.
61. *Ibid.*, 276-277.
62. *Ibid.*, 277, f.n. 1.
63. *Ibid.*, 277, f.n. 2., SnA., 204-205; CBhA., 97.
64. *Ibid.*, 277.
65. *Ibid.*, 277.
66. *Ibid.*, 277, f.n. 3; Clv., tr. I, 19, 4.5.
67. *Ibid.*, 277., Mhv, xxxvii, 189-198.
68. *Ibid.*, 277; Mhv., li, 80-81.
69. *Ibid.*, 277.
70. *Ibid.*, 278., Mhv., li, 79.
71. *Ibid.*, 278., *ibid.*, lii, 80.
72. *Ibid.*, 278.
73. *Ibid.*, 278; Mhv., xlvi, 5.
74. *Ibid.*, 278, f.n. 3.
75. *Ibid.*, 278.
76. *Ibid.*, 278.
77. *Ibid.*, 278., Miln., 119.
78. *Ibid.*, 278; D.A., 707.
79. *Ibid.*, 278; f.n. 6.
80. *Ibid.*, 279.
81. *Ibid.*, 279; DA., 707.
82. *Ibid.*, 279.
83. *Ibid.*, 279.

84. *Ibid.*, 280.
85. *Ibid.*, 280, f.n. 1.
86. *Ibid.*, 280, f.n. 1.
87. *Ibid.*, 280; Dāṭhā, 114, 119.
88. *Ibid.*, 280., *ibid.*, 340., Mhv., xxxvii, 92.
89. *Ibid.*, 280., Dhātu, 6.
90. *Ibid.*, 280., *ibid.*, 6.
91. *Ibid.*, 280.
92. *Ibid.*, 280., Dāṭhā., , 284, 286, 289, 295, 296.
93. *Ibid.*, 97., Mhv., xxxvii, 95-97; Dāṭhā, 405-406., Fa Hien, 106-107.
94. *Ibid.*, 97, f.n. 1.
95. *Ibid.*, 97.
96. *Ibid.*, 97.
97. *Ibid.*, 280; Dāṭhā, 406.
98. *Ibid.*, 280; Fa Hien, 104.
99. *Ibid.*, 280; Hiun Tsiang BK. XI.
100. *Ibid.*, 281; Fa Hien, 105-107.
101. *Ibid.*, 281; Fa Hien, 105-107.
102. *Ibid.*, 281; *ibid.*, 105-107.
103. *Ibid.*, 281; *ibid.*, 105-107.
104. *Ibid.*, 281; Hiun Tsiang BK., XI, 248.
105. *Ibid.*, 282.
106. *Ibid.*, 282.
107. *Ibid.*, 282.
108. *Ibid.*, 282.
109. *Ibid.*, 282; Mhv., xxxvii, 66-89.
110. *Ibid.*, 282; *ibid.*, xxxviii, 58-59.
111. *Ibid.*, 282; f.n. 2.
112. *Ibid.*, 283; Fa Hien, 108-109.
113. *Ibid.*, 120; Mhv., xlviii, 5., xlix, 15.
114. *Ibid.*, 283; *ibid.*, xxxviii, 66.
115. *Ibid.*, 283; *ibid.*, xxxix, 6-7.
116. *Ibid.*, 283; *ibid.*, xxxix, 40.
117. *Ibid.*, 283.
118. *Ibid.*, 284; Dpv; xxi, 11, 14-15., xxii, 6.
119. *Ibid.*, 284; MA, 888, AA., 256.
120. *Ibid.*, 284; f.n. 2.
121. *Ibid.*, 284; f.n. 2., Dpv., xxi, 10.
122. *Ibid.*, 284; f.n. 3.
123. *Ibid.*, 118; f.n. 1.
124. *Ibid.*, 284; DA., 129; M.A., 207; VbhA, 245.
125. *Ibid.*, 284.
126. *Ibid.*, 284.

127. *Ibid.*, 284; DA., 757; VbhA, 360.
128. *Ibid.*, 285.
129. *Ibid.*, 285; Dpv., xxi, 25; EZ., I, 58, 62.
130. *Ibid.*, 285.
131. *Ibid.*, 285.
132. *Ibid.*, 285; Mhv, xliv, 48.
133. *Ibid.*, 285; Fa Hien, 107-108.
134. *Ibid.*, 285-286; *ibid.*, 107-108.

6

Buddhist Literature of Sri Lanka

The people of Sri Lanka believe that "the preservation of the Theravāda canon in the Pāli language is the greatest contribution that the Sinhalese people had made to the intellectual heritage of mankind."[1] Several works in old Sinhalese had developed around this canon and they were exegetical texts, religious stories and historical accounts of India as well as of Sri Lanka. The historical traditions of the Mahāvihāra had been arranged together in the Dīpavaṁsa in Pāli verse. A Sinhalese another in his first attempt wrote it in that language.[2] In other countries where the Theravāda form of Buddhism flourished, the people were unable to understand the Sinhalese language. For this reason, the great Buddhist scholar Buddhaghosa translated into Pāli these exegetical works of the Mahāvihāra in the form of commentaries to the Vinaya and the Nikāyas of the Suttapiṭaka.[3] He came to Sri Lanka in the last years of the reign of Mahānāma. He also wrote the Visuddhimagga, in which he explained the Buddhist doctrines. A poem on the Tooth Relic was composed in Sinhalese in the reign of Sirimeghavaṇṇa, when it was brought to Sri Lanka.[4]

Buddhaghosa Thera compiled the Pāli Aṭṭhakatha (commentaries) and this was an important event in the annals of Sri Lanka. This indicates the development of Buddhism in the Island. The Pitakas or the teachings of the Buddha were handed down orally and in 397 B.E. (89 B.C.) they were committed to writing. At this time the commentaries on these in Sinhlalese were committed to writing.[5] In about 410 A.D. when king Mahānāma ruled at Anurādhapura, the fame of Sri Lanka's Buddhist literature was well-received in India and the Sinhalese Buddhist monks visited India, China and other countries and there they introduced the literature of Sri Lanka. Buddhaghosa Thera in the reign of Mahānāma (410-432 A.D) came to Sri Lanka. He wrote the Pāli commentaries. The Samantapāsādikā on the Vinaya Piṭaka was the first of such commentaries.[6] The Kankhāvitaraṇī on the Pātinokkha of the Vinaya Piṭaka was compiled later. Then he wrote the commentaries on the four Nikāyas namely the Sumangalavilāsini on the Dīgha Nikāya, the Papañcasūdanī on the Majjhima Nikāya, the Sāratthappakāsinī on the Saṁyutta Nikāya and the Manorathapūraṇī on the Aṅguttara Nikāya.[7] He also compiled the Dhammapadaṭṭhakathā on the Dhammapada, the Jātakaṭṭhakathā on the Jātaka and the Paramatthajatikā on the Khuddakapātha and the Suttanipāta of the Khuddaka Nikāya.[8] He compiled the Atthasāliṇī on the Dhammsaṅganī, the Sammohavinodanī on the Vibhaṅga and the Pañcappakaraṇaṭṭhakathā on the other five books of the Abhidhamma Piṭaka.[9] After the tenth century A.D. the old Sinhalese commentaries were completely lost and for this reason Buddhaghosia's commentaries became very important and his activities gave inspiration to the Buddhist world of Sri Lanka. He played a great role to inspire the Buddhist scholars of Sri Lanka to popularise the learning of Pāli in Sri Lanka and it helped to produce many other Pāli commentaries and other literary works in Sri Lanka.

Some time before and after the compilation of the Pāli commentaries by Buddhaghosa two importanat literary works of a different type were composed in Pāli metrical verses in Sri Lanka. They are the Dīpavaṃsa and the Mahāvaṃsa.[10] These two works are the earliest extant literary records narrating a continuous history of the reigns of the kings of Sri Lanka from pre-Buddhistic periods up to the end of the reign of king Mahāsena.[11]

The Dīpavaṃsa

Among the well-known Pāli works written in Sri Lanka, the Dīpavaṃsa, "the History of the Island" is the oldest one and it deserves special attention.[12] Several scholars opined that the Dīpavaṃsa was produced in Sri Lanka on the basis of the commentaries Aṭṭhakathās).[13] It is a historical poem and is written in Pāli verses. We do not know the name of its author from it. But several scholars say that it mentions nuns (Theris) in it.[14] "The Dīpavaṃsa while giving an account of the Therīs, first of all, speaks of the well-known Therīs headed by Mahāpajāpati Gotamī who became well-versed in Vinaya (Vinayaññu) in Master's life-time. In the second stage it mention the Therīs, headed by Saṅghamittā, who went to the island of Ceylon in Devamampiya Tissa's time and recited the five Vinaya books and the seven Abhidhamma treatises in Anurādhapura...."[15] Some scholars conclude that it was compiled by nuns and from time to time they compiled it. G.P. Malalasekera states, "Nevill in his Manuscript Catalogue draws attention to the 'unique consequence given to nuns' all throughout the Dīpavaṃsa and is of opinion that it seems to afford a clue to its authorship."[16] It is not a work of one individual author but "it is the outcome of several previous works to which additions have been made from time to time, taking its present form about the fourth century A.D."[17] According to Oldenberg, this was written between the beginning of the 4th and the first third of the 5th century A.D.[18] G.P. Malalasekera[19] agrees with H. Oldenberg.[20] He describes, "It could not have been closed before the beginning of the fourth century, because its narrative extends till about A.D. 302. . . . Buddhaghosa quotes sevearl times from the Dīpavaṃsa, but his quotation differ in some details from our version. In the Mahāvaṃsa we are told that Dhātusena (459-477 A.D.) ordered the Dīpavaṃsa to be recited in public at the annual Mahinda festival, so that by that time the Dīpavaṃsa had been completed. After that date it fell into disuse, its glory outdone by the more brilliant work of Mahānāma, but it seems to have been studied till much later, because Dhammakitti III of the Āraṇyakarāsi sect, quotes it in his Saddhamma-Saṅgaha with great respect as a work of much merit and immense importance."

The Dīpavaṃsa has taken its materials from several sources of which the Sīhala Mahāvaṃsaṭṭhakathā, also called the Sīhalaṭ ṭhakathā or the Porānaṭṭhakathā or merely Aṭṭhakathā was pre-eminent.[21] The Mahāvaṃsa-ṭīkā mentions that the Dīpavaṃsa and the Mahāvaṃsa also obtained their materials from the Uttaravihāra-aṭṭhakathā and the Uttaravihāra-Mahāvaṃsa, the Vinayaṭṭhakathā, the Dīpavaṃsaṭṭhakathā, the Sumedha-Kathā and the Sahassavatthu-aṭṭhakathā but these are not available to us now.[22]

The Dīpavaṃsa describes the political history of Sri Lanka from Muṭasiva to Mahāsena. It mentions the activities of the Kings of Sri Lanka from pre-Buddhistic times up to the end of king Mahāsena's reign.[23] According to B.C. Law, "Its narrative is dull and its diction is in some places unintelígible. Repetitions are also found here and there. This chronicle, however, contains germs of historical truth buried deep under a mesh of absurd fables and marvellous tales. It should be critically read so as to enable us to find out germs which go to make up facts of history."[24] From the description of the Dīpavaṃsa it is known that its main theme is "the conquest of Laṅkā, both politically and culturally."[25]

The Dīpavaṃsa has twenty-two chapters.[26] It discusses the three visits of the Buddha to Sri Lanka, the ancestry of the Budha, the genealogy of the old royal families of India and Sri Lanka, the three Buddhist councils, the rise of the different Buddhist schools after the Second Council, the important role played by king Aśoka for the progress of Buddhism and the Colonisation of Sri Lanka by Vijaya and his successors.[27] It also deals with the introduction of Buddhism in Sri Lanka in the reign of king Devānaṁpiya Tissa by Mahinda and Saṅghamittā and the reigns of king Devānaṁpiya Tissa's successors, especially,

Duṭṭhagāmaṇī, Vattagāmaṇī and Mahāsena.[28] The Dīpavaṃsa's accounts end with the reign of Mahāsena.

The Mahāvaṃsa

The Mahāvaṃsa[29] the "great Dynasty of Sinhalese kings" was another important work of Sri Lanka. Mahānāma was its author.[30] He probably belonged to the last quarter of the fifth century A.D. or the early sixth centutry A.D. The Mahāvaṃsa is the work of a poet Mahānāma. It is a perfect epic.[31] Wilhelm Geiger says, "The Mahāvaṃsa is a work of art creted by a man who well deserves to be called a poet, and who mastered the frequently crude material, if not with genius, yet with taste and skill."[32] He describes further, "The Mahāvaṃsa is already worthy the name of a true epic. It is the recognised work of a poet, and we are able to watch this poet at work in his workshop. Although he is quite dependent on his materials, which he is bound to follow as closely as possible, he deals with them critically, perceives their shortcomings and irregularities, and seeks to improve and to eliminate."[33] G.P. Malalesekera refers to Mahānāma's work Mahāvaṃsa. He states, "When Mahānāma came to write his work the Mahāvaṃsa, 'replete with information on every subject, comprehending the amplest details of all important events, like unto a splendid and dazzling garland strung with every variety of flowers, rich in colour, taste and scent.........avoiding the defects of the ancients," we find that he could not rise above his material. He strove to confine himself to his sources to the best of his power. Often he adopted the Pāli verses of the originals unchanged in his work, especially when they appeared to him to be of an authoritative character. He went to the same sources as the Dīpavaṃsa, and in many passages the two works agree word for word."[34] He narrates further, "Mahānāma was no genius, he was too much hide-bound by tradition, and his work cannot rank as a literary performance of the first order; yet his services to the cause of

Pāli literature, and to historical studies of later generations, were immense, and to us invaluable."[35]

The Mahāvaṃsa covers the same period of history and its material has taken from the same sources as the Dīpavaṃsa, but, yet, it has much more additional material produced in a better form.[36] It has 37 chapters in all. They discuss the same events as those of the Dīpavaṃsa but there are much longer accounts and greater details of the activities of several kings such as Paṇḍukābhaya and Duṭṭhagāmaṇī and the facts relating the establishment and development of Buddhism and the rise and growth of new schools in Sri Lanka.[37]

The Mahāvaṃsa begins with the story of Gotama Buddha.[38] It mentions his three legendary visits to the island of Sri Lanka. "It says how the Exalted one surveyed the whole world with his 'Buddha-eye', how a Terrible war broke out between the shake princes Great-Belly and Small-Belly, how the Buddha in his boundless goodness felt pity, flew over to the island accompanied by gods, and let the light of his doctrine shine forth, whereupon hosts of shanke demons and other demons were converted to the pure doctrine."[39] It then gives an account of the ancestry of the Buddha, the history of Buddhism in India, the three Buddhist Councils, the reign of Aśoka, his important role for the propagation of Buddhism in India and abroad, the colonisation of Sri Lanka by Vijaya with 700 companions, the introduction of Buddhism in Sri Lanka by Mahinda and Sanghamitta's arrival in the reign of Devānampiya Tissa of Sri Lanka.[40] It then refers to the reigns of Paṇḍukābhaya, Duṭṭagāmaṇī and Vattagāmaṇī of Sri Lanka.[41]

The Mahāvaṃsa in its comprehensiveness, arrangement of facts and high literary standard in better work.[42] B.C. law narrates "the Mahāvaṃsa certainly stands as a masterpiece produced by the poetically gifted Thera Mahānāma in the Vaṃsa literature of Ceylon. It is undoubtedly the more finished product of the literary and poetical art employed in the earlier works of the same type, particularly in the Dīpavaṃsa."[43] H. Oldenberg informs, "....the two works, viz., the Dīpavaṃsa and the Mahāvaṃsa, were based on the historical introduction to the great commentary of the Mahāvihāra, each of them representng their common subject in its own way, the first following step by step and almost word for word the traces of the original. The second work proceeding with much greater independence and perfect literary mastery."[44] The Dīpavaṃsa and the Mahāvaṃsa discuss many mythological and legendary stories, but they give useful information on political and religious matters. To trace the history of the ancient periods of the island of Sri Lanka, these informations in then world be useful no doubt. The Mahāvaṃsa was the work of the Thera Mahānāma who wrote it in the reign either of Moggathāna I or of his successor Kumāradhātusena.[45] Mahānāma was also the author of the Saddhammappakāsinī.[46] In it he specifically mentions that in the third year after the death of Moggathara I he was able to complete the commentary. He ignored the reigning king, Kumāradhātusena, "probably because he was not persona grata with him."[47] Mahānāma, the author of these two works, has been identified with the thera Mahānāman of Sri Lanka, who established a Buddhist shrine at Bodh Gaya.[48] This was known from an Indian inscription dated in 518 A.D.[49]

It may be noted here that in the early part of the fifth century A.D. Buddhaghosa Thera compiled the Pāli commentaries. Before he finished the entire work, the illness of his teacher Revata in India had compelled him to leave Sri Lanka.[50] Several other Pāli scholars finished the work which Buddhaghosa was unable to do and they compiled commentaries to the rest of the texts of the Pāli canon in the succeeding years.[51] The commentator Dhammapāla Thera compiled the commentaries to the Udāna, Itivuttaka, Vimānavatthu, Petavatthu, Theragāthā, Therīgāthā and Cariyāpiṭaka of the Khuddaka Nikāya and these commentaries become known by the name Paramatthadīpanī.[52] Upasena Thera compiled the Saddhammappajjotikā on the Niddesa, Mahānāma thera compiled the Saddhammappasinī on the Paṭisanbhidāmagga, and Buddhadatta Thera compiled the Maduratthavilasini on the Buddhavaṃsa.[53] The Visuddhajanavilāsinī is commentary on the Apadāna. But its author is not known.[54] The commentator Buddhadatta was a contemporry of Buddhaghosa. But Upasena and Mahānāma belonged to the latter part of the sixth century A.D. and Dhammapāla flourished in the latter part of the tenth century A.D.[55]

The political disturbances from the time of king Dhātusena until the reign of Vijayabahu I greatly disturbed Sri Lanka's literary activities and for this reason, during this period only a few religious works were written. About the end of the tenth century A.D. Khema, a thera, wrote an expository work on the Abhidhamma and this was the Paramatthadīpani.[56] Kassapa V patronised scholars who wrote in Pāli. The Pāli Mahābodhivaṃsa belongs to the tenth century A.D. It refers to the history of the sacred Bodhi-tree at Anurādhapura.[57] A poem entitled Anāgatavaṃsa on the future Buddha Matteyya also belongs to this period.[58] A Pāli poem of 98 stanzas called the "Tela-Kaṭ āhagāthā," in the form of religious exhortations of a great elder named Kalyāya Thera who was condemmed to be cast into a cauldron of boiling oil, belongs to the tenth or the early part of the eleventh century A.D.[59]

The Mahābodhivaṃsa or the Bodhivaṃsa

The Pāli Mahābodhivaṃsa or the Bodhivaṃsa[60] "The History of the Bodhi Tree" is a prose work. M. Winternitz sees Gāthāas only "at the end of the chapters and towards the end of the whole work."[61] According to him, Upatissa, a Buddhist monk, in the first half of the eleventh century A.D. wrote this work.[62] But Wilhelm Geiger opines that in the tenth century A.D. it was compiled.[63] D.M. dez Wickramasinghe agrees with him.[64] S. Arthur Strong edited it in 1891 and he thinks that the author of the Mahābodhivaṃsa belonged to the period of Buddhaghosa.[65]

Both D.M. dez Wickremesinghe and Wilhelm Geiger state that the Mahābodhivaṃsa was written in the last quarter of the tenth century A.D.[66] The Mahābodhivaṃsa begins with the account of Buddha Dipaṅkara.[67] It discusses the existence of the Bodhisattva under previous Buddhas, the life of Gotama, the attainment of his enlightenment at the foot of the Bodhi Tree, the attainment of Bodhi by Ānanda, the Mahāparinibbāna of the Buddha and the first three Buddhist Councils.[68] It also narrates the history of Mahinda's mission, the introduction and the establishment of Buddhism in the island of Sri Lanka, the arrival of the Buddha's relics and a branch of the Bodhi Tree in Sri Lanka and the introduction of the Bodhi-pūjā there.[69]

The only work of the Abhayagiri-vihāra was the Saddhammopayana, a poem which discusses the doctrines of Buddhism.[70] It gives us an idea that the Abhayagīri-vihāra "did not deviate from the orthodox school in important matters of doctrine."[71] Although the language of Sri Lanka's Buddhism was Pāli, yet, Sanskrit, the sacred language of the Brahmaṇas, was studied by the Sinhalese during this period. The earliest evidence of the knowledge of Sanskrit in Sri Lanka is given by several inscriptions of Mahāyānistic content: and the monks of the Abhayagiri-vihāra, who studied the Mahāyāna and who took interest in the Mahāyāna ideas, knew that language well.[72] But a poem named the Jānakiharaṇa in Sanskrit was found in Sri Lanka and it given the story of the Rāmāyaṇa.[73] Although it was in Sanskrit, but it had no connection with the Mahāyāna ideas. A literary tradition has mentioned that king Kumāradāsa (512-520 A.D.) was the author of this work. Because he was referred to as a friend of the celebrated Indian poet Kālidāsa.[74] Manuscripts of the original poem were discovered in Malabar and they show that the poet of the Jānakīharaṇa was Kumāradāsa. He was not a king but a member of the Sinhalese royal family, the son of a prince named Māmita who was killed by his enemies on the very day the poet was born.[75] According to scholars, the Jānakīharaṇa belongs to the seventh century A.D.

Most probably, its author was the son of the Yuvarāja, named Māna, of Aggabodhi III (633-642 A.D.).[76]

The Pāli commentaries were based on old Sinhalese exegetical works and they were kept in the Mahāvihāra as late as the tenth century A.D. The Rasavāhinī got its material from the stories which existed in the old Sinhalese language. The Pāli chronicles were based on the Sinhalaṭṭakathā Mahāvaṃsa, a historical work.[77] Moggallāna II and Kassapa V were emiment poets. Under the patronage of Aggabodhi I (575-608 A.D.) several poets flourished in his reign. A king styled Saamevan who may be Sena IV 954-956 A.D. wrote the Siyabaslakara, a work on rhetoric and this is the earliest Sinhalese literary work.[78] It has been kept up to the present time. A glossary compiled by Kassapa V and two works on Vinaya rules "have no literary pretensions, but are invaluable to the student of philology and of the history of the Sinhalese language."[79] One of the Kassapa V's inscriptions referred to a poem which was written by Kassapa V and it highly praised the Buddha.[80] The Sasadāvata, the only Sinhalese poem, was composed in the Polonnaruva poet and its subject is the Sasa Jātaka.[81] The Muvadevudāvata and the Kausiluminạ, the two other works of the same kind, belonged to the twelfth century A.D.[82] According to many scholars, the latter is a century later.[83] Guruḷugomi flourished in the twelfth century A.D. and he was the author of the two prose works, the Dharmapradipikā and the Amāvatura.[84] The former employed pedantic language and brittled with Sanskrit tatsamas, while the language of the latter was very simple and was unaffected by Sanskritism. The two works in style and subject are very dissimilar.[85] The Butsaraṇa is the work of the twelfth century A.D.[86] The Sadalakuṇu is a Sinhalese grammar and it belonged to twelfth century A.D. It is now lost.[87] The Sidat-Saṅgarā is a work of the thirteenth century A.D. It is a Sinhalese grammar.[88]

Vijayabāhu I was great patron of literature and was a scholar of high repute. There was a great intellectual re-awakening in his reign. He was the author of many Sinhalese works including a Sinhalese translation of the Dhammsanganī. But not a single of them is available to us today. Now not a single one exists today.[89] At that time, Anuruddha, a monk, wrote the Anuruddhasataka, the Abhidhammattha-Sangaha, the Nāmarūpa-pariccheda and the Paramattha-Vinicchaya.[90] The first is a Buddhist devotional poem of 101 stanzas in Sanskrit. The second one is summary work on the teachings of the Abhidhamma. All Buddhists of the southern school spoke highly of it. The third and the fourth are two works in verse on the Abhidhamma. They are short works.[91]

The reign of king Parākramabāhu the great marked an important period not only in the history of Buddhism but also in the history of literary world. Great attention was given to the study of the Abhidhamma. Intensive literary activity took place in the study of Buddhist philosophical analysis. During this period the people used to think that "critical analysis was more prominent than creative literary effort."[92] Mahākassapa-thera of Dimbubāgala-vihāra, Moggallāna thera and Sāriputta-Thera flourished in the reign of Parākramabāhu the Great.[93] The king for the purpose of purifying the Buddhist Saṃgha convoked a Council and Mahākassapa-Thera presided over it. The latter for his scholarship in Pāli and Sanskrit was a well-knwon person in Parākramabāhu the Great's reign. He wrote a Sinhalese paraphrase (sanne) to the Samantapāsādika. But it is now lost.[94] He was the author of a sub-comentary to the Abidhamattha-Sangaha. He also wrote several other works such as the Moha-Vicchedanī, which is a treatise on the Abhidhamma and Vimativinodanī, which is a commentary on the Vinaya.[95] Moggallāna-thera, another famous scholar, was a contemporary of Mahākassapa-thera. He wrote the Moggalānavyākaraṇa, a Pāli grammatical work.[96] Another learned Thera, also named Moggallāna, wrote the Abhidhānappadipikā, a Pāli lexicon. It is the only ancient Pāli dictionary in Sri Lanka.[97] Sāriputta-thera was the most well-known write of the reign of Parākramabāhu the Great. He was a Sanskrit scholar also. He wrote two works on Sanskrit grammar. He compiled the Vinaya-Sangaha, which was a summary of the Vinaya Piṭaka.[98] He also wrote a ṭikā and Sinhalese paraphrase on this work. He also composed the Sāratthadīpanī, a sub-commentary on Buddhaghosa's Samantapāsādikā.[99] He wrote further a Sinhalese paraphrase (sanne) to the Abhidhammattha-Sangala of Anuruddha Thera.[100] He was also the author of two other tīkās the Sārattha-mañjūsā on the Manorathapūraṇī and the Linatthappakāsinī on the Papañcasūdanī, which ware commentaries by Buddhaghosa on the Anguttara Nikāya and the Majjhima Nikāya.[101] He established a large school of learning at the Jetavana monastery in Polonnaruva and he became known as "Sāgara-mati", "like to the ocean in wisdom"[102] It should be noted here that the ṭikās mentioned above formed one of the major groups of Pāli literature compiled during this period."[103] Mahākassapa-thera and several other monks met at the Jetavana Vihāra at Polonnavuva and there they took a decision to write exegetical commentaries because the existing sub-commentarsie on the old Aṭṭhakathās were unintelligible.[104] Then they wrote tīkās, namely the Sāratthadīpanī on the Vinaya Piṭaka, the Sāratthamañjūsā in four parts on the first four nikāyās on the Sutta Piṭaka and the Paramattha-duipanī in three parts of the Abhidhamma Piṭaka.[105] It is known that several tikās were written either by Mahākassapa-Therra or under his supervision.

Several religious works written in Sinhalese also belong to this period. There were the collections of the Jātaka stories and the stories of the Dhammapada in the Sinhalese language.[106] A collection of stories from which the Pāli Rasavāhini took its material and the Sīhalaṭṭhakathā Mahāvaṃsa on which the Pāli chronicles were based also existed in the Sinhalese language.[107] Many Sinhalese religio-literary works which were written in or about the twelfth century A.D. are popular even today. Among them are the Sasa-dāvata which is a poem on the Sasa Jātaka, the Muvadevadāvata which is a poem on the Mukhādeva Jātaka and the Kavsilumia which is a poem on the Kusa Jātaka.[108] Most probably, Gurulogomi's Amāratura and the Dharmapradipikāra and Vidyācakravarti's Butsaraṇa were written in the twelfth century A.D.[109]

The Dāṭhāvaṃsa or the Dantadhātuvaṃsa

The Dāṭhāvaṃsa or the Dantadhātuvaṃsa,[110] "the History of the (Buddha's) Tooth" was written in partly Sanskritized Pāli (with long compound words). It is an epic.[111] It has five chapters. It is very rich in vocabulary.[112] The Dāthāvaṃsa narrates a history of the Tooth-Relic of the Buddha. It refers to "Pāli as a medium of epic poetry."[113] It was written during the reign of Queen Lilāvatī (1210 A.D.) at the request of a minister named Parākrama by Dhammakitti-thera, a pupil of Sariputta Thera.[114] "It is an eleborate composition, very much influenced by Sanskrit, and is generaly regarded as one of the best extant Pāli poems."[115]

The Dāṭhāvaṃsa mentions the history of the Tooth-Relic of the Buddha which was brought to Sri Lanka from Dantapura, the capital of Kaliṅga in the ninth regual year of Sirimeghavaṇṇa by Hemamālā and Dantakumāra, the daughter and the son-in-law of Guhasīva, king of Kaliṅga.[116] It bagins with an account of the Buddha Dīpankara. It gives us the history of Gotama, the attainment of his enlightenment, his visit to Laṅkā, his Mahāparinibbāna and the distribution of his bodily relics by a Brahmin named Doṇa. It then supplies us with an account of the Tooth Relic of the Buddha at Dantapura, the genealogy of the Kaliṅga kings from Brahmadatta to Guhasīva and the latter's conversion to Buddhism. Then the Dāthāvaṃsa discusses the war of the king of Pātaliputra with Guhasīva on account of the possession of the Tooth Relic which the latter possessed and the marriage between Hemamālā, the princess of Kaliṅga and Dantakumāra, son of the king of Ujjain. It then informs us the history which was respossible for bringing the Tooth-Relic to Sri Lanka. It then describes the arrival of the Tooth-Relic in Sri Lanka in the reign of Sirimeghavaṇṇa and the construction of a temple for the Tooth-Relic at the cost of nine lacs.[117]

During the Polonnarura period Sanskrit played a great role both as an independent classical study and as a powerful influence on the growth of the Pāli language and literary styles. At that time Sri Lanka had close contacts with South India and the arrival of large number of Tamils into Sri Lanka had helped to cultivate Sanskrit learning which had already started in earlier times.[118] Kauṭilya (or Kauṭalya), Man and several other Sanskrit scholars were frequently referred to in Sri Lanka's literature and this shows the influence of Sanskrit not only in the political world but alsoin social spheres.[119] Several inscriptions of the period begin or end with Sanskrit stanzas and these facts indicate that their authors had good knowledge in that languagae.[120] Mahākassapa-thera of Dimbulāgala was well-versed with Sanskrit grammar and he wrote the Bālāvabodhana.[121] Sāriputta-thera wrote a Tikā and a concise Sanskrit grammar.[122] About six or seven other Sanskrit works now extant were written during the Polonnaruva period.[123]

The Cūlavaṃsa

The Cūlavaṃsa, the "Lesser Dynasty of Sinhalese kings" is a continuatation of the Mahāvaṃsa.[124] It describes a connected history of the island of Sri Lanka up to modern times. This continuation occurred under the able guidance of different authors from time to time. We learn from different texts that after the death of Mahānāma, the Mahāvaṃsa's author, the Cūlavaṃsa was continued by the Theras who belonged to different periods with an idea of narrating a continuous history of the island up to modern times.[125] B.C. Law states, "The Mahāvaṃsa proper with Duṭṭhagāmaṇi as its hero was composed by Mahānāma, the Cūlavaṃsa with Parākramabāhu-Parakamabāhu) the Great as its hero was composed by Dhammakitti, the second portion of the Cūlavaṃsa with Kittisiri as its hero was composed by Tibbotuvāve Siddhatha and concluded with a chapter added by Itikkāduve Siri Sumaṅgala. A laudable attempt has been made by the venerable Yogirala Paññānanda to bring it down to modern times". [126] The first part brings the history down to the twelfth century A.D., the second part discusses the history down to the fourteenth century A.D., and the third part gives the history up to modern times.[127] B.C. Law mentions that the first portion of the Cūlavaṃsa consists of forty-three chapters (XXXVII-LXXIX).[128] He narrates further that just after the account of Parākramabāhu I's reign, Wilhelm Geiger finds a great change in the chronicle of the kings who captured the throne after Parākramabāhu I.[129] Sirima Wickremasinghe agrees with Wlhelm Geiger.[130] According to her, chapters XXXVII to LXXIX contain two parts and were written not by a single author but by two different authors.[131] From a tradition we learn that a part of the cūlavaṃsa was written by a thera named Dhammakitti during the reign of Parākramabāhu II, which, Sirima Wickremasinghe "is inclined to believe, could be the second part of this work devoted to the reign of Parākramabāhu."[132] B.C. Law informs that the Cūlavaṃsa's second portion comprises eleven chapters. He states that it begins at chapter LXXX and ends with chapter XC.[133] This portion refers to the history of Sri Lanka from the reign of Vijayabāhu II to that of Parākramabahu IV.[134] According to B.C. Law, a monk who belonged to the Coḷa country was the author of this portion of the Cūlavaṃsa.[135] Sirima Wickremasinghe opines that the third part of the Cūlavaṃsa begins with the reign of Vijayabāhu II, i.e., from chapter LXXX.[136] This part begins at chapter Lxxx and ends with the reign of Parākramabāhu IV at verse 102 or 104 of chapter XC.[137] It was written by a different author. B.C.Law informs that the Cūlavaṃsa gives a continuous history of Sri Lanka up to the reign of Kitti-Siri-Rājasiṃha who ascended the throne of Sri Lanka in the second half of the eighteenth century A.D.[138] Tibhotuvare Siddhattha Sumaṅgala Thera was the author of this part of the Cūlavaṃsa.[139] Hikkaduve Siri Sumaṅgala and Baṭuvantudāve Paṇḍita wrote the concluding chapter which narrates the history of Sri Lanka down to A.D. 1815.[140]

Parākramabāhu II brought the religious revival in Sri Lanka and it continued up to the fifteenth century A.D. But during that period there was not much stability in the political world in the island. Several religio-literary works were compiled during this time. Parākramabāhu II took interest to bring from India to Sri Lanka to teach the monks of Sri Lanka. He was the author of the Sinhalese translation to the Visuddhimagga and the Vinaya Vinicchaya, the Sinhalese poem Kav-Silumina, the masterpiece of Sinhalese poetry, based on the Kusa Jātaka and the Sinhalese from Daladā-sirita.[141] In his reign lived the thera Dharmakīrti who wrote the Dāṭhāvaṃsa, the Pāli poem, and the first part of the Cūḷavaṃsa.[142] The Thūpavaṃsa on the erection of stūpas in Sri Lanka, the Hattha-Vanagalla-Vihāra-Vaṃsa on the hisory of the ancient vihāra at Attenagalla, the Rasavāhinī which is a collection of stories about ancient India and Sri Lanka, the Samantakūtavaṇṇanā on the Buddha's visit to Sumanakūṭa (Adam's Peak), the Kesa-dhātuvaṃsa on the history of the hair-relic of the Buddha, the Pārami-Mahāsataka on the ten perfection (pāramitā), the Saddhamma-Sangaha which deals with history and progress of Buddhism in Sri Lanka are the religious works which were written in Pāli from the time of Parākrambāha II until the fifteenth century A.D.[143]

The Thūpavaṃsa

The Thūpavaṃsa "the History of the Topes" is a work in Pāli and it was written in the thirteenth century A.D.[144] It discusses the thūpas or stūpas or dāgobas (relic-shrine) (dhātucetiya) which were erected over the relics of Buddha in India and Sri Lanka up to the reign of Duṭṭhagāmaṇī of Sri Lanka.[145] It describes the reign of Duṭṭhagāmaṇī who constructed the Mahāthūpa, the great Thūpa at Anurādhapura in Sri Lanka.[146] It has sixteen chapters. During the reigns of Vijayabāhu III and Parākramabāhu II the Thūpavaṃsa was written in Pāli by Vacisserā-thera.[147] He was a well-known scholar and was well-versed in the Tipiṭaka. He wrote the Limaṭṭhadīpanītīkā on the Paṭisambhidamagga, the Saccasaṅkhepaaṭṭhadīpanā and the Visuddhimaggasaṅkhepa-aṭṭhappakāsanā in Sinhalese.[148] According to the Cūlavaṃsa, Vācissara, who belonged to the reign of king Vijayabāha III, father of Parākramabāhu II, was the leading thera of his time and was one of the heads of the Buddhist Saṇgha.[149] He was the leader of the theras of Sri Lanka who visited the kingdoms of Pāṇḍya and Coḷa for the search of the Buddha's Tooth-Relic and Bowl with a hope to bring them to Sri Lanka.[150]

The Thūpavaṃsa opens with a detailed account of the earlier Buddhas.[151] It mentions the history of the life of Gotama from his birth to the attainment of his Mahāparinibbāna, the distribution of the Buddha's bodily relics by a Brahmin named Doṇa, the construction of a great Thūpa (stūpa) at Rājagaha over the bodily relics of the Buddha by king Ajātasatru Ajātasation) of Magadha, the erection of 84,000 vihāras over the relics of the Buddha by Asoka, the Maurya emperor, the latter's religious missions to several countries for the program of Buddhism and the arrival of Mahinda and Sanghamittā in Sri Lanka.[152] It then describes the reign and activities of king Duṭṭhagāmaṇī of Sri Lanka and the building of the Mahāthūpa by king Duṭṭhagāmaṇī at Anurādhapura in Sri Lanka.[153]

The Hatthavanagallavihāravaṃsa

The Hatthavanagallavihāravaṃsa was written in simple Pāli in the reign of Parākramabāhu II in the middle of the thirteenth century A.D.[154] It discusses the life and career of Siri-Saṅghabodhi and the history of the Hatthavanagallavihāra or the history of the ancient temple at Attanagala of the western province of Sri Lanka.[155] It was composed mostly in verse but prose narrative is also there. It is a poem "with a strong influence of Sanskrit, displaying at the same time a fair degree of literary merit."[156] It has eleven chapters. It is a historical novel. We do not know the name of its author. But in the introductory verses the author says that his teacher Anomadessi requested him to write a history of the Hatthavanagalavihāra and he wrote it.[157] Anomadessi belonged to the reign of Parākramabāhu II.[158] The Hatthavamagalla-vihāra was built by Goṭhābhaya-Maghavaṇṇa.[159] King Parākramabāhu II constructed a three-storeyed building for Anomadessi Mahāsāmi at the Hatthavanagalla-vihāra "at great cost" under the supervision of his minister Devepatirāja.[160] The king repaired this vihāra and also built a cetiya and an octagonal image house. This Anomadessi Mahāsāma most probably was the same Anomadessi who told one of his pupils to write a history of the Hatthavanagalla-vihāra. The Hatthavanagallavihāravaṃsa ends with the reign of Parākramabāhu II.

The Halthavanagallavihāravaṃsa describes the Hatthavanagalla-vihāra, a monastery which was built at Attanagalla of western province of Sri Lanka.[161] According to a tradition, this monastery was built on the spot where the ex-king, Siri-Saṅghabodhi of Anurādhapura, offered his head to a poor man.[162] The first eight chapters of the Hatthavanagalla-viharāvaṃsa gives the life of Siri-Saṅghabodhi.[163] The remaining three chapters refer to a history of the Hatthavanagallavihāra and the endowments and the various meritorious deals performed by successive kings of Sri Lanka.[164] We learn from the text that after abdicating his throne the king went to a forest to lead a life devoted to meditation. There he offered his head to a poor man, because Goṭhābhaya, his rival for the throne, announced that any body would receive a reward from him who would secuie Siri-Saṅghabodhi's head. This pious king thought that other people would suffer for him. For this reason, he sacrificed his life for the benefit of others. Most probably, this vihāra was the place where the cremation of the ex-king took place. But several scholars opined that the cremation took place not in Attanagalla of the western province, but to the south of the Issarasamaṇa-vihāra in Anurādhapura.[165] The Hatthavanagal-lavihāravaṃsa mentions that family history of Siri-Saṅghabodhi, his meritorious activities, the life of his queen and it says that she left the palace to follow him where he abdicated the throne but died on the spot where her husband donated his head to a poor man.[166] It describes certain aspects of social conditions in mediaeval Sri Lanka.

The Rasavāhini

The Rasavāhinī is a collection of Buddhist stories in simple Pāli prose.[167] In the first half of the fourteenth century A.D. Vedeha Thera wrote it. It belonged to the Dambadevi period in Sri Lanka. The author in the open stanza says that his work "is a revision of an old Pāli translation, made from an original compilation by Raṭṭhapāla Thera of the Taṅgutta-Vaṅka Parivena of the Mahāvihāra."[168] Raṭṭhapāla Thera has taken his material from the ancient Sahassa-Vatthu-aṭṭhakathā (commontary of the Thousand Stories), which is a collection of legends of folktales.[169] The Rasavāhinī was based on Raṭṭhapāla's work. But Vedeha Thera revised it thoroughly and gave new ideas in it and then he wrote the Rasavāhinī. G.P. Malalasekera describes, "Vedeha, who was of a poetic temperament, and, therefore, loved beauty of diction, was not satisfied with such an inartistic presentation of these homely stories, and he proceeded to clothe then in a new garb. The result is the Rasavāhinī, exquisite in its simplicity, charming in its naivete and delightful in its innocence."[170]

The Samantakūṭa-Vaṇṇanā

The Samantakūṭa-Vaṇṇanā is a Pāli poem of 800 verses.[171] Vedeha Thera of the Vanavāsi fraternity wrote it at the request of Rāhula, another member of the vanavāsi school.[172] This poem describes the beautiful peak known as the Samantakūṭa (Sumaṇakūṭa or Adam's Peak).[173] It is known from this work that the Buddha on his third visit to the island of Sri Lanka imprinted the work of his left foot on this beautiful peak.[174] The poem discusses the Buddha's birth, his enlightenment and his three visits to Sri Lanka. It also describes the hills, mountains, rivers, forests and valleys of many parts of the island.[175] G.P. Malalasekera narrates, "The Samanta-Kūtavaṇṇanā is undoubtedly the work of a poet, rich in his gifts and inspired with love and reverence for the subject of his poem. The opening verses of adoration, enchantingly sweat in their beautiful cadences, are sung even today, by many thouasnds who love never heard his name and know nothing of his work."[176] The Samantakūṭa-Vaṇṇanā like the Rasavāhinī was a work of the Dambadeṇi period. Vedeha Thera flourished in the reign of Parākramabāhu II's period.

The Nalāṭadhātuvaṃsa or Lalāṭadhātuvaṃsa

The Pāli Naḷātadhātuvaṃsa or the Lalātadhātuvaṃsa or simply Laḷātavaṃsa refers to a history of the frontal bone relic of the Buddha.[177] It has five chapetrs.G.P. Malalasekera mentions, "It is a work, undoubtedly, of great antiquity, and evidently belongs to the cycle of sages and legends of Rohaṇa and Malaya. It therefore, contains many popular traditions not found elsewhere, especially grouped round the family and contemporaries of the Kākavaṇṇa-Tissa, father of Dutugamuṇu."[178] It discusses Buddha Dīpaṅkara,Gotama, his life, his enlightenment, his three visits to Laṅkā, his mahāparinibbāna and the distribution of his bodily relics.[179] The third chapter gives an account of the frontal bone relic and the Mallas who received it at the time of the distribution of the Buddha's relics.[180] It then mentions its arrival in Sri Lanka in the reign of Mahānāga of Mahāgāma who received it with great honour. The last two chapters inform Kākavaṇṇa-Tissa's family, the construction of a dāgopa (stūpa) at Seruvila for this holy relic, its dedication and the enshrinement of relics.[181] This work does not say anything about its date and its author's name. According to G.P. Malalasekera, it was written in the tenth or eleventh century A.D.[182]

A large number of Sinhalese works on religious subjects also belonged to this period. The Saddharmaratnāvalī which describes the stories of the Pāli Dhammapadaṭṭhakathā in Sinhalese, the Pūjavalī which refers to the honours and offerings received by the Buddha, the Pansīya-panas-Jātaka based on the Pāli Jātaka commentary, the Sinhala Bodhivaṃsa on the history of the Bodhi tree, the Elu-Attanagalu-vaṃsa which is a translation of the Pāli work, the Saddharmalaṅkāra, based on the Pāli Rasavāhini, the Guttilakāvyaya based on the Guttila Jātaka, the Kāvyasekharaya based on the Sattubhatta Jātaka, the Buduguṇālankāraya which narrates the dispelling of the calamity in Vesāli by the Buddha and the Loveda-Sangarāva containing religious instruction for the laity are important works of this period.[183] Apart from these works, there are also other works in Sinhalese. These are the Rājavaliya, the Rājaratnākarya, the Daḷadā-Sirita, the Daḷadā Pūjāvaliya, the Dambodeṇi Asna, the Kandavurusirita, the Saddharma Ratnākaraya etc.[184] They not only give useful information on political matters but also discuss religious history of the island. The Pāli and the Sinhalese works are very important for the reconstruction of Sri Lanka's history. The Kavsilumina (crest-gem poetry) in classical Sinhalease is attributed to Parakramabāhu II of Dambadeniya. In the poem itself the authoer is called a Paṇḍu king who had the title The Pujaualiya of Kali-kal-savani (Kalikāla sarvajña). The Cūlavaṃsa says that Parakramabāhum III had that title.

The Pūjāvaliya

The Pūjāvaliya, "the History of offerings" was written by Mayūrapāda Thera or Buddhaputra Sthavira of the Mayūrapāda Pariveṇa, the monastic college at Vatagiri (Vākīrigala or Vāgirigala) in the Kagalla District.[185] The author belonged to the reign of Parākramabāhu II. The latter patronised this monastic college. In the thirteenth year of the reign of Parākramabāhu II, the Pūjāvaliya was written.[186] Most probably, it was in A.D. 1266 or 1270. Patirājadeva, the Prime Minister of Parākramabāhu

II, requested Mayūrapāda to compose it to justify the Bodhisattva status attained by Parākramabāhu II.[187] The author then completed it and gave it to the minister to present it to the king. The latter became very glad to receive it "as if a second kingdom had been bestowed upon him, and that he listend to its praise of the virtues of the Buddha during the period covered between two uposatha days, setting aside his royal duties. Further, we are told that the book was placed on the back of the royal elephant with banners flying and was taken round the city amidst great festivity."[188] The Pūjāvaliya has 34 chapters. It narrates the history of Sri Lanka from the earliest times up to the end of the reign of Parākramabāhu II. It gives stories about honours and offerings received by the Buddha to justify the epithet of arhat by which the Buddha is mentioned. The book is of historical value as there are chapters dealing with the offerings to the Buddha by the kings of Sri Lanka and mentioning information about religious activities of king Parakramabāhu II.

The Kanadavurusirita or the Kandavuru Sirita

The Kandavurusirita is an important work in the reign of Parākramabāhu II. It does not mention the name of its author. For a study of the reign of Parākramabāhu II it is valuable no doubt.[189] It gives the daily routine of Kalikāla Sāhitya Sarvajña Paṇḍita Parākramabāhu, "the all-knowing sage Parākramabāhu II of the dark (Kali) age of literature."[190] It informs that the king used to begin his day "with meditation on anicca, dukkha, and anātura followed by concentration on the suttas."[191] It refers to his observation of the sila and the great homage paid by him to Tooth-Relic "as part of the daily routine."[192]

The Saddharmaratnāvalī

Dharmasena-sthavira of the Dambadeniya period wrote the Saddharmaratnāvalī, a Sinhalese work.[193] It may belong to the twelfth century A.D. It describes in Sinhalese the stories of the

Pāli Dhammapadaṭṭa-Kathā but it is not a mere translation. "The stories are related with great gusto, the narration being enlivened with homely proverbs and similes drawn from life."[194]

The Pansiya-panes-jātaka

The Pansiya-panas-jātaka in Sinhalease was written in the reign of Parākramabāhu IV.[195] It is based on the Pāli Jātaka and its commentary. Several hands must have co-operat in this monumental literary undertaking, because "its styles is not uniform throughout."[196] This work is not a mere translation from the Pāli, the stories were told in such a way as to attract the attention of the reader, or rather the listener. The Pansiya-panas-jātaka from the time of its composition up to the present day has got great populaity with the average Sinhalease Buddhist and "has had no small influence in shaping his character by setting before him a standard of conduct."[197]

Vilgammuḷa-mahāsāmi in the reign of Parākramabāhu IV wrote the Sinhalese Bodhivaṃsa and Anāgatavaṃsa, but both were translation of Pāli originals.[198] He was very formal in style.

The Daḷadāsirita of Devrada

A Sinhalese prose work of the reign of Parākramabāhu IV was written in A.D. 1318 or 1326. It was the Daḷadāsirita of Devrada (Devarāja).[199] It mentions the history of the Tooth Relic as an introduction to the rules promulgted for its shrine by the king." The rules themselves are in the usual legal phraseology, while the rest of the work, written for the most part in pure Sinhelse, is highly ornate in style and often makes use of alliteration."[200] The Daḷadā-Sirita "History of the Tooth Relic" or "the ceremonial of the Tooth Relic" was written in the Saka year 1240 (A.D. 1318) in Parākramabāhu IV's reign.[201] Some scholars say that it was written in A.D. 1325. Amaradasa Liyanagamage informs that its author is known as Devradadampasangināvan.[202]

G.P. Malalasekera opines that Parākramabāhu IV wrote it.[203] The king used to pay great homage to the Tooth Relic. For his great devotion to the Tooth Relic, he wrote the Daḷadā-Sirita. In the concluding portion the work describes the rules of conduct towards the Tooth Relic. It also informs the king's conduct in connection with the Tooth Relic. It gives us an account of bringing of the Tooth Relic to Sri Lanka, and informs the history of the island from the earliest times up to the reign of Parākramabāhu IV. It supplies a list of kings from Sirimeghavaṇṇa to Parākramabāhu IV.[204]

A pupil of Vilgammula who lived at the Laṅkā-tilaka-vihāra wrote the Vimmkti-Sangraha.[205] The book is an exposition of certain aspects of the Buddhist doctrine. The Eḷu Attamagalu-vaṃsa was written in A.D. 1382. It is a translation of the Pāli work.[206] Dharmakīrti, the second Saṅgharāja of that name, who resided at Gaḍalādeniya temple, wrote the Saddharmalaṅkāra.[207] This work, for the most part, discusses in Sinhalese the stories mentioned in the Pāli Rasavāhinī.

The Nikāya-Saṁgraha

Dharmakīrti was the author of the Nikāya-Saṁgraha, a concise history of Buddhism in Sri Lanka.[208] This work is of great value as a source book for the history of Sri Lanka, particularly of the Gampala period. It narrates a history of Buddhism from the earliest times up to the reign of Bhuvanakabāhu V of Gampola.[209] In its colophon the author says, "This brief history of the religion was composed by the learned monk, Devarakkhita, known and renowned over the world as Jaya-Bāhu and celebrated as the Mahā Thera Dhammakitti, who attained the rank of Saṇgharāja and glorified the religion."[210] Dharmakirti, the author of the Nikāya-Saṇgraha, was the Saṅgharaja in the reign of Bhuvanakabāha V and Virabāhu II (A.D. 1372-1410).[211] He reformed the Buddhist Saṃgha in the reign of the latter king.

The Nikāya-Saṃgraha is an important work for a study of the reformation of the Buddhist Saṃgha in the reign of Parākramabāhu II.[212] It mentions Buddhism and the problems of the Buddhist Saṃgha in the reign of Kaliṅga Vijayabāhu who had the first name Magha.[213] It gives the names of fifteen kings who occupied the throne of Sri Lanka after Parākramabāhu I and it says that Kaliṅga Vijayabāhu who was also known as Māgha ascended the throne after their death.[214] G.P. Malalasekera informs, "it gives much valuable information about schisms in the Buddhist church, and is an authentic record, specially of events which took place in the thirteenth and fourteenth centuries, where the Mahāvaṃsa accounts are often unreliable and seem to want supplementation."[215]

The Saddharmaratnākara

Vimalakīrti-Sthavira, the pupil of Dharmakīrti the second, wrote the Saddharamatnākara.[216] From the literary point of view, this work, written in early years of the reign of Parākramabāhu VI, is the least meritorious of the series of Sinhalese prose works noticad so far.[217] The Saddharmaratnākara was written in the fifteenth century A.D.[218] It is "a collection of Buddhist stories, not an attempt to set out the history of these events connected with the Sāsana. Nevertheless it gives a brief historical outline, evidently following the Nikāya Saṃgraha."[219] Dhammadinna Vimalakitti Thera who was also known as Siddhttha was its author.[220] It narrates the history of Sri Lanka from the earliest times up to the reign of Parākramabāhu VI.

The Dambadeṇi Asna

The Dambadeṇi Asna gives information on the social condition and political life in mediaeval Sri Lanka.[221] It mentions various types of jobs in the royal court, the different departments of the army and a description of musical instruments.[222] In the concluding portion it refers to the names of Parākramabāhu (II),

Bhuvanakabāhu, Vathimirāja and Prākramabāhu.[223] It does not say anything about the name of its author. C.E. Godakumbura states that it was written in the reign of Parākramabāhu IV.[224] He opines, "the names of kings appended to the work are an addition by a later scribe."[225]

The Daḷadā-Pūjāvaliya

The Daḷada-Pūjāvaliya deals with a history of the Tooth-Relic.[226] In the opening passage the author states that in order to help the three Prime Ministers, Alagakkonara, Patirāja and Jayasiṁha to gain merit, he wrote this work.[227] In it there is a reference to Bhuvanekabāhu, who, according to scholars, was Bhuvanekabāhu V of Gamapola (A.D. 1378-1398).[228] C.E. Godakumbura remonks that the Daḷadā-Pūjāvaliya was written in the reign of this king.[229] But in the list of kings this work does not give the names of kings who followed Parākramabāhu IV up to Bhuvanekabāhu V.[230] It inform that Parākramabāhu IV used to pay homage to the Tooth Relic.[231] It says him as apage Siri-Parākramabāhu', our (king) Siri-Parākramabāhu'. B.C. Law thinks that in his reign it was composed.[232]

The Rājavaliya

The Rājāvaliya gives a history of Sri Lanka from the earliest times to the end of the reign of Vimaladhammasuriya II.[233] According to B.C. Law, it was written in the beginning of the eighteenth century A.D.[234]

NOTES

1. CHC, 115.
2. *Ibid.*, 115.
3. *Ibid.*, 115.
4. *Ibid.*, 115.
5. BC., 33.
6. *Ibid.*, 35.

7. *Ibid.*, 35.
8. *Ibid.*, 35.
9. *Ibid.*, 35.
10. *Ibid.*, 36.
11. *Ibid.*, 36.
12. BACSEA., 2.
13. BIA., 5.
14. BACSEA., 3; PLC, 135-36.
15. BACSEA., 3; OLC, 7-8.
16. BACSEA., 4; PLC, 135-136.
17. BC., 36.
18. DPV., 8-9; HIL, II, 2310; OCC, 1-2.
19. PLC., 138.
20. *Ibid.*, 138.
21. BC., 37; PLC, 133; BACSEA., 2, f.n. 5.
22. *Ibid.*, 37; *ibid.,133; ibid.* 2, f.n. 5.
23. *Ibid.*, 36.
24. BACSEA., 5. DV, 5.
25. DV., 5.
26. *Ibid.*, 1; Bc, 37; BACSEA., 5.
27. *Ibid.*, 1; *ibid.*, 37; *ibid.*, 5-6.
28. *Ibid.*, 10-11; *ibid.*, 37; *ibid.*, 6; OCC, 6-7.
29. BACSEA., 6-7., OCc, 12.
30. *Ibid.*, 7; *ibid.*, 15; HIL., 211; PLC, 139.
31. BACSEA., 8; HIL, II, 211.
32. *Ibid.*, 8; *ibid.*, 212; Dipmah, 19.
33. BACSEA., 8; DIPMAH, 2; PLC., 141.
34. *Ibid.*, 9; *ibid.*, 14; *ibid.*, 139.
35. *Ibid.*, 9; PLC., 141.
36. BC., 37.
37. *Ibid.*, 37.
38. BACSEA., 9; HIL. II, 212-213.
39. *Ibid.*, 9; *ibid.*, 212-213.
40. *Ibid.*, 9; *ibid.*, 213.
41. *Ibid.*, 9; *ibid.* 213.
42. *Ibid.*, 10; BC, 37.
43. *Ibid.*, 10; OCC, 36.
44. *Ibid.*, 10; *ibid.*, 14; DPV, 7.
45. CHC., 174.
46. *Ibid.*, 174.
47. *Ibid.*, 174.
48. *Ibid.*, 174.
49. *Ibid.*, 174.

50. BC., 43.
51. *Ibid.*, 43.
52. *Ibid.*, 43.
53. *Ibid.*, 43.
54. *Ibid.*, 43.
55. *Ibid.*, 43.
56. *Ibid.*, 43.
57. *Ibid.*, 43.
58. *Ibid.*, 43.
59. *Ibid.*, 43-44.
60. OCC, 19-20; PLC, 142; HIL, 218; DPRD., 6-7.
61. HIL, 218.
62. *Ibid.*, 218.
63. DIPMAH, 79.
64. Wickremasinghe, xiv.
65. PLC., 157.
66. *Ibid.*, 157.
67. *Ibid.*, 157.
68. *Ibid.*, 157.
69. *Ibid.*, 157.
70. CHC., 175.
71. *Ibid.*, 175.
72. *Ibid.*, 175.
73. *Ibid.*, 175.
74. *Ibid.*, 175.
75. *Ibid.*, 175.
76. *Ibid.*, 175.
77. *Ibid.*, 175.
78. *Ibid.*, 176.
79. *Ibid.*, 176.
80. *Ibid.*, 176.
81. *Ibid.*, 266.
82. *Ibid.*, 266.
83. *Ibid.*, 266.
84. *Ibid.*, 266.
85. *Ibid*., 266-267.
86. *Ibid.*, 267.
87. *Ibid.*, 267.
88. *Ibid.*, 267.
89. BC., 44.
90. *Ibid.*, 44.
91. *Ibid.*, 44.
92. CHC., 267.

93. *Ibid.*, 267; BC., 44.
94. BC., 44.
95. *Ibid.*, 44.
96. *Ibid.*, 44; CHC., 267.
97. *Ibid.*, 44; *ibid.*, 267.
98. BC., 45.
99. *Ibid.*, 45; CHC., 267.
100. BC., 45.
101. *Ibid.*, 45.
102. CHC., 267-268.
103. BC., 45.
104. *Ibid.*, 45.
105. *Ibid.*, 45-46.
106. *Ibid.*, 46.
107. *Ibid.*, 46.
108. *Ibid.*, 46.
109. *Ibid.*, 46.
110. BACSEA., 16; DTV, 109; DIPMAH., 88t; HIL., 218.
111. BACSEA., 16; HIL., 218.
112. HPL., II, 580.
113. *Ibid.*, II, 579.
114. CHC., 268; BACSEA., 17.
115. CHC., 268.
116. HPL., II, 581; PLC., 66-67.
117. BACSEA[illegible]8.
118. CHC., 26[illegible]
119. *Ibid.*, 268.
120. *Ibid.*, 268.
121. *Ibid.*, 268.
122. *Ibid.*, 268.
123. *Ibid.*, 268.
124. DPRD., 5.
125. PLC., 141-142; BC., 38.
126. OCC., 12.
127. BC., 38.
128. OCC., 17.
129. *Ibid.*, 17.
130. DPRD., 5.
131. *Ibid.*, 5.
132. *Ibid.*, 5.
133. OCC., 17.
134. *Ibid.*, 17.
135. *Ibid.*, 17.

136. DPRD., 5.
137. *Ibid.*, 6.
138. OCC., 17; PLC., 142.
139. *Ibid.*, 17; *ibid.*, 142.
140. *Ibid.*, 19-20; *ibid.*, 142; BACSEA., 14.
141. BC., 49.
142. *Ibid.*, 49.
143. *Ibid.*, 49.
144. BACSEA., 18; HIL, II, 218; OCC., 24.
145. *Ibid.*, 18; HPL., II. 562; OCC., 24.
146. *Ibid.*, 18; OCC., 24.
147. *Ibid.*, 18; HIL., II, 219; DPRD., 6; PLC., 217.
148. *Ibid.*, 19; PLC., 217; OCC., 24.
149. *Ibid.*, 19; *ibid.*, 217; *ibid.*, 25; CV., LXXXI, 20-23.
150. *Ibid.*, 19; OCC., 25.
151. *Ibid.*, 19; PLC., 216., HPL., II, 566.
152. *Ibid.*, 19; HPL., II, 566-575.
153. *Ibid.*, 19; *ibid.*, I, 576-579; PLC., 216-217.
154. *Ibid.*, 19; PLC, 218-219; DPRD., 6., SHVGV., 1.
155. *Ibid.*, 20; *ibid.*, 218-219; *ibid.*, 6; HPL., II, 579; Wickremasinghe, 70-71.
156. *Ibid.*, 20; DPRD., 16.
157. *Ibid.*, 20; *ibid.*, 16; PLC., 219.
158. *Ibid.*, 20; PLC., 219.
159. *Ibid.*, 20; OCC., 25.
160. *Ibid.*, 20; DPRD., 16., CV; Lxxxvi, 37-39; PLC, 219.
161. *Ibid.*, 21; DPRD., 16; PLC, 218.
162. *Ibid.*, 21; *ibid.*, 16; *ibid.*, 218; OCC., 25.
163. *Ibid.*, 21; *ibid.*, 16; *ibid.*, 218.
164. *Ibid.*, 21; *ibid.*, 17; *ibid.*, 218-219.
165. *Ibid.*, 22; *ibid.*, 16; HC., 1, 190, n. 26.
166. *Ibid.*, 22; DPRD., 17.
167. *Ibid.*, 22; PLC., 162 and 224.
168. *Ibid.*, 22; *ibid.*, 224.
169. *Ibid.*, 22; *ibid.*, 225.
170. *Ibid.*, 22; *ibid.*, 225.
171. *Ibid.*, 23; *ibid.*, 223-224.
172. *Ibid.*, 23; *ibid.*, 223.
173. *Ibid.*, 23; BC., 49.
174. *Ibid.*, 23; PLC., 223.
175. *Ibid.*, 23; *ibid.*, 224.
176. *Ibid.*, 23; *ibid.*, 224.
177. *Ibid.*, 23; *ibid.*, 255; OCC., 25.

178. *Ibid.*, 23; PLC., 255.
179. *Ibid.*, 23; *ibid.*, 255.
180. *Ibid.*, 24; *ibid.*, 255.
181. *Ibid.*, 24; *ibid.*, 256.
182. *Ibid.*, 24; *ibid.*, 256.
183. BC., 49.
184. BACSEA, 24-25.
185. *Ibid.*, 25; OCC., 26; DPRD., 11 and 176; CC., 333.
186. *Ibid.*, 25; DPRD., 11-12.
187. *Ibid.*, 25; *ibid.*, 15.
188. *Ibid.*, 25; *ibid.*, 15.
189. *Ibid.*, 25; *ibid.*, 28.
190. *Ibid.*, 26; *ibid.*, 28.
191. *Ibid.*, 26; *ibid.*, 28.
192. *Ibid.*, 26; *ibid.*, 24.
193. CHC., 333.
194. *Ibid.*, 333.
195. *Ibid.*, 334.
196. *Ibid.*, 334.
197. *Ibid.*, 334.
198. *Ibid.*, 334.
199. *Ibid.*, 334.
200. *Ibid.*, 334.
201. PLC., 214 and 232; DPRD., 25; BACSEA., 26.
202. DPRD., 25; BACSEA., 26.
203. BACSEA., 26; PLC, 214 and 232.
204. BACSEA., 27.
205. CHC., 334.
206. *Ibid.* 334.
207. *Ibid.*, 334
208. *Ibid.*, 334.
209. BACSEA., 27; DPRD., 30.
210. BACSEA., 28; PLC., 242-243.
211. *Ibid.*, 28; *ibid*, 242.
212. *Ibid.*, 28; DPRD, 30.
213. *Ibid.*, 28; *ibid.*, 117.
214. *Ibid.*, 28; *ibid.*, 117.
215. BACSEA; 28., PLC., 243.
216. CHC., 334.
217. *Ibid.*, 334-335.
218. BACSEA., 28; DPRD., 117.
219. *Ibid.*, 28., *ibid.*, 117.
220. *Ibid.*, 28., PLC., 253.

221. *Ibid.*, 27; DPRD., 27; DA., 30-39.
222. *Ibid.*, 27; DPRD., 27-28.
223. *Ibid.*, 27; *ibid.*, 28.
224. *Ibid.*, 27; *ibid*, 28.
225. *Ibid.*, 27; *ibid.*, 28.
226. *Ibid.*, *27; ibid.*, 26; f.n. 8.
227. *Ibid.*, 27; *ibid.*, 26; f.n. 8.
228. *Ibid.*, 27; *ibid.*, 26; f.n. 8.
229. *Ibid.*, 27; *ibid.*, 26; SL., 114-115.
230. *Ibid.*, 27; *Ibid.*, 26.
231. *Ibid.*, 27; OCC., 26.
232. *Ibid.*; 27; *ibid.*, 26.
233. *Ibid.*, 29; DPRD., 239.
234. *Ibid.*, 29; OCC., 28.

7

The Buddhist Monastery of Sri Lanka: Its Administrative System

The administration of a Buddhist monastery in Sri Lanka was under the management of the Buddhist Saṃgha. A Nevāsika Mahathera (Resident Chief Mank) of each monastery looked after its discipline and order and it was under his control.[1] The Buddhist Saṃgha used to appoint the chief monk of a monastery. Most popularly a monk of outstanding ability, knowledge and character was selected to such posts. No individual monk on the ground of pupillary succession or śiṣyānuśiṣya-paramparāra as to-day had no power to claim incumbency of a monastery. The first evidence of incumbency through pupillary succession was found in the Buddhannchāla Pillar Inscription during the resign of Kassapa V (913-923 A.D.)[2] A Nevāsika Mahāthera had the capacity to give his judgment in matters of emergency. For example, on one occasion, Abhaya Thera, the chief monk of the Cetiyagiri (Mihintale), received and treated hospitably a rebel and his followers who went to a monastery to carry off the goods of the monastery by using force.[3] Although the action of the Mahāthera did not agree with the original rules of the Vinaya, yet, he understood that in order to save the valuable property of the monastery he did the right thing. Other monks at the begining criticised him for his action. But they discussed the matter with him and the they accepted his vices.[4]

In the early days when there were no temporalities, the administration of a monastery in order to maintain the discipline of the inmates and to keep the place clean and in order was very simple.[5] But after some time, when many monks lived in a monastery and the establishment of large religious endowments brought huge incomes, then the administration of a monastery took the shape of a complete department with several branches.[6] From inscriptions we get an idea about the administrative system of a monastery in ancient Sri Lanka.[7] Those inscriptions are the Jetavanārāma Sanskrit Inscription (EZ., I, 4), the two Tablets of Mahinda IV at Mihintale (EZ. I, 4), the Jetavanārāma Slab (No. 2) of Mahinda IV (EZ., I, 232), and the Slab of Kassapa V (EZ., I, 43).[8] They throw flood of light on the administrative system of a monastery. Most of these lithic records belong to the 9th and 10th centuries, but the system mentioned in these records was based on similar earlier schemes. The inscription of Mahinda IV at Mihintale informs that after consulting the earlier rules that were current at Mihintale and the Abhayagiri, the present rules were framed.[9] "........Conferred with competent persons as to the expediency of selecting such of the rules as pleased him out of those (in force) at his own Abhayagiri-vihāra and out of those formerly instituted at Catiyagiri-vihāra (Mihintale)." "Seygiri-veherhi pere tubū sirit......Abahay-giri-veherhi sirit sija rusvā genā me veherat me sirit tuluva vaṭi nisiyan hā sasāndā.....".[10]

The lithic records relating to monastic administration available to us belong to monasteries which came under Mahāyānistic influence.[11] The Jetavanārāma Sanskrit Inscription refers to rules for the administration of certain minor monasteries.[12] During the time of Mahāsena in the 4th century A.D. Mihintatle was under the influence of Mahāyānism and the Dhammarueikas occupied it. It was under the occupation of the Dhammarusikas.[13] A fragmentary Sanskrit hymn of the 8th century A.D. in praise of the three bodies (trikāya) of the Buddha was found on a rock near the Sahautiya at Ambasthala in Mihintale. This show that it was under the influence of Mahāyānism.[14] The two Tablets of

Mahinda IV were discovered at Mihintate. They deal with the rules that helped to govern a monastery under Mahāyānistic influence.[15] But no record, which discusses the administration of the Mahāvihāra or any other Theravāda monastery at that time, was found.

There were rules relating to the monks, the employees, and the serfs, and the administration of temporalities. The king after taking the advice and the approval of the Buddhist Saṃgha introduced these rules. Not only duties but also payments and remunerates attached to them were referred to. All administrative works of various departments and servants were arranged after discussing with the Buddhist Saṃgha. With the approval of the Buddhist servants were punished or dismissed and no individual monk was allowed to interfere in such matters.[16] Monks, who were in charge of the revenue, used to receive from the villages and lands granted to the monastery. Accounts were maintained daily and at the end of each month they were again kept in the monthly sheet.[17] At the end of the year for approval the annual statement of accounts were placed before the Buddhist Saṃgha and if they found any irregularities and shortcomings relating to the accounts, then the theras who kept the register (paṇ̃jikā) made an enquiry into this matter.[18] From its revenues all employees of the monastery were regularly paid. Every little detail of work which was necessary for the upkeep of the monastery was taken very carefully and remnueration was assigned for each piece of work.[19] Even such minor servants as flower-gather used to receive regularly definite sums of money.[20] The monks themselves for their works were paid. The monks, who used to teach the Vinaya, the Sutta and the Abhidhamma and those who used to look after the monastery, used to receive different grades of look after the monastery, used to receive different grades of payments and these payments were fixed for them.[21] There was a communal kitchen within the monastery premises and food was prepared there.[22] The monks in order to receive their ration used to go to the place where their ration was distributed. No raw rice was distributed to monks.[23] The teaching of the Vinaya and the Suttas prohibited the Buddhist monks from accepting raw rice.[24] Ghee and other medicines also were distributed at the monastery and the monks in order of seniority usually went to the appointed place to receive them.[25]

There were monks who used to lead improper lives and for this reason they were not permitted to live in the monastery. For example, there were some monks who had agricultural and commercial interests, others who had lauded property, who did some works which were against religion and society, who evaded their duties, who committed offences and were expelled from their monasteries, such monks were not permitted to remain in the monastery.[26] There were monks who created disturbances and generals in the monastery.[27] One inscription mentions that if there was a dissension, then the food should not be given to monks and it should be given to dogs and crows.[28] If there was a dispute between one monk and another, then the one who spoke improperly and did not behave in a proper way, he was not allowed to remain in the monastery.[29] The inmates of one monastery had no right over another monastery.[30] The Jetavanārāma Sanskrit inscription informs that those who give help or associate themselves with other monasteries should not stay in that monastery.[31] "anyavihāra-sāhāyyaṃ kurvatā'pi na vastavyam."[32] This may be noted "as a sign of sharp difference and jealousy among the various nikāyas at the time."[33] Lodgings were not given to any outsiders in the building known as "Water-Pavilion-at the Gate" either in the upper floor or in the ground floor.[34] Outsiders' belongings should not be kept there. If anything other than the belongings of servants was kept there, then the servants in charge were dismissed from their services and were not allowed to keep the maintenance lands (divel) in their possession.[35] This prohibition was applied to royal officers who frequently used monastic buildings as temporary residences.[36] Labourers, cows, carts and buffaloes belonging to the monasteries were not allowed by anyone to take as one's own.[37] After making due inquiry fines exacted in the villages belonging to the monastery were handed over to the monastery and the state was not allowed to take as one's own.[38] Trees on monastery grounds could not be felled.[39] Sometimes people would come to the Vihāra and would ask for trees. The monks, on the ground that they belonged to the Buddhist Saṃgha, refused them. But if the layman insisted on getting them or threatened violence, then, they, after paying as compensation a reasonable inpost or doing some work for the monastery, were allowed to take the trees.[40] "Even a tree of the size of a needle is a major article (garu-bhaṇḍa)."[41] Even without permission trees could be used for building a residence for monks. Even leaves or flowers or fruits were not allowed to give to lay people.[42] In order to protect monasteries from intruders from outside the Buddhist monastery has introduced this sort of prohibition.

Many monks in the monasteries like the Mahāvihāra, the Abhayagiri, the Jetarama, Mihintale and the Tissamahārāma used to live. Fa-Hien, the Chinese pilgrim, visited Sri Lanka in the fifth century A.D. He says that there were about 5,000 monks at the Abhayagiri, 3000 at the Mahāvihāra and 2000 at Mihintale when he came to Sri Lanka.[43] Further he describes that there were about 60,000 monks in the kingdom who used to get their good from their common stores and that the king, besides, arranged elsewhere in the city a common supply of food for five or six thousand more.[44] Hiuen Tsiang visited Sri Lanka in the seventh century A.D. He mentions that at his time there were about 20,000 monks in the country.[45] Their records show that the number of Buddhist monks in Sri Lanka was very large.

The Buddhist monks themselves looked after their own personal needs and cleaned their own cells and courtyards. But for the maintenance and upkeep of the monasteries a large number of servants and workers was required. From the Mihintale Inscription of Mahinda IV we learn that in the monastery at Mihintale about 20 servants were permanently employed and they used to perform various duties and activities connected with that monastery.[46] Many kings and queens gave ārāmikas and servants to the Buddhist Saṃgha and the monasteries.[47] King Silāmeghavaṇṇa in the seventh century A.D. captured Tamil soldiers as prisoners and he gave them to several monasteries as slaves.[48] Sometimes poor people became attendants in monasteries and they took the help of monks to maintain themselves. "Duggatamanussā saṅghaṃ missāya Jivissāmāti vihāre kappiyakārakā honti."[49] These men did odd jobs in the monastery. There was another class of people known as bhikku-bhatikas and in the vihāra they used to live with monks and for their living they depended on monks.[50] An inscription of the tenth century A.D. informs that certain attendants known as uvasu or upāsaka used to reside in the monastery.[51] South Indian Tamil inscriptions describe a class of temple attendants known as upāsakas (EZ., III, 228). Even today in the Buddhist monasteries in Sri Lanka there are elderly men who do temple duties and help monks who want their services. Generally they are known as upāsakas. Originally, any devout by Buddhist became known as upāsaka, irrespective of his status in life. But later on the term indicates an elderly person, "very often a poor elderly person, given to religious activities and frequenting Buddhist temples."[52] Apart from these community servants there were also the personal attendants of the important chief monks.[53] The Buddhist monasteries employed many servants for the service of the monasteries and the number was so great that the kings, in addition to general grants, gave villages and resources for the specific purpose of maintaining the servants.[54] A regular and substantial income was necessary to maintain and to upkeep a big monastery. From various sources this was taken. These permanent endowments can be classified into four categories: first, the grant of lands and field and village; second, tanks and canals; third, the deposit of paddy and other grains and money to be kept in trust for the monastery; fourth, the levying of taxes and the collection of fines.[55] If may be noted here that it was impossible for private individuals alone to maintain large monasteries when several thousand monks used to reside in monasteries. For this reason an income of a permanent character was considered essential, helpful and important and such revenues should bring no hardship to the people. These endowments were first established not very such later than the introduction of Buddhism to the Island.[56] There is a reference to a grant to a monastery in the first century B.C. when Vaṭṭagāmaṇī granted saṃghabhoga to the Kupikkala vihāra of Mahātissa thera.[57] A ketaka leaf was used to write the grant. It is difficult to say anything about Sangha-bhoga. Most probably, it was a grant of lands or fields or tanks or even income from a village.[58] W. Geiger states that the word Saṅgha-bhoga was "lands for the use of the brotherhood." But there is no justification for the assumption that the grant was of lands. Saṇgha-bhoga literally means "possession", "revenue" or "wealth for the community."[59] Many kings and queens throughout the centuries gave lands, fields and maintenance villages to religious bodies.[60] Fa Hien mentions, "He (king) then endowed the community of the monks with the population, fields and houses, writing the grant on plates of metal (to the effect) that from the time onwards, from generation to generation, no one should venture to annual or alter it."[61] Fa Hien their visited Sri Lanka in the fifth century A.D. From his record we learn that how some of these lands were granted in the fifth century A.D. Temple lands, fields and villages were free from government taxes and on official business no officers of state were allowed to enter them.[62] If anyone for protection or asylum entered these lands, no body had right to arrest him there. No officers within the boundaries of these lands could arrest any body. When there was any unworthy of protection, then they could be arrested only after their departure from the temple lands.[63] Once king Bimbisār a proclaimed that nothing should be done to a person who was a member of the Buddhist Saṃgha.[64] Everybody tried to follow this law and to honour it. Even an all-powerful king never had the courage to violate this law and he knew that it was very dangerous to violate it even for him. During Udyoa III, (934-937 A.D.) time some officials of the court fled to Taporana "The Ascetic Grove" for fear of the king.[65] The king at the uparāja went there and their heads were cut off by them. On seeing this unlawful act, the ascetic monks who used to live there left the place and went to Rohaṇa to stay there. After this incident the people and the troops revolted against the king, climbed the Ratana-pāsāda in the Abhayagiri-vihāra and the heads of some of the officials were cut off by them. The Yuvarāja and his friend Ādipāda in fear went to Rohaṇa and they met the ascetic monks, they cried and lamented and requested the monks to pardon them for their acts and behaviour. Through the intervention of the ascetic monks as well as the other monks of the three nikāyas, there was a reconciliation between the king and the people and the army and peace was established there.[66] No one was allowed to violate or to discontinue these religious grants. Some inscriptions refer to warnings to those persons who might disturb these grants. One inscription describes: "If there be any one who shall create disturbance to the fields......may they not receive food to eat; may they be born as dogs and crows in their next birth."[67] The figures of a dog and a crow were carved in illustration at the end of some of these inscriptions.[68] Another inscription informs: "Anyone who shall discontinue this (charity) may not be able to raise his hands (in adoration) even if the Perfect Buddha Matteyya (Metā) were to pass by his door."[69] Such warnings brought great results and these warnings kept the credulous villagers away from the temple hands. Most probably, in times of distress these lands were sold or mortgaged. King Udaya I's queen brought back and recovered such lands by payment.[70] It may be noted here that kings and queens and private individuals granted many tanks and canals to monasteries and their member was very large.[71] King Dhātusena granted eighteen tanks to the Theriya Sect.[72] Most of the tanks given to monasteries were village-tanks and these tanks and canals "formed a valuable source of income, and the revenue derived therefrom by way of water-tax must have been considerable."[73] In order to book after ancient dilapidated buildings and to give help for repairing these buildings many grants were made.[74] Several grants were made for offering some particular varieties of food to the Buddhist Saṃgha. An inscritpion at Rāssahela says that curd, oil and milk should be provided from the income of a certain land.[75]. "There are some devotees who wish to offer to monks and monasteries things they (devotees) themselves like most, so that they may be endowed with those things in abundance in their future births. The benefactors in this instance perhaps had a particular fondness for curd, oil and milk. It may also be that this kind of stipulation was necessary to prevent any misuse of the grant."[76]

From several inscriptions of the 4th and 5th centuries A.D. we learn that there was a great change in the formation of religious endowments. From about the 4th century A.D. apart from the old practice, some of the religious endowments refer to the form of deposits both in kind and in money. This new development took place owing to Sri Lanka's trade with foreign countries, especially with the Roman Empire. Sri Lanka used to supply pepper, spices, precious stones, perfumes etc. to foreign countries. Many Roman coins were found in various seaports in the island. During this period Sri Lanka has trade relations not only with Rome but also with Greece and Persia.[77] The Toṇigala Inscription, dated the 3rd year of Śrī Meghavaṇa (362-389 A.D.)[78] mentions that a person named Deva, son of a Minister of state, deposits with the merchants' guild (niyama tama), called Kalahumma, situated in the northern district of the city, two cart loads and ten amuṇas of paddy, six amuṇas of undo (a species of flemiṅga) and ten amuṇas of beans. The capital was not allowed to be spent or decreased, but the interest thereon, which was 50% on paddy and 25% on other kinds of grain per annum, should be spent for the Ariyavaṃsa-festival which was held annually at a new monastery called Yahisapavaya. Boiled rice, eatables between breakfast and lunch (atarakaja), curd, honey, sweets, sesame, butter, salt, green herbs and other things needed in the kitchen should be given from this income. From this inscription we get an idea of a deposit in kind as a religious endowment. An inscription from Lahuatabandigala[79] informs that a person called Sirinaka, son of a Minister of State, deposited 100 Kahāpaṇas with the guild of Mahatabaka situated in the eastern district of the city for the use of a great monastery called Devagiri. Here also the interest on the capital was to be spent towards the expenses for the Ariyavaṃsa-festival annual. A fragmentary inscription from the same place[80] describes that another man called Niṭalaviṭiya Siva deposited 20 Kahāpaṇas for the use of the Devagiri monastery. Here too the interest was utilized for the Ariyavaṃsa-festival. An inscription from Kaludiyapokuṇa of the 9th century A.D.[81] states that a man named Daḷanā deposited 23 Kaḷaṇdas of gold for the purpose of arranging meals for the community of monks at the Dakkhiṇāgiri monastery. A Kaḷanda is a weight equivalent to about 70-72 grains Troy.[82]

The Buddha did not allow Buddhist monks to accept male or female slaves (dāsi-dāsa).[83] But when the number of monks and temporalities was great, then slaves were employed in the Buddhist monasteries. The Samantapāsādikā[84] narrates that kings gave slaves to monasteries. "Vihāresu rājūhi ārāmikadāsā nāma dinnā honti, tepi pabbājeṭuṃ na vaṭṭati, bhujisse katvā pana pabhājetuṃ vaṭṭati."[85] King Silāmeghavarṇa gave Tamil prisoners of war as slaves to monasteries.[86] But they were not admitted into the order of the Saṅgha. After they were freed, then they were admitted. The Buddha did not permit Buddhist monks to accept slaves. "As the acceptance of slaves was against the injunction of the Buddha, the Majihima-nikāya commentry[87] bid down that it was not proper to accept slaves as such, but that it was proper to accept them when one says: "I offer a Kappiya-kāraka, I offer an ārāmika." "Kappiyakārakas are generally speaking layman who undertake the responsibility of providing monks with their needs. A Kappiyakāraka offers his services voluntarily and if his patronage is accepted, the monk thereafter feels himself free to inform the Kappiyakāraka of his needs without any reserve. The monk is also thereby entitled to feel confident that a Kappiyakāraka will never give him any gift except in strict accordance with the rules of the Vinaya and the conventions of the people. The Kappiyakārakas mentioned in this context, however, seem to have been people provided by others to do the work of the temple, and therefore, in the nature of servants. Ārāmikas are attendants and servants of the monastery."[88] It may be noted here that farm early days slaves, both male and female, were employed in monasteries and large sums of money were kept for their maintenance. Eight short inscriptions at Anurādhapura[89] dating from the 6th to the 7th century A.D. mention some grants in money (Kahavaṇas) by several people for the maintenance of slaves at the Abhayagiri Vinhāra at Anurādhapura. Their names are referred to. Six of these men had deposited 100 Kahāpaṇas each, one of them had kept 1,000, while the other had deposited 2,000. Whatever merit they gained by these gifts was transferred to all beings. The word vaharala was translated by S. Paramavitana as "slaves" or "slavery." It has several variant forms such as Vaharila, Vaherila, Veherala, Viherila, Vahala, Varala etc., in then and other inscriptions. But D.J. Wijayaratna (Interpretation of vaharala etc., in Sinhalese Inscriptions, UCR, X, No. 1, 103) discusses the validity of S. Paramaistama's translation on several grounds, and describes the term vaharala etc. as "timber." According to him, Vaharala etc. from Skt. Visara Tla meaning "wood" or "timber". "Whether the terms vaharala etc. in the inscriptions mean "slaves" or "timber",[90] the historical fact that slaves were employed in Buddhist monasteries in ancient Sri Lanka remains the same on the strength of the commentarial and chronicle evidence, as seen above. The money paid for vaharala, whether it meant "slaves" or "timber", was an income to the monastery......"[91] The Anāgatavaṃsadesanāra was written by

Vilgammula Mahāthera at the beginning of the 14th century A.D. It informs that "in order to liberate oneself from evil tendencies one should liberate slaves."[92]

When a person offered himself as a servant to the Buddha, Dhamma and Saṇgha, then it was considered highly religious and meritorious.[93] According to some people, it was an attempt to practice the virtue of humility. Many Buddhists have taken their personal names as Buddhadāsa (servant of the Buddha). King Devānampiya Tissa played the role of a gatekeeper for three days to honour the Bodhi branch immediately after it was brought from India.[94] This way he expressed his honour and respect towards the Buddha, Dhamma and the Saṃgha. Mahādāṭ hika Mahānāga (67-79 A.D.) offered himself, his queen, his two sons, his state-elephant and his state-horse to the Buddhist Saṃgha, "in spite of their (Saṃghis) remonstrance, and then redeemed himself and the rest by giving to the order of monks various suitable gifts worth six hundred thousand and to the order of Nus things worth one hundred thousand."[95] Aggabodhi VIII (801-812 A.D.) "made his mother offer him in his own person to the Saṃgha, then paid "a sum equal to his own value (dhaman attagghamaṇ" and thus became a free man."[96] The king did this "as a punishment for his having called one of his servants 'slave' (dāsa)."[97] The king's mother offered the king to the Saṃgha as a "slave". Kīrti Nisiaṅka Malla (1187-1196 A.D.) offered his son and daughter to the Tooth Relic and the Alms Bowl of the Buddha and then by "offering wealth including a golden casket" he freed them.[98] "Ghana ran dāgalak atuḷuvū dhana puda."[99] From these instances we learn that some of the "slaves" freed were not real slaves. Four rock inscriptions from Vessagiriya inform that various people received freedom from slavery for themselves and for their relatives.[100] One of then from slavery liberated his wife. Two people liberated their children from slavery. Two others liberated themselves. Whatever merit they acquired was transferred to all beings. This clearly indicates that "to become a slave at a monastery and to obtain even one's own manumission was regarded as being religious and meritorious."[101] The two persons paid 100 kahapaṇas to the monastery because they liberated themselves together.[102] An inscription of about the 7th century A.D. found at Madagama vihāra in the Tisāra Korale of the Kuruṇāgala District says that a man from slavery liberates his daughters (dariyana, Pāli dārika).[103]. This shows that female slaves at the time used to work in monasteries. From the Minintale Inscription of Mahinda IV we get information that in the 10th century A.D. in that monastery female servants were employed.[104] An inscription of the time of Dalla Moggallāna (611-617 A.D.) discovered at Nilagama in the Mātale District describes that eight persons in company, on the New Moon day in the month of Vesak by paying hundred Kahāpaṇas each to Tissārāma at Nilagama, liberated themselves from slavery.[105] This indicates that sometimes several people together became "slaves" and they themselves together "freed." This gives us an idea that the "traffic in slaves", both genuine and sham, was a lucrative source of income to monasteries."[106] At this time many monasteries had slaves and they engaged them to do work there. This system had helped monasteries to increase their income.

From religious records we learn that the monasteries had another source of income. An inscrption of the 10th century A.D. mentions that for the maintenance of the Mahāpāli, the great common refectory of the Saṃgha, a tax was levied at a rate of one pata (Skt. prastha) from each sack of paddy brought into Anurādhapura.[107] We do not know whether in other towns also similar taxes were introduced. When persons committed officers within the villages and lands of a monastery, then fines were collected for these offences and the monasteries used to get those fines.[108] Many individuals, both layman and bhikkhus, made smaller contributions towards the maintenance and upkeep of the monasteries, e.g. by establishing a pillar or by constructing a flight of steps or granting a stone-boat (gel-nāv).[109] Even from kings distinguished monks used to receive special remnueration.[110]

The Vibhaṅga commentary says that the Cittala-pa-bhata as well as the Tissamahā-vihāsa each had enough paddy for the maintenance of twelve thousand monks for three years.[111] Sometimes, monasteries used to help the kings when they were in difficulty. When Saṇghatissa II (611 A.D.) during a troublous period of his reign was spending his days without food, at that time the Mahāpāli refectory came forward and gave him food.[112] Fa Hien, the Chinese pilgrim, describes, "In the treasuries of the monkish communities there are many precious stones and priceless manis. Even a king was tempted to take the priceless pearls by force. He confessed this sinful thought later to the monks and desired them to make a regulation that from that day fourth the king should not be allowed to enter the treasury and see (what it contained), and that no bhikshu should enter it till after he had been in orders for a period of full forty years."[113] This clearly indicates that the monasteries in Sri Lanka were wealthy in about the 5th century A.D. Although the larger monasteries were rich but the smaller monasteries were not so rich. During the time of Aggabodhi IX (828-831 A.D.) the Buddhist monks from small monasteries used to go to the Mahāvihāra to receive their gruel. When the king knew it, he then offered grants to those monasteries also.[114]

Nunneries were in existence in Sri Lanka from the time of the introduction of Buddhism to the Island. Devānampiya-Tissa himself for Anulā and her women constructed a nunnery in Anurādhapura.[115] Both Jeṭṭhā, the queen of Aggabodhi IV (658-674 A.D.) and Kassapa V (913-923 A.D.) built nunneries.[116] Most probably, the system of the administration of a nunnery was the same as that of the monasteries.

Two inscriptions of the 10th century A.D. discovered at Maḍirigiriya in the Tamankaḍura District of the North-Central Province reveal that a hospital was attached to a monastery.[117] This place had the ruins of the famous ancient Maṇḍalagiri-Vihāra.[118] Many kings built buildings at this Vihara. One of the two inscriptions informs that "the (dead) (?) goats and fowls should be assigned to the hospital of the vihāra."[119] (Ma)ḷa elu kukulan veher ved-halat bahā lanu koṭ."[120] The other inscription refers to such terms as "ved-hal-ka-miyan" "employees of the hospital", "ved-hul-dasun" "serfs of the hospital", "ved-samdaruvan" "state physician," "ved-halbadgambim," "villages and lands attached to the hospital," "ved-halbad-kudīn", "tenants attached to the hospital".[121] Most probably, "these hospitals had villages and lands set apart for their use, and there were tenants and employees and serfs attached to them under the supervision of state physicians."[122] The Kukurumahandamana Pillar Inscription[123] of the 10th century A.D. mentions a hospital attached to a nunnery called the Mahindārama. It is very probable that nuns used like the nursing sisters of today used to look after the sick. The Buddha himself praised that attending on the sick was a great virtue. Archaeological remains such as stone medical baths (medicine boats) were unearthed near Mihintale and Thūpārāma at Anurādhapura and other places and these facts throw flood of light on the existence of hospitals which were attached to monasteries.[124] But it is difficult to say whether these temple hospitals were built only for monks and other inmates or whether lay people from outside were allowed to admit into them for treatment. Thus it was clear that in ancient Sri Lanka the Buddhist monasteries were autonomous institutions. They were great centres of learning and culture. They played a great role not only for the progress of Buddhism but also they became well-known as inportant centres of learning where people from different parts of the country used to come to receive education under the supervision of learned teachers.

The Buddhist Monastery and Its structure: Manner of Building or Butting together or Manner of Organisation of a Buddhist Monestry

There were caves in Mihintale, Vessagiriya, Situlpavvas (cittalapabbata), Riṭigala (Ariṭṭhpabbata) and Rājagala or

Rāssahela in the Batticaloa District and the earliest Buddhist monks used to live there.[125] Mahinda and other arahants in the caves of Mihintale spent their first vas retrent in Sri Lanka.[126] In early days the natural cave was used as a residence for monks. In the Mahātaṇhāsaṅkhaya-sutta the Buddha mentions that a virtuous monk lives in a cave (giriguhaṇ).[127] The Buddha himself did his meditation in a cave named Indaslaguhā on the Vedika mountain.[128] Maha-Kassapa used to go very often to a cave named Pipphaliguhā near Rājagaha.[129] Tālapuṭa thera expressed his earnest desire to live alone in a cave.[130] According to the lay people, the cave-dwelling monks were more spiritually-minded and religious than the others. The commentary on the Vibhaṅga[131] refers to a king named Tissa who thought that the monks at the Cetiyagiri (Mihintale) were better than those at Anurādhapura. Fa Hien mention a "śramaṇa of great value" who used to live at Mihintale early in the fifth century A.D.[132] Buddhaghosa reveals that people accepted Dakkhiṇāgiri, Hatthikucchi, Cetiyagiri and Cttalapabhata as abodes of arahants.[133] The Cūlanāga-lena of Tambapaṇṇidipa was an ideal place for meditation.[134] Udumbaragiri (Dimbulāgala) was another place where many monks used to visit for meditation.[135] Most probably, certain theras received the caves for their own use and later they gave them to the Buddhist Saṃgha. Some relatives of some theras had made the caves and then they on theras' behalf offered them to the Buddhist Saṃgha and the names of these theras as donors were inscribed.[136] Even Buddhist monks were referred to as donors.[137] Sometimes several members of the same family each separately expressed desires to grant caves.[138] The king was the owner of most of the caves, but the people got permission from the king to clean them and prepare them as dwelling places for the Buddhist monks, and they also inscribed their own names as donors.[139] Thus the caves were ideals places for deep meditation. Apart from the caves there were also huts which were built for the residence of early monks.

After Buddhism became the religion of the state and the people, then the kings and the common people did not want the

Buddhist monks to live alone in lonely caves and huts in jungles and on mountain and they wished thenmto live near their places. Because they need their advice and guidance. Gradually, in the neighbourhood of flourishing cities and prosperous villages the Buddhist monasteries began to grow. When the rise of Buddhist monasteries took place near these places, then a good relation was established between the Buddhist Saṃgha and the lay people. The Tissārāma in the Mahāmeghavana of Anurādhapura was the first monastery in Sri Lanka and it was established by Devānampiya-Tissa.[140] This later became the Mahāvihāra, the great Monastery. At the begining for the residence of the Buddhist monks there was only a clay-built house and this was as Kālapāsāda-pariveṇa.[141] Later on, the king and his ministers for the use of the Buddhist monks built several other houses in the Mahāmaghawana.[142] After the Thūpārāma Dāgiba was constructed and the Bo-tree after the Bodhi-branch from Buddhagayā was planted at the Mahāmeghavana, then the cetiya was introduced as a feature of the Buddhist monastery of Sri Lanka during the reign of Devānamapiya Tissa.[143] Gradually, in Rohaṇa and in other parts of the Island large monasteries began to appear.[144] By the second century B.C. during the reign of Duṭṭha-gāmaṇī, the Mahāvihāra at Anurādhapura had many new buildings and many monks at that time used to live there.[145] The Abhayagiri vihāras and the Jetavanārama, the two other important monasteries, were constructed in the first century B.C. and the fourth century A.D. respectively.[146]

A monastery was also known as an ārāma or a vihāra. There was a building called Doratu-pan-maḍiya at the entrance to a large monastery. This was "Water-Pavilion-at-the-Gate".[147] Pots of water (pan-kaḷa) were kept at this place. Before the pilgrims entered the holy places they used to perform their ablutions and they used to sprinkle water on flowers and sometimes they used to drink water. The "Water-Pavilion-at-the-Gate of the Jetavanārāma was a storeyed building of a big size. No outsider was permitted to stay in the building either in the upper storey or in the lower one or in the place where pots of water were kept.[148] This pavilion was very large in size. Because many pilgrimes from distant places used to wash themselves and used to change their clothes and used to wear clean clothes. At the entrance to the courtyard of some dāgabas at Anurādhapura some blocks of stone with basin-shaped hollows scooped in them were found near the flight of steps.[149] A donative inscription was found on one such stone-basin at the Pankuliya monastery near Anurādhapura. It mentions the term pa-doni (P. pādadhovanī) which means "foot-washer."[150] This indicates that there were stone basins in which water was kept for the worshippers to wash their feet before they entered the sacred areas.[151] Within the precincts of the monastery the cetiya or the dāgaba in which relics of the Buddha were enshrined was the most important object. Round the cetiya then were two courtyards. The outer one was Vālikaṅgaṇa or sand-court. The inner courtyard was Hatthipākāra which was decorated with figures of elephants.[152] At the four main entrances there were gateways called toraṇa.[153] The dome of the cetiya rose from the circular terraces called Vedikā-bhūmi or pupphādhāna which formed the base of the cetiya.[154] The uppermost terrace became known as Kucchi-Vedikā-bhūmi and the lowest terrace had sixteen monks of footsteps and became known as pādapiṭhika.[155] There was a structure called Cetiya-ghara or Cetiya-house round the cetiya. It sometimes called Cetiya-geha as well.[156] Over small dāgabas like the Thūpārāma and the Ambatthala, the cetiya-ghara was found. But no cetiya-ghara was found at any of the large dāgabas like the Ruvanvali, the Abhayagiri or the Jetavana. The cetiya-ghara was like a shelter not only for the cetiya but also for its worshippers who took a walk round it in sun and rain. It protected the monument no doubt, but sometimes on a moonlight might it disturbe very much to see its majestic beauty. Sometimes a cetiya was decorated with painting (cittakammaṃ). Aggabodhi II (601-611 A.D.) adormed the Thūpārāma with paintings after its restoration.[157] Saddhā Tissa (77-59 B.C.) painted the

Ambatthalathūpa. Its colour was golden with manosilā or red arsenic powder.[158]

In a monastery the Bodhi-tree occupied an important place. There were four toraṇas or gateways on the four sides of the courtyard of the Bodhi or Bo tree,[159] and round the tree there was a stone platform or a Vedī.[160] There was a Bodhi-ghera or Bodhi-geha near it.[161] The paṭimā-ghera or image-house became an important feature of the monastery of Sri Lanka. The image of the Buddha was kept there. The Mahāvaṃsa mentions that a great and beautiful stone image was placed by Devānampiya Tissa in the Thūpārāma.[162] It is very probable that Sri Lanka has the earliest Buddha-image in the world. King Jeṭṭha-Tissa (323-333 A.D.) from the Thūpārāma removed it and established it at a monastery called Pācīnatissapabhata.[163] Mahāsena (334-362 A.D.) removed it from that place and kept it at the Abhayagiri-vihāra.[164] Buddhadāsa (about the end of the 4th century A.D.) in the eye-sockets of this image set jewels.[165] But the gems had been lost and Dhātusena (460-478 A.D.) gave jewels for a pair of eyes. Sīlāmeghavaṇṇa (617-626 A.D.) renovated its old shelter and decorated it with various gems.[166] Sena II (851-885 A.D.) repaired the ruined temple of the image and his queen gave a blue diaden on it.[167] This image became known by various names such as urusilāpaṭimā[168], mahāsilāpaṭimā[169], silāsatthu[170], silāsambuddha[171], silāmayabuddha[172], silāmayamuminda[173], and silāmayamahesi.[174] Wherever the reference to this image was made, the world sīla (stone) was used. There were other stone images, but this one was known as "the great stone image." The Mihintale Inscription of Mahinda IV (956-972 A.D.) mentions mangul-maha-sala-piḷina (manala-mahā-silā-paṭimā) "the auspicious great stone image".[175] The Jetavanārāma Slab Inscription of the same king deal with a maha-salapiḷima" "great stone image" in highly eulogistic terms.[176] All these facts stated above indicate that there was an ancient stone image of the Buddha and the people honoured it as a relic of great value. According to scholars, the stone image of the Buddha referred to in the inscriptions of Mahinda IV was probably the one which was established at the Thupārāma by king Devānaṃpiya Tissa[177] and most probably, the image was the same which Fa Hien, the Chinese pilgrim, found it in the fifth century A.D. at the Abhayagīrivihīra.[178] King Vasabha (127-171 A.D.) made four Buddha-images and for them he constructed a house.[179] Voharika-Tissa (269-291 A.D.) made two bronze-images and in the eastern Bodhi-ghara of the Mahābodhi he kept them.[180] From the fourth century A.D. onwards the Mahāvaṃsa narrates that many kings not only built images-houses but also made Buddha-images.[181]

All Buddhist monasteries had an uposatha-house where the Buddhist monks on full-moon and new-moon days assembled there to do acts of the Vinaya.[182] The nine-storeyed Lohapāsāda of the Mahāvihāra at Anurādhapura was the Uposatha-house.[183] There were other uposatha-houses at other monasteries such as Thūpārāma, Maricavaṭṭi and Dakkhiṇa-vihāra in Anurādhapura.[184] In later times, in some monasteries there was a dhātu-sālā or dhatu-geha, "a house for keeping the relics of the Buddha."[185] The Dāṭhādhātughara or the Tooth Relic chamber at Anurādhapura was a beautiful building "of very great religious importance." There was also a building known as the Ratanapāsāda in some monasteries like the Mahāvihāra, the Jetavana, and the Abhayagiri-vihāra.[186] There was a refectory, called bhattasālā in every monastery. Here the Buddhist monks used to get meals.[187] King Devānaṃpiya Tissa erected the bhattasālā at the Mahāvihāra. This was known as Mahāpāli.[188] The refectory was a common distributing centre for all monks of the chief monasteries at Anurādhapura "irrespective of their sect, even after separation of the sects had taken place."[189] In the Mahāpāli hall there were stone camoes or troughs for crooked rice (bhattanāvā).[190] The Buddhist monks from the salākagga (sinh. labāg) used to take tickets which were made of wood before they went to the refectory for getting their ration of food.[191]

The living quarters of the Buddhist monks became known as vihāras, ārāsas or pariveṇas.[192] In ancient Sri Lanka the people used to call the pariveṇas the the living quarters of the Buddhist monks. The term pirivena derived from Pāli pariveṇa is now used in Sri Lanka to indicate only a monastic college where Buddhism and "oriental" languages as the principal subjects of study are taught. Vihāra can be taken only for an image-house. Ārāsa is only a small residence for a few Buddhist monks, without other features of a monastery.[193] A monastery had many parivenas and they were cells for the Buddhist monks. The Thūpārāma had many periveṇas and Cūlanaga Thera used to live in the Asiggāhaka pariveṇa.[194] The Mahāvihāra at Anurādhapura had 364 pariveṇas and prāsādas.[195] Most probably, these prāsādas were assembly and confession halls on the model of the Lohaeāda. There were 363 pariveṇas in the Tissa-mahā-vihāra in Rohaṇa in the 9th and 10th centuries A.D.[196] The Padhānaghara was another important building in the Buddhist monasteries.The name shows that it was a house for meditation. In later times the Padhānaghara was used as the residence of the chief monk of the monastery. Buddhaghosa met Saṅghapāla Thera, the chief monk of the Mahāvihāra at the Mahāpadhānaghara.[197] The Samantapāsādikā informs that on festive occasions people used to go to pariveṇas and padhānagharas and used to invite the Masters of the Tripiṭaka (tipiṭaka) and preachers (dhammakathika) even with a hundred other monks.[198] Sometimes in the padhānaghara sermons were delivered.[199] The uposatha-house in modern Sri Lanka is a necessary feature of a monastery, but it is used as a residence and no uposatha-ceremony is performed regularly there.[200] In modern Buddhist temples in Sri Lanka the Uposatha-houses are used for the Vinaya acts only during the Vassa season.[201] In certain monasteries even a caṅkamana is a feature of the monastery, but it is not used for the purpose of meditation.[202] There was the vaccakuṭi or the latrine in every monastery.[203] There were separate sheds for brooms (sammajjaniaṭṭa) and fire-wood (dārmaṭṭa). There was a pānīyamālaka or a place for keeping pots of water for the common use.[204]

The Monastic Life: Life of a Buddhist Monk in a Monastery: His Way of Life

In early days the Buddhist monks were only paiṃsukūla cīvara "rag-robes," i.e., "robes made of pieces of cloth thrown away as useless."[205] But, after some time, the well-known physician, Jīvaka requested the Buddha to allow the Buddhist monks to take robes from the laity.[206] When the Buddha permitted it, then the common people began to offer robes to the Buddhist monks. Then a rule was laid down by the Buddha that a cīvara-paṭiggāhaka (robe-receiver) would be a Buddhist monk who would accept robes given by the pious persons.[207] Then the office was created for the robe-receiver. With the permission of the Buddha a cīvara-nidahaka (robe-depositor) was appointed to deposit the robes.[208] According to the instruction of the Buddha, a store-room (bhaṇḍāgāra) was made and the post of a store-keeper was created to supervise the store. The store-keeper was the bhaṇḍāgārika.[209] The Buddha then appointed a cīvara-bhājaka (robe-distributor) for the distribution of the robes equally among the Buddhist monks. Gradually, the rules relating to robes increased in number.[210] To meet new situations the original rules were changed and supplementary rules were introduced in their places. The rules relating to gaṇabhojana (communal meal) was changed and was modified no less than seven times.[211] On the request of his disciples, the Buddha changed several rules not only for Aranti, but also for all the countries outside the limits of the Mid-country. Then with the permission of the Buddha, the Buddhist monks outside the Mid-country performed the Act of the upasampadi with five monks, including one who knew the Vinaya well. The Buddhist monks used sandals made of more than one piece of leather, and they took frequent baths as they liked and they used skins for seats.[212] During the famine at

Rājagaha the people gave necessary foodstuffs to the Buddhist monks. But they were not allowed to keep these foodstuffs inside their living rooms and they kept them outside. Cats, rats and various other animals ate them and thieves and hungry people stole and ate them. For this reason, the Buddha permitted the Buddhist monks to keep foodstuffs inside their living quarters. He allowed the Buddhist monks to cook their meals inside their living quarters.[213] He also allowed them to prepare their own food by themselves. During the famine at Rājagaha several rules relating to food were changed. But when it disappeared, the old rules were introduced again.[214]

The Mahāparinibbāna Sutta mentions that the Buddha told Ananda that it was never in his mind that he "managed" the Saṃgha" or "the Saṃgha depended on him."[215] "Tathāgatassa kho Ānanda na evaṃ hoti: ahaṃ bhikkhu-saṅghaṃ pariharissāmīti va manuddesiko bhikkhusaṅghoti vā." (Mahāparinibbāna-sutta, D.I, 62).[216] He also "advised the bhikkhus to depend on themselves and the dhamma and not on anything or anyone else as their refuge."[217] "Attadīpā viharatha attasaraṇā anaññasaraṇā, dhammadīpā dhamma-saraṇā anaññasaraṇā." (Mahāparinibbāna-Sutta, D, II, 62).[218] "Probably, as a member of the class which favoured democratic constitution, the Buddha because imbued with democratic ideas. He wanted to see his Saṃgha grow on democratic lines and formed the rules accordingly."[219]

The first century B.C. was regarded as the most important period in the history of Buddhism in Sri Lanka. During the latter part of that century certain radical changes relating to the life of the Buddhist monks as well as to the Buddhist doctrines took place in Sri Lanka.[220] At this time the country was disturbed not only by a foreign invasion but also by a famine. In this situation it was difficult to continue the oral tradition of the Tripiṭaka. Then the Mahā-Theras of Sri Lanka took a decision to commit the Tripiṭaka to writing at Alu-vihāra, "so that the teaching of the Buddha might prevail."[221] During this period only one monk knew the Mahā-Niddesa, the Pāli text. He was a peson of very bad character. The learned and the virtuous monk-theras did not like him. But they used to learn it from him so that the text with his death might not be lost.[222] After the famine, a conference of several hundreds of Buddhist monks was held at a monastery called the Maṇḍalārāma in Kallagāma Janapada and a new question was asked—what was the basis of the Sāsana—learning or practice?[223] "Pariyatti nu kho sāsanassa mūlasiṁ udāhu paṭipattiti."[224] "According to the original teaching of the Buddha, the practice of the dhamma (paṭipatti) is of greater importance than mere learning (pariyatti)."[225] Even the Theras asked this question. The Paṃsukūlikas opined that practice was the basis of the Sāsana. But the Dhammakathikas mentioned that learning was the basis.[226] The Paṃsukūlikas wore only rag-robes. The Dhammakathikas were preaches or teachers. They knew the Dhamma very well. In support of their ideas and theories, both sides gave reasons and arguments. At the end the theras took a decision that "learning was the basis of the Sāsana, and not practice."[227] The Paṃsukūlikas did not utter a single word, and the Dhammakathikas became victorious.[228]

The commentary on the Aniguttara-nikāya[229] following this decision describes, "Even if there be a hundred or a thousand bhikkhus practicing vipassanā (meditation), there will be no realization of the Noble Path if there is no learning (doctrine, pariyatti)". "Āraddhavipassakānaṃ bhikkhunaṃ satepi sahassepi saṃvijjamāna pariyattiyā asati ariyamaggapaṭivedho nāma na hoti"[230] The same idea is stated in the commentaries on the Dīgha and the Majjhima Nikāyas in the following words: "There may or may not be realization (patiredha) and practice (patipatti) learning is enough for the perpetuation of the Sāsana. The wise one, having heard the Tripiṭaka, will fulfil even both........Therefore, the Sāsana (religion) is stabilized when learning endures."[231] "Paṭivedho ca paṭipatti ca hoti'pi na hoti'pi sāsanaṭṭhitiyā pariyatti pamāṇaṃ. Paṇḍito hi tepiṭakaṃ sutrā dve;pi pūreti.....Tasmā pariyattiyā thitāya sāsanaṃ thitaṃ hoti."[232] The vibhaṅga commentary also mentions that "it is a great mistake to belittle the value of learning."[233] All able and intellectual monks took interest in learning. Because learning produced great results and its importance was of greater than practice and realization was established very firmly.

There are references to the two terms gantha-dhura and vipassanā-dhura in the Pāli commentaries of the 5th century A.D. and other non-canonical works. Gantha-dhura was more important than Vipassanā-dhura. "....All able and intelligent monks applied themselves to gantha-dhura while elderly monks of weak intellect and feeble physique, particularly those who entered the Order in their old age, devoted themselves to vipassanā-dhura."[234] Cakkhupāla Thera told, "I entered the order in my old age; I am not able to fulfil gantha-dhura. So I will practice Vipassanā-dhura"[235] "Ahiṃ mahallakakāle pabhajito; ganthadhuraṃ S/CNO. 266 pūressāmi."[236] The author of the DhpA refers to these words to Cakkhupāla as speaking in front of the Buddha. But we know that no such division of vocation took place at the time of the Buddha. It was clear that after the theory of gantha-dhura and Vipassanādhura was introduced this was written.[237] Milakkha-Tissa, a hunter of Rohaṇa in Sri Lanka in his old age joined the order. He spoke to his teacher: "Sir, learning is a vocation for an able one. My faith is based on suffering. I shall fulfil Vāsa-dhura (Vipassanā)."[238] "Bhante, gantho nāma paṭibabassa bhāro Mayhaṃ pana dukkhāpanisā saddhā, vāsadhuraṃ pūressāmi."[239] Milakkha-Tissa from his teacher received a topic of meditation and he engaged himself in meditation and he used to go to holy places such as Cittala-pabbata, Gameṇḍavāla Mahāvihāra, Katāragama and other places of worship.[240] Even to-day there are monks who try to follow this kind of life. Ganthadhura or the vocation of "books" indicates the learning and teaching of the dhamma, while vipassanā-dhura or the vocation of meditation narrates reflecting on life as impermanent, suffering and without permanent entity.[241] Sometimes vipassanā-dhura is known as Vāra-dhura.[242] When these new ideas developed, the Buddhist monks devoted themselves to study and only secondly to meditation. Originally, gantha-dhura signified only the learning and teaching of the Tripiṭaka. But after sometime the idea was widened and it implied languages, grammar, history, logic, medicine and other fields of study as well. Not only literature, but also the fine arts were included in the field of interest of the Buddhist monks who devoted themselves to gantha-dhura.

When Buddhism became the religion of the country many people took interest in the religion of the Buddha and they joined the Buddhist Saṃgha as monks and began to live in monasteries. When the community of monks grew numerically, the large and several endowments were offered to the monasteries for their maintenance. "If the monks were to make use of the landed property of monastery with an easy conscience, it had to be "religionized."[243] In order to regularize the new situation, the Buddhist Saṃgha argued upon a new Vinaya convention and tried to invent new practice known as "labha-sīmā".[244] The Samantapāsādikā describes, "As for lābha-sīmā (income area), it was neither allowed by the Buddha nor established by the theras who collected the dhamma (in Council). But kings and ministers after building a vihāra define (boundaries within a distance of) a gāvuta, half a yojana or a yojana around (the place), and set up pillars inscribed with the names saying "this is the income-area (or limit) of our vihāra", and fix boundaries saying "whatever is produced within this, all that we give to our vihāra." This is called lābha-simā."[245] "Lābhasīmā vāma neva Sammā-sambuddhena amuññātā, na dhammasaṅgāhakattherchi ṭhapitā: api ca kho rājarājamahāmattā vihāraṃ kāratvā gāvutaṃ vā aḍḍhayojanaṃ vā samantato vā samantato paricchinditvā ayaṃ anuhākaṃ Vihārasa lābhasīmā'ti nāma-likhitake thambe nikhaṇitvā, yaṃ etthantare uppajjati sabbaṃ taṃ aṇhākaṃ Vihārasse demā'ti Sīmaṃ ṭhapenti, ayaṃ lābhasīmā nāma."[246] It may be noted here that there is no reference to the term lābha-sīmā in any one of the numerous ancient inscriptions which grant lands to monasteries. But some of these lithic records mention the words Sīmā atuḷu koṭ "having defined the boundaries" and most probably, they could be defined as giving the idea of lābha-sīmā.[247] The Vinaya conventions recognised and sanctioned the landed property of the monasteries and the Buddhist monks took interest in the income and expenditure of the monasteries. For approval they used to submit annual statements of accounts to the assembly of the Buddhist Saṃgha.[248]

The new situation demanded many new practices which were against the original Vinaya. The Vinaya says that a Buddhist monk should not dig or tell another to dig the earth. When he does so, then an offence called the pācittiya will be committed by him.[249] But this was very difficult to follow when "There was regular landed property attached to the monastery."[250] It is not proper to say, "dig this place, dig a pond in this place." It is proper to say "dig yams, dig roots" without specifying.[251] It is not proper to state "dig this creeper, dig yams or roots in this place."[252]

Irrigation tanks formed one kind of endowments to monasteries and it brought considerable income. If one offered a tank to the Buddhist Saṃgha, then it should not be accepted. A tank should be taken when it was given to the Buddhist Saṃgha in order to enjoy the four requisites (cattāro paccaye).[253] Certain inscriptions giving tanks to monasteries, in conformity with this convention, had the required words mentioning the intention that for the purpose of the four requisites they were given to the Buddhist Saṃgha.[254] "Pālumākiccāva Inscription of Gajabāhu I (174-196 A.D."bukasagahaṭaya catiri pacaṇi." (EZ. I, 211). "Thūpārama Slab Inscription of Gajabāhu —"catara paca paribujana koṭu dine." (EZ, III, 116). "Nāgarikanda Rock Inscription of Kumāradāsa (513-522 A.D.)."bikasagahiṭa catarapaccayaṭa dine." (EZ. IV, 123). Some of these grants of tanks and canals were made, but they did not mention any specific purpose.[255] Those inscriptions are EZ, III, 154, Inscription of Bhātikam Abhaya (38-67 A.D.); p. 165, Vihāregala Rock Inscription (2nd century A.D.); EZ.IV, 217, Habassa Rock

Inscription (2nd century A.D.); p. 227, Timbirivara Rock Inscription (4th century A.D.).[256] Most probably, when the grant was made orally the "proper" words were mentioned, though the inscriptions do not refer to them.[257]

Once ecclesiastical property was accepted as a necessity for the progress of the religion for a very long time and the Buddhist Saṃgha's duty was to protect it. For this reason, the Buddhist monks are requested to receive and to treat hospitably even rebels and robbers and rowdices with the property of the Buddhist Saṃgha, if it was thought necessary to do so in order to save the wealth of the monastery.[258] Once Abhaya Thera, the chief monk of Mihintale, entertained a rebel who came to disturb and to damage the monastery by using force. Other monks criticised the thera for his action. Afterwards, they were happy when he talked to them that by doing it he saved the property of the monastery from the rebels and that "what he spent in treating them was even less than the value of one rug spread in the cetiyaghara there. The critics were convinced."[259]

When a layman came to a Buddhist monk and requested him to treat a patient and to prepare some medicine, then the request should be ignored. But "if a layman were to inquire from a monk as to what is given for a certain ailment, then it is proper to tell him. If a man says to a monk: "Sir, my mother is ill; please prescribe some medicine", he should not be told anything."[260] The Buddhist monks had a talk among themselves about what they gave to a ceratin monk when he suffered from identical illness. If the man was there when their conversation took place and he heard it and accordingly he treated his mother, then there is nothing wrong.[261]

In ancient Sri Lanka, two great convocations were held twice a year before and after the Vassa season (rainy season) in two central places.[262] One was the Mahāvihāra at Anurādhapura and the other was the Tissamahāvihīra in Rohaṇa. The monks who belonged to the north of the Mahāvaligaṅga held a meeting at the Mahāvihāra and those monks who belonged to the south of the river assembled at the Tissamahāvihāra.[263] Before the Vassa season they met and they cleaned and whitewashed the cetiya and after their meeting with the Mahātheras they received topics of meditation from them. After the end of the vassa season they met again and declared their spiritual attainments during the "retreat" and recited and raised their learning of the dhamma. On these occasions they discussed difficult points and problems with experts and in this way, they cleared their doubts. In the time of the Buddha himself a great convocation twice a year was started and it was held from that time.[264]

The Monastic Life (Its Activities, Life of a Buddhist Monk in a Monastery, His Way of Life, Monk's Actvities in a Monastery)

Generally, the Buddhist monks should arise from bed early in the morning before sunrise.[265] Then they should engage themselves in meditation on the Buddha, mettā (loving kindness), asubha (impurity of the body) and earth. These four topics of meditation became known as caturārakkhā (Sinhalese Siyu arak "four protections").[266] In the tenth century at Mihintale this practice was followed.[267] "There is no reason to think that it was not so in other places, both before and after the 10th century, for it has come down as a tradition among the Saṃgha up to the present day."[268] After their meditation they should clean their teeth and should perform their ablutions. Several commentaries mention that they should sweep and clean their compounds and other places and they should worship at the cetiya and the Bodhi.[269] But the Mihintale Inscription of Mahinda IV does not refer to this.[270] According to it, after ablutions the monks should dress and drape their robes carefully. They should follow the instruction given in the Sikha-Karaṇī (Rules of Sekhiyā). They should go to the Ration Room (Lahāg) and should recite the Metta-Sutta (Met-Pirit).[271] Met-Pirit in only another name for the Metta-sutta in the Suttanipāta. It is included in the Parittas as well, and the term Met-Pirit is used when this sutta is used as a paritta.[272] Then the monks should take their breakfast or morning meal at the refectory. If the monks owing to illness were unable to go to the Ration Room, then their share should be sent up if the physicians recommended it.[273] One account in the Aṅguttara Commentary does not say anything about the morning meal.[274] But it mentions that the Buddhist monks were busy to engage themselves in meditation. They are advised to go on with their meditation till they get up to more for the alms-round. Then again after their meal they should make themselves ready for meditation till they attended to their other duties in the evening at the cetiya and towards the elders. After this, the first watch of the night should be spent again in meditation.[275] By beating a drum (bheri) or gong (yāma-gaṇḍi) the time for going-out for piṇḍapata was announced.[276] The Kalyāṇī-Mahāvihāra announced the time by beating a drum. But the Vajagaragri-vihāra announced it by striking a gong.[277] During the day the time was measured by taking the help of a Kālatthambha "time-pole" ("must probably a pole with a sun-dial fixed on it").[278] There was also yāma-yanta "watch-machine." Even during the night, when properly set, it announced the time. Like a clock (yāma-yantaṇ paṭati) it helped to strike hours.[279] There were the attendants (ārāmikā) or some monks who used to announce the various items of the time-table. At Kalyāṇi, the attendants used to do it, and at the Vajagaragiri-vihāra a thera called Kāladeva took the charge of beating the gong, particularly during the vas season. The thera announced the three watches of the night.[280]

Distribution of Food of the Buddhist Monks in a Monastery

A monk spent a considerable portion of the foremen to collect his food and in several ways he used to get it.[281] The Mahāvihāra, the Abhayagiri-vihāra and Mihintale had common refectories and several thousand monks used to go to these places for food.[282] Fa Hien describes, "They get their food from their common stores. The king, besides, prepares elsewhere in the city a common supply of food for five or six thousand more. When any want, they take their great bowls, and go (to the place of distribution), and take as much as the vessels will hold, all returning with them full".[283] About two centuries later, Hiuen Tsiang narrates, "By the side of the kings palace there is built a large kitchen, in which daily is measured out food for eight-thousand priests. The meal-time having come, the priests arrive with their pātras to receive their allowance. Having received and eaten it, they return, all of them, to their several abodes. Ever since the teaching of the Buddha reached this country, the king has established this clarity and his successors have continued it down to our times."[284] The Rasavāhinī mentions that monks and nuns from five great monasteries (pañca-mahāvāsa) used to collect alms at Mahā-pāli.[285] But some monks used to go round from house to house for alms. They did not want to go to the common refectory for food. Even some monks took a walk from Mihintale to Anurādhapura for Piṇḍapāta.[286] A thera called Mahā-Tissa after taking a walk from Cetiya-pabbata (Mihintale) to Anurādhapura collected his piṇḍa-pāta. Most probably, the capital was extended near Mihintale. The city of Anurādhapura was not far away from Mihintale.[287] A monk does not walk fast when he goes on piṇḍapāṭa. He is advised not to do it.[288] Certain monks used to go on piṇḍapāta twice a day—early in the morning and once again before noon.[289] Pious laymen often invited the Buddhist monks for meals at their homes also. Particularly for ghee or oil a monk went on piṇḍapāta and for this reason he carried a small bowl (thālak) and he did not take with him the usual alms-bowl.[290] "Sahassavatthu: Saṅghāmaccassa Vatthu." There was light refreshment between the two meals. This light refreshment was some shacks called antara-khajjaka.[291] Honey (madhu) and jaggery (sakkhara) were included in it. Sometimes preparation of meat were included in it.[292] The Rasavāhī informs how a seṭṭhi invited monks and gave delicious preparations including hare (sasa-maṃsa) to them three times in the forenoon.[293] A special preparation of hare was included not only in the antara-khajjaka but also in the other two meals.[294] The Toṇigala Inscription records that curd (di), honey (miyavaṭa), treacle (paṇi), seasame (tila), butter or ghee (bu (ja) matela), salt (loṇa) and green herbs (palahavaṭa) were included in the diet of monks in Sri Lanka in the 4th century A.D.[295] It may be noted here that a monk became known as eka-bhattika "one-mealer." Generally a monk takes one meal a day. According to the commentarial interpretation, there are two meals—breakfast (pātarāsa-bhatta) and super (sāyamāsa-bhatta). "Breakfast is confined to the forenoon. The other meal is confined to the period between the noon and the sunrise."[296] The commentary describes that if a monk during the forenoon eats even ten times, he is mentioned as an eka-bhattika, taking only one meal a day.[297] There were some monks who took only one meal a day even in later times. But the vast majority of them during the forenoon had more than one meal. The monks in the evening usually as refreshment took some drink or even ghee or treacle.[298]

Various Duties of the Buddhist Monks

The Buddhist monks not only made their robes, but also washed, cleaned and dyed them properly. They also had duties at the cetiya, Bodhi and uposatha houses. They made brushes (koccha) and ladders (nisseṇi) and white-washed (sudhā-kamma) the cetiya.[299] They did not spend their whole time for these activities only. Then they would be guilty of Kammārāmatā "addiction to activities."[300] For tis reason they spent their time properly in studies, recitation, meditation and duties at the cetiya and other activities.[301] It is not the duty of a monk to allow his hair or nails to grow too long. The Vinaya says that a monk must shave his head before his hair is two inches long or before two months elapse.[302] He should take care of his body and he must not neglect it. He must not allow it to be soiled with sweat and dirt. He should take his bath regularly and keep it clean.

He should always clean his robes and should have well-stitched, washed and dyed.[303] He should look after his lodgings properly and should be kept clean and tidy.[304] In order to look after the cleanliness of his system he should take laxatives and other medicines. When he needed these medicines he should take them.[305]

The Visuddhimagga[306] mentions that the living quarters of some monks at least about the 5th century A.D. were very dirty. "Carpets were full of dust and fouled by the droppings of lizards (gharagolika); the rooms smelt of bats and rats; the floor was dirty with the excreta of pigeons; there were dry leaves and grass on the compound scattered by the wind; sometimes the compound was soiled with excreta, urine and spittle of young sāmaṇeras who were ill and unable to go to the lavatory; on rainy days the compound was muddy and full of puddles." Generally, the Buddhist monastery is regarded as the cleanest place in the village. It was the place of all good and beautiful things. For this reason, the monks played a great role to make their monasteries models of refinement and sources of inspiration to the people. A beautifully maintained courtyard "acts like a foil to the inner peace and calm of the monastery."[307]

Evening Duty of a Buddhist Monk

The Buddhist monks used to sweep the courtyard of the cetiya daily and after worship, they sat together there and enjoyed the serenity of the moment and recited the suttas (sajjhāya) and offered prayers and showed their devotion to the Buddha.[308] Nuns and others also were present there and they listened "to the melody of the devotional recitation on these occasions."[309] The elders gave a religious sermon to the younger monks at the end of this recitation and then on various questions of the dhamma a free discussion took place.[310] This was the daily routine of the Buddhist monks in the evening. Apart from this communal recitation (gaṃa-sajjhāyanā) the individual monks in the night recited the suttas in their residences. It is said that two deities (devatā), who listened to the recitations of the Mahāsamaya and the Mahādhammasamādāna Suttas by two young monks (daharā) in two different places—one at Nāgaleṇa in Koṭa-pabbata-vihāra and the other at Paṅgura-vihāra in the south—were very happy and they spoke highly of the recitation of these two monks.[311]

Preaching

The Buddhist monks delivered sermons when their turn came. In monasteries sermons were delivered on full noon and new moon days and also on quarter noon days (aṭṭhamiyaṃ). The preachers used a fan (Vījanī). The Buddhist monks were present to hear the sermon when the time for preaching was announced. If anybody did not attend the sermon when it was announced, then it was accepted as disregard and disrespect for the dhamma.[312] Sometimes certain monks used to travel long distances to hear sermons preached by famous preachers.[313]

Communal Duty

The relation between the teacher and the pupil was that of father and son. The Buddha stated that the teacher (ācariya) accepted his pupil (antivāsika) as his son, and the pupil accepted his teacher as his father. So the same relation existed between the preceptor (upajjhāya) and co-resident (saddhivihārika).[314] Ācariyo bhikkhave antivāsikamhi puttacittaṃ upaṭṭhapessati, antevāsiko āacariyamhi pitucittaṃ upaṭṭhapessati."[315] "Upajjhāyo bhikkhave saddhivihārikamhi puttacittaṃ upaṭṭhapessati, saddhivihāriko upajjhāyamhi pitucittaṃ upaṭṭhapessati."[316] Both spiritually and materially, the pupil looked after his teacher and the teacher looked after his pupil. The pupil always took care of his teacher. But if the pupil fell ill, then the teacher attended on him. He prepared his bed, and supplied him with warm water and other things. In this way they used to lead a smooth communal life, loyal and devoted.[317] The Buddhist monks in the presence of elderly monks knew the proper behaviour and etiquette. They should not move about or sit down pushing the elderly monks. When the elders have taken their seats on lower ones, they should not manage to sit on higher seats. When the elders had not sandals they should not use sandals. While talking to elders, they should not gesticulate with their hands. Without the permission of the elders who were present, it was not their duty to deliver a sermon or answer a question. In the most humble manner a monk should go to a teacher to receive a topic of meditation (Kammaṭṭhāna) from him. He should not go with an attendant or a pupil and he should not carry an umbrella (chatta) and should not wear a pair of sandals. When the elder brought the water, he should not use it. He should wash his feet in a place where his teacher cannot see it. Before he received the topic of meditation he should act as a most humble attendant to the elder.[318] When a monk as a guest went to a vihāra, the resident monks received him in a very kind manner, took his alms-bowl, robe and fan, arranged a seat for him and gave attention to see what he needed. When the guest wanted to leave the place, the resident monks asked him to stay on. If the resident monks did not attend on their guests kindly, then it would be very bad for them and they would become known as ill-mannered, and unfaithful, unpleasant and morose and other Buddhist monks would never visit such a place even if they went that way. That would be very bad for the vihāra and the residents because they would not be able to meet with the learned and holy monks.[319] Sometimes the younger monks behaved with other people in a very light-hearted manner.

Spiritual Standard of the Buddhist Monks

In ancient Sri Lanka the spiritual standard of some monks was not very high. In the third century A.D. king Vohārika-Tissa in order to free some monks from debt paid 300,000 pieces of money.[320] From the records of the Pāli commentaries we learn that in the 5th century A.D. the life of some monks was full of jealously, hypocrisy and pettiness.[321] When a monk went to get Kammaṭṭhāna from a famous teacher, he was told to go direct to the teacher himself, and asked him not to go to other's quarters to take rest before his meeting with the teacher took place. Because if he went to the quarters of some monks ill-disposed towards this particular teacher, they might tell against him and the new-comer's mind might be affected and he would form an opinion against him.[322] Dīgha-bhāṇaka Abhaya Thera of Rohaṇa was a great preacher. Once he delivered a sermon on the Ariyavaṃsasutta and the whole of Mahāgama on this occasion arrived there to listen to him. A certain mahā-thera was very much jealous of Dīgha-bhāṇaka Abhaya Thera's fame and popularity and commented: "Well, the Dīgha-bhāṇaka on the pretext of preaching the Ariyavaṃsa creates a great disturbance throughout the whole night."[323] Both of them left the place and went out for their respective vihāras. The Maha-thera all the way made insulting remarks about the Dīgha-bhāṇaka but the latter kept quiet and did not say anything against him. At the junction when their separation took place, the Dīgha-bhaṇaka Abhaya thera saluted the Mahā-thera and remarked: "That's your road, Sir." But the Mahā-thera did not say anything and moved away as if he did not hear his word.[324]

There were some Buddhist monks who did not want other Buddhist monks coming to their vihāras as guests. They were very much jealous of their guests. Because they got in touch with their supporters (dāyakā). They did not wish to divide even things belonging to the Buddhist Saṃgha among other monks. There were some monks who did not like others' education, and they were jealous of it.[325]

On festival days when the people visited the vihāra, a monk then engaged himself to sweep the courtyard of the catiya, clean the place, wash the flower altars and water the Bo-tree so that the people may form an opinion about him that he was a good monk. In the presence of laymen a monk may ask an elderly monk such questions as "Sir, when I was sweeping the yard some blades of grass were broken. What happens to me?"[326] But the elder stated that you have not done anything wrong. There was no transgression. Because there was no intention. But, even then, the monk asked, "It appears to me a grave offence. Please inquire about it carefully."[327] Ignorant laymen listened to it and thought, "well, if this monk is so worried about such a minor matter, how conscientious he must be with regard to more important matters."[328] When people approached the monastery a monk then pretended that he was meditating. Another person in the presence of others posed as a great scholar, though he was not a learned person.[329] The commentaries record that how hypocritical monks tried to show others with virtues which they did not possess.[330] There were monks who showed their interest in their pupils' matters and their belongings (satta-saṅkhra-kaḷāyana-puggalā). They never allowed their pupils to do anything for others and also they never allowed others to use their things.[331]

The Jetavanārāma Sanskrit Inscription and the Mihintale Tablets of Mahinda IV mention that in the 9th and 10th centuries the spiritual standard of some monks was very poor. There were some monks who showed their interests in agricultural and commercial matters, who were landlords and had landed property, who did wrong thing against religion and society, whose speech was coarse and who were not truthful persons. The Buddhist monasteries did not allow such monks to stay in the monasteries or did not allow them to receive food or raiment there.[332] An inscription of the 9th century offered some grants to a monastery, but it mentions a condition that "if there be any discussion in the monastery, the good should be thrown to crows and dogs."[333] "Vehara Viyagurak ata me bat Kavuḍu ballanat onā isa"— Kaludiya-pokuṇa Cave Inscription, EZ, III, 258.[334]

Buildings and Repairs

The Jetavanārāma Sanskrit Inscrption says that whatever place the monks had some connection with it, they should allow it to keep it in good condition. They should not neglect it to become dilapidated.[335] "Yatra ye miyaktās tatrāvināṣ- as taireva deyah."[336] If a Buddhist monk lived in a monastery but he did not take any interest in the work on new buildings or on repairs to old ones, then other people for neglecting his duty blamed him and criticised him.[337] "Naravihāre bahuṃ narakammaṃ hoti: akarontaṃ ujjhāyanti." (Vsm. 88) "Jiṇṇavihāre pana bahuṃ paṭijaggitabbaṃ hoti. Antamaso attano scñasanamattampi apaṭijaggantaṃ ujjhāyanti." (Ibid., 89).[338] Every monk living in a monastery tried to improve the place and did some kind of work in connection with it. In order to devote his full time for meditation and study he was exempted sometimes from this kind of word.[339] For the purpose of doing repairs on the cetiya or thatching the Bodhighara or Uposatta-house some monks occasionally used to call other monks by sounding a drum (bheri) or gong (gaṇḍi).[340] According to the Mahāvaṃsa, the plan of the nine-storeyed Lohapāsāda was done by eight arahants at the request of king Duṭṭa-Gāmaṇī.[341] An arahant named Indagutta supervised the construction of the relic chamber of Ruvanvali-saya.[342] Even the Buddhist monks brought bricks for the construction of the Mahācetiya.[343] The Majjhima-nikāya commentary mentions a monk who white-washed the Mahācetiya. He was a satāpanna.[344] A slab inscription[345] at Kataragama (1st or 2nd century A.D.) describes a Thera named Nanda helped to enlarge the cetiya there (Nada tera ceta vadita), and at the four entrances built the steps (catara-dorahi patagaṭa ataṭḍui). Nanda Thera might have built this, just as Saraṃaṇkara Saṅgharāja's pupils repaired dilapidated vihāra in the 18th century or as Nāranviṭa Sumanasāra Thera restored Ruvanvali-saya at the end of the 19th century.[346] An inscription on the stone canoe at the Mahāpāli Refectory narrates that the Buddhist monks in order to restore the Jetavana Dāgaba sacrificed their ration of food at the Mahāpāli.[347] "Me Machapela) bat (ga)nnā tāk denamo a (pa) lada bat (ko) ṭas bat Denāvehe (ra) dāgaba karena (kam) vāvāmaṭa dunmo." (EZ, III, 132). Most probably, the Buddhist monks lived by piṇḍapāta. Because they gave their share to this work. A sāmaṇera did the three stone steps to climb the Akāsacetiya and the Mahāvaṃsa praises their work as meritorous.[348] A monk was busy with the construction of a building and that was regarded as helpful in getting rid of kilesas permanently.[349] This type of work as a means of getting rid of kilesas was prescribed only for those who were spiritually backward. For a person genuinely showed his keen interest in his spiritual attainments, this was mentioned as a great hindrance (palibodha) and this was to be avoided.[350]

Affairs of the Heart: Love Affairs between a Monk and a Nun and a Monk and a Woman

The Mahātheras always played their great roles to protect their pupils from falling victims to temptations and dangers. Even during the great famine, Bāmiṇiṭiyā sāya, a mahā-thera wanted to punish a sāmaṇena "for creating a suspicion in his mind." In later life the sāmaṇera became well-known as Vattabhaka-Nigrodha and he knew the Tripiṭaka very wall. Before dawn he went to the jungle to fulfil his vow of āraññikaṅga. But his teacher had no idea what happened to the sāmaṇera.[351] The principal of the Kāḷadīghavāpidvāravihāra agreed to guide a young student monk only on condition that the latter would not visit the village. Because this village had a very bad reputation. The teacher feared that he would not be able to protect his young student from falling victim to temptation and dangers.[352] But this young monk, after his studies, on his way back home, went through this village. A young girl, wearing a yellow cloth, gave some gruel into his alms-bowl. At first sight she fall in love with him. She then told her parents that her life would come to an end if she could not win the love of the young monk. Her parents then invited this young monk to come to their place to take his meal. But he refused to go to their place. He at once thought of his teacher's advice and he knew that he would be in trouble and he left the place. The girl then died of grief.[353] After some time the young monk knew this story from another monk and he died of grief. He felt sorry for this matter. He thought that he had missed a great chance of getting a sincere and devoted wife.[354]

A young monk of Lohapāsāda and a lady of King Saddhā-Tissa's retinue loved each other and they died of love for each other.[355] Another monk called Citta of Cetiyagiri joined the Buddhist Saṃgha when he was advanced in age (Buddha-pabbajita). He was very much made with love for the young Tamil queen (Damiḷa-devī) of king Mahādāṭ-hika-Mahānāga (67-79 A.D.) and he "became a butt for the clumsy ridicule of the younger monks at Mihintale."[356] Some Buddhist monks fell in love with nuns. Once young monks at the Mahācetiya (Ruvanvali-saya) in the evening recited suttas (sajjhāyaṃ). Immediately behind them some young nuns were there and they listened to the recital.[357] According to some scholars, this was a class. But, in the evening after their worship at the cetiya the Buddhist monks used to recite the suttas (Sajjhāya). Up to this day the Buddhist monks follow this practice. Sometimes men and women, also sit down and listen to this.[358] One of the young monks, who sat down there, stretched his hand backward and touched the body of a young nun. She then placed his hand on her breast. They fell in love with each other and later they left the Buddhist Saṃgha.[359]

At the consecration ceremony of the Maricaraṭṭi-vihāra (1st century B.C.) many monks and nuns were present at Anurādhapura. A little sāmaṇera carried a bowl of hot gruel. But it was very hot. A little nun saw it and gave him a plate (thālaka), saying: "Take it on this." Then there was a famine in Sri Lanka. Many monks and nuns, including the two mentioned above, went to a "country beyond the seas" (parasamuddaṃ), most probably to India. The nun went there with an earlier group of nuns. There she met this young monk. The old memories were refreshed and for each other they developed a love and then they left the Buddhist Saṃgha.[360]

The Dharmapradīpikā mentions that "a man and a woman wearing robes" (Sivuru perevi strī-puruṣa Kenekun) had physical relation in a park at Anurādhapura in the 2nd century B.C.[361] Guruḷugomi did not call them monk and nun, but mentioned them as "a men and a women wearing robes."[362] When a Buddhist monk fell in love with a woman and it was not possible for him to overcome the temptation, then the normal course was for him to leave the Buddhist Saṃgha honourably and to merry her, which was perfectly justifiable and allowed.[363]

Pilgrimages

The Buddhist monks in Sri Lanka used to 20 on pilgrimage to places of worship in the Island and also in India. Generally, on these trips they visited those places in groups. Because it was very safer for then to go in groups. When great teachers like Dhumadinna of Tissamahā vihāra near Talaeṇgara-pabbata and Tipiṭaka cūlabhaya went on pilgrimage, then large number of Buddhist monks, as many as 500, used to go with them.[364] Small groups of 7, 12, 30, 50 or 60 Buddhist monks were very common.[365] Usually, in these groups there were teachers and students or co-celibates from neighbouring vihāras. But the Paṃsukūlikas and the Piṇḍapātikas went alone.[366] Groups of pilgrims, sometimes including laymen and lay women went on pilgrimage to Buddhagayā in India. But the whole journey from Anurādhapura to Buddhagayā took about ten or eleven months.[367] (From Anurādhapura to Koṭṭapaṭṭana 4 months; from Koṭṭapaṭṭana to the other shore (paratira) by sea 3 months; from there to the Bodhi at Buddhagayā 3 months).[368] Sri Lanka had several well-known places of pilgrimage. The Mahbodhi and the Mahācetiya (Ruvanvalisaya) at Anurādhapura were very popular places of pilgrimage.[369] Nāgadīpa (in modern Jaffna Peninsula) was also very popular place.[370] Tissamahā-vihāra in the south[371] and Kalyāṇī-cetiya in the west were well-known places of pilgrimage.[372] Samantakūṭa (Śrī-Pada) was also an important place where many people visited there.[373] Generally, the Buddhist monks used to travel with learned teachers. Because all along the way they could talk important religious matters with them. It was like a peripatetic school. The Buddhist monks on pilgrimage gave valuable services to the people. Just like the Buddha and his disciples on Cārikā, these pilgrim monks used to give advices to the people in the villages to lead good and holy lives. They stopped and delivered sermons at several places where they felt that it was necessary and good for the people to do so.[374] A Buddhist monk on a journey generally carried with him three robes, alms-bowl, and water-strainer, an oil-can, a pair of sandals and a case to keep them in when not in use, a fan, an umbrella and a walking stick.[375] He had also a knapsack (thavikā) containing the apparatus for generating fire (araṇisahitādiṁi), sipāṭikāc a case?), ārakaṇtaka (pim?), pipphalaka (pair of scissors?), nakhacchedana (nail-clipper), and sūci (needle). There was also a note-book wherein for occasional references the virtues of the Buddha and the Dhamma were written.[376]

The interest of the Buddhist monks in social work and social service

The Buddhist monks should take interest in social service and humanitarian activities. Apart from their educational and cultural activities, they should be interested in social work. There were some Buddhist monks who tried to engage themselves in meditation and they had no interest in the welfare of the people. But other class of monks took interest in the welfare of the people—both spiritual and material in addition to their own salvation.[377] This attitude was very good no doubt and it was better than the first one. Many people likė the attitude of the Buddhist monks who showed their interest in the welfare of the people.

The traditional and popular attitude of the Buddhist Saṃgha is clearly stated in the advice given to them in the following verse:

"gihīnan upakarantānaṃ niccaṃ āmisadānato.
Karotha dhammadānena tesaṃ paccupakārakaṃ."[378]

"Render help in return by spiritual gifts to lay people who always support you with material gifts."[379]

The Sigāla-sutta of the Dīgha Nikāya referred to the same idea.[380]

In the verse mentioned above, all spiritual, educational and cultural services can be included in the term dhamma-dāna. Thus the Buddhist monks understood that it was their duty to help the lay people with spiritual, cultural and educational gifts and these lay people always felt for their material comforts.[381] Certain stories inform that the Buddhist monks wanted to lead a holy life themselves and they wished to serve the people.[382] The lay people will be impaired to see their holy life and they would try to follow their righteous life as fast as possible. The Buddhist monks are requested to help and to look after their parents when they are in need of material help.[383]

Buddhist sects or Nikāyas of Sri Lanka

The chronicles mention three nikāyas (Nikāyattaya) in Sri Lanka.[384] King Mahānāga (556-568 A.D.) rebuilt the three great cetiyas (Mahācetiyattaya) and offered gifts of cloth to the three nikāyas.[385] The three cetiyas were the Suvaṇṇamālī (Ruvanvalisaya), the Abhayagiri and the Jetavana dāgabos at Anurādhapura, and these three were the three chief monastic establishments.[386] The three nikāyas stated in the chronicles were the Mahāvihāra, the Abhayagiri and the Jetavana.[387] There were two other sects and they were the Dhammaruci and the Sāgaliya sects.[388] But they were included in the Abhayagiri and the Jetavana sects respectively. But sometimes they became known by their former names.[389] The Mahāvaṃsa describes that Aggabodhi IV (658-674 A.D.) gave many maintenance villages to the vihāras of the two nikāyas and 1,000 villages to the three nikāy as.[390]

"tathā dvinnaṃ nikāyānaṃ vihāre mandapaccaye
dirvā vā'pi ca sutrā vā bhogagāme bahū adā
bahunā kintu vuttena mikāyesu'pi tisu'pi
adā gāmasahassaṃ so bahuppādaṃ nirākulaṃ."[391]

It is very difficult to say whether these two nikāyas were included in the three great nikāyas or whether they were the Dhammaruci and the Sāgaliya or some other two nikāyas. According to W. Geiger, perhaps they were the Thūpārāma and the Mirisavaṭi-vihāra.[392] From records of about the latter part of the first century it was known that two groups known as the Dhamma Kathika and the Paṃsukūlika flourished.[393] Most probably, they were not two different nikāyas but only two groups of the same community and they led two ways of life. The Dhammakathika signifies a "preacher." The learned monks, who were teachers, belonged to this group. The Paṃsukūlikas were monks who were only rag-robes. There were three grades of them: the first grade used to wear robes made out of rags packed up in cemeteries; the second grade collected all kinds of rags left in various places by the lay people for the use of monks; the third grade took even robes left by the lay people at the feet of those monks. But none of them at their will and pleasure accepted robes given by the lay people.[394] Several kings in the 8th and 10th centuries offered robes to the Paṃsukūlikas. The Mahāvaṃsa accounts record that they belonged to the third grade.[395] There were the Paṃsukūlikas who belonged to the Mahāvihāra as well as to the Abhayagiri-vihāra.[396] But the Paṃsukūlikas of the Abhayagiri-vihāra in the 20th year of Sena II (851-885 A.D.) formed themselves into a special group.[397] The Paṃsukūlikas used to live in the Thūpārāna as well as in forest-dwellings like the Tapovana, and mountain caves like Riṭigala.[398]

The Āraṇyavāsī or the Vanavāsī monks used to dwell in jungle areas, but the Grāmavāsī monks used to reside in towns and villages. From about the 6th century A.D. they are mentioned as a distinctive group, though not as a separate nikāya.[399] The Āraṇyaka monks belonged to the Mahāvihāra.[400] Mahāvihāra bhikkbūnaṃ vane nivaratam adā."[401] "From about the 6th century onwards the forest-dwelling monks became known as tapassi "hermit" or "ascetic" and this term may not be applied to the Buddhist monks.[402] In the 10th century there was a monastery called Tapovana "Ascetic-Grove" near Anurādhapura and the forest-dwelling monks used to reside there.[403] The Paṃsukūlikas also lived in this monastery.[404] Paṃsukūlika and the Āraṇyaka were only two of the 13 dhutaṅgas.[405] There were monks who observed other dhutaṅgs like piṇḍapātika.[406] The thirteen dhutaṅgas are: paṃsukūlika, tecīvarika, piṇḍapātika, sapadānacārika, ekāsanika, pattapiṇḍika, khalupacchabhattika, āraññika, ukkhamūlika, abbhokāsika, sosānika, yathāsanthatika, nesajjika.[407]

The Araṇyavāsis used to live in quiet, forest areas, devoted chiefly in meditation, while the Grāmavānis used to live in towns and villages, and they were busy in activities connected with cultural and educational development. In later times, the Āraṇyakas, also, like the grāmavāsins, showed greater interest in intellectual activities, and they used to write non-religious works. The Bālāvabodhana, a Sanskrit grammar, was written by Araṇyavāsī Dimbulāgala Mahā-kāsyapa. By that time the difference between the Araṇyavāsis and the grāmavāsins was only in the name, and not in practice. The Araṇyavāsins were attracted by the way of life of the grāmavāsins. These two groups in later times became known as labhaya-vāsa "two residences," i.e., grāma (village) and araṇya (forest).[408] Modern Malavatta and Asgiriya, the two chief vihāras in Kandy, were the descendants of the old Ubhaya-vāsa, the former being the gramavāsa and the latter the araṇyavāsa.[409] Another group of monks known as Lābhavāsi belonged to the 10th century and later. But little is known about them.[410] The Samantapāsādikā refers to "five great monasteries" (pañca-mahāvihāra).[411] The Rasavāhinī also describes pañcamahāvāsa, "five great residences."[412] It is difficult to say what are these. But it is quite certain that they were not sects or nikāyas.[413]

The Buddhist Nuns of Sri Lanka

We know very little of the activities of nuns in Sri Lanka. The Kukurumahandamana Pillar Inscription of the 10th century records that there was a hospital (Ved-hul) in front of the nunnery known as Mehindārāma on the High Street (Mahavaya) of the Inner city (of Anurādhapura).[414] Some people wanted to know whether the Buddhist nuns (bikkhunīs) worked as nurses in these hospitals. Various sources gave information that the kings and the queens of Sri Lanka established richly endowed nunneries for the maintenance of the Buddhist nuns.[415] The Dīparaṃsa refers to a list of prominent nuns, but nothing is mentioned about their activities, except that the Vinaya was taught by them.[416]

NOTES

1. HBC., 135; AA., 23.
2. HBC., 135; EZ., I, 194-196.
3. HBC., 135; Smp (SHB), 338-339.
4. *Ibid.*, 135; *ibid.*, 338-339.
5. HBC., 135-136.
6. *Ibid.*, 136.
7. *Ibid.*, 136.
8. *Ibid.*, 136, f.n. 1.
9. *Ibid.*, 136.
10. *Ibid.*, 136; EZ., I, 91, II, 6-7.
11. *Ibid.*, 136.
12. *Ibid.*, 136.
13. *Ibid.*, 136.
14. *Ibid.*, 136., CJSC., G. II, 42.
15. *Ibid.*, 136.
16. *Ibid.*, 137; EZ., I, 85.
17. *Ibid.*, 137.
18. *Ibid.*, 137; EZ., I, 4.87.
19. *Ibid.*, 137.

20. *Ibid.*, 137; EZ., I, 87.
21. *Ibid.*, 137; *ibid.*, I., 85, 87.
22. *Ibid.*, 137.
23. *Ibid.*, 138; EZ., I, 85; III., 268.
24. *Ibid.*, 138, f.n. 1.
25. *Ibid.*, 138; Smp. III (col. 1900), 340.
26. *Ibid.*, 138; EZ., I, 4-5, 86.
27. *Ibid.*, 138.
28. *Ibid.*, 138; EZ., III., 258-259.
29. *Ibid.*, 138; *ibid.*, I, 5.
30. *Ibid.*, 138; *ibid.*, III, 103.
31. *Ibid.*, 138; *ibid.*, I. 4.
32. *Ibid.*, 138; f.n. 7.
33. *Ibid.*, 138.
34. *Ibid.*, 138.
35. *Ibid.*, 138; EZ., III, 227.
36. *Ibid.*, 138-139; *ibid.*, III, 228., n. 6.
37. *Ibid.*, 139.
38. *Ibid.*, 139; EZ., II, 10-13.
39. *Ibid.*, 139; *ibid.*, I., 87.
40. *Ibid.*, 139.
41. *Ibid.*, 139.
42. *Ibid.*, 139; VbhA., 234.
43. *Ibid.*, 139; Fa Hien, 102, 105, 107.
44. *Ibid.*, 139; *ibid.*, 107.
45. *Ibid.*, 139; Hiuen Tiang BK, XI, 247.
46. *Ibid.*, 140.
47. *Ibid.*, 140; MHv., xlvi, 10, 14, 28; 1.64.
48. *Ibid.*, 140; *ibid.*, xliv, 73.
49. *Ibid.*, 140; Smp. III (Colombo. 1900), 177.
50. *Ibid.*, 140; *ibid.*, III, (Col., 1900), 222.
51. *Ibid.*, 140; EZ., III, 227.
52. *Ibid.*, 140; f.n. 7.
53. *Ibid.*, 140-141; Mhv., xxxvii, 173.
54. *Ibid.*, 141; *ibid.*, xxxvii, 63., xlii, 23.
55. *Ibid.*, 141.
56. *Ibid.*, 141; Mhvg., 256.
57. *Ibid.*, 141; Mhv., xxxiii, 50.
58. *Ibid.*, 142.
59. *Ibid.*, 142., f.n. 1.
60. *Ibid.*, 142; MhV., xxxiv, 63., xxxv, 83, 117; xlvi, 14-16; xlix, 21; EZ., 1, 254-255; III, 198; IV, 114, 143, 173-174, 182-184.
61. *Ibid.*, 142; Fa Hien, 109.

62. *Ibid.*, 142; EZ., I, 167-169; 173-174; II, 3-4, 28; III, 103-105, 200.
63. *Ibid.*, 142; *Ibid.*, I, 203, 205; II, 6-8, 23, 29.
64. *Ibid.*, 142; Mhvg., 87.
65. *Ibid.*, 142.
66. *Ibid.*, 142-143., Mhv; liii, 14.
67. *Ibid.*, 143; EZ., III, 198.
68. *Ibid.*, 143.
69. *Ibid.*, 143; EZ., III, 258.
70. *Ibid.*, 143; MhV., xlix., 76.
71. *Ibid.*, 143; *ibid.*, xxxv, 48; xxxvi, 3; EZ., I, 211, 254-255; III, 116, 154, 165; IV, 123, 217, 221; EZ, IV, 227.
72. *Ibid.*, 144; MhV., xxxviii, 44-51.
73. *Ibid.*, 144.
74. *Ibid.*, 144; EZ., I, 69, 254-255., III, 218.
75. *Ibid.*, 144; *ibid.*, IV, 173-174.
76. *Ibid.*, 144, f.n. 3.
77. *Ibid.*, 145.
78. *Ibid.*, 145; EZ., III, 177.
79. *Ibid.*, 146; *ibid.*, III, 250.
80. *Ibid.*, 146; *ibid.*, III, 251.
81. *Ibid.*, 146; *ibid.*, III, 258.
82. *Ibid.*, 146; f.n. 4.
83. *Ibid.*, 146; DN., I, 49.
84. *Ibid.*, 146; Smp, III (*Colombo* 1900), 177.
85. *Ibid.*, 146; f.n. 6.
86. *Ibid.*, 146; f.n. 7; MHV., xliv, 73.
87. *Ibid.*, 147; MA.,404
88. *Ibid.*, 147; f.n. 2.
89. *Ibid.*, 147; EZ., IV, 139-140.
90. *Ibid.*, 147, f.n. 3.
91. *Ibid.*, 147, f.n. 3.
92. *Ibid.*, 148, AVDN, 42.
93. *Ibid.*, 148.
94. *Ibid.*, 148; MHV., xix, 32.
95. *Ibid.*, 148-149; *ibid.*, xxxiv, 86-88.
96. *Ibid.*, 149; *Ibid.*, xlix, 62-64.
97. *Ibid.*, 149.
98. *Ibid.*, 149; EZ., II, 107.
99. *Ibid.*, 149, f.n. 3.
100. *Ibid.*, 149, EZ., IV, 132-133.
101. *Ibid.*, 149.
102. *Ibid.*, 149.

103. *Ibid.*, 150; EZ., IV, 134.
104. *Ibid.*, 150.
105. *Ibid.*, 150; EZ., IV, 294-295.
106. *Ibid.*, 150.
107. *Ibid.*, 150; EZ., III, 133.
108. *Ibid.*, 150; EZ., I, 44: Slab-Inscription of Kassapa V.
109. *Ibid.*, 150; *ibid.*, III, 122; IV, 145, 149.
110. *Ibid.*, 150; MHV., xxxvii, 150, 173.
111. *Ibid.*, 151; VbhA., 314.
112. *Ibid.*, 151; Mhv., xliv., 11, 12.
113. *Ibid.*, 151; Fa Hien, 104.
114. *Ibid.*, 151; Mhv., xlix, 88-90.
115. *Ibid.*, 151; Smp (SHO), 53.
116. *Ibid.*, 151; Mhv., xlvi, 27., EZ., I, 47.
117. *Ibid.*, 152; EZ., II, 25.
118. *Ibid.*, 152; Mhv., xxxvi, 17; xlvi, 29; li, 75; lx., 598.
119. *Ibid.*, 152.
120. *Ibid.*, 152, f.n. 3.
121. *Ibid.*, 152.
122. *Ibid.*, 152.
123. *Ibid.*, 152; EZ., II, 22.
124. *Ibid.*, 152.
125. *Ibid.*, 112.
126. *Ibid.*, 112.
127. *Ibid.*, 112; MN., I, 271.
128. D.N., II, 162; *Ibid.*, 112; DPPN., I, 313.
129. *Ibid.*, 112, f.n. 4; DPPN., II, 204.
130. *Ibid.*, 112, f.n. 4, Thera., 316.
131. *Ibid.*, 112; VbhA., 335.
132. *Ibid.*, 113; Fa Hien., 107.
133. *Ibid.*, 113; Vsm., 89.
134. *Ibid.*, 113; *ibid.*, 94.
135. *Ibid.*, 113; RSV., II, 126.
136. *Ibid.*, 113.
137. *Ibid.*, 113; EZ., I, 144, No. 4.
138. *Ibid.*, 113; *ibid.*, I, 18.
139. *Ibid.*, 114.
140. *Ibid.*, 115.
141. *Ibid.*, 115; MhV., XV 203-204.
142. *Ibid.*, 115; *ibid.*, XV, 205-213.
143. *Ibid.*, 115.
144. *Ibid.*, 115.
145. *Ibid.*, 115.

146. *Ibid.*, 115.
147. *Ibid.*, 116.
148. *Ibid.*, 116; EZ., III, 227.
149. *Ibid.*, 116-117.
150. *Ibid.*, 117.
151. *Ibid.*, 117.
152. *Ibid.*, 117; MhV., xxxiii, 31., xxxiv., 70; MA., 699; Mhv., xxxviii, 10.
153. *Ibid.*, 117; MA., 699; Mhv., xxxviii, 10.
154. *Ibid.*, 117; M.A., 699; Mhv., xxx, 51, 56, 60., xxxiii, 22.
155. *Ibid.*, 117.
156. *Ibid.*, 119; Smp., III (Col. 1900), 279, 314. Mhv, xxxv, 87; 90-91; xxxvi, 9, 106; xlviii, 66.
157. *Ibid.*, 120; Mhv., xlii, 56.
158. *Ibid.*, 119-120; RSV., II, 10., Mhv., xxxvi, 24.
159. *Ibid.*, 120; Mhv., xxvi, 103, 126.
160. *Ibid.*, 120., *ibid.*, xxxvi, 52, 103; xlii, 19.
161. *Ibid.*, 120-121; *ibid.*, xv, 205., xxxvii, 15; xxxviii, 43, 69; xli, 65; xlii, 19, 66; xlviii, 70; xlix, 15; li, 54., Smp. III, 279, 314 (Col. 190).
162. *Ibid.*, 122; Mhv., xxxvi, 128.
163. *Ibid.*, 122-123; *ibid.*, xxxvi, 129.
164. *Ibid.*, 123; *ibid.*, xxxvii, 14.
165. *Ibid.*, 123; *ibid,* xxxvii, 123; xxxviii, 61-62.
166. *Ibid.*, 123; *ibid.*, xxxviii, 61-64.
167. *Ibid.*, 123; *ibid.*, li, 77, 87.
168. *Ibid.*, 123; *ibid.*, xxxvi, 128.
169. *Ibid.*, 123; *ibid.*, xxxvii, 123.
170. *Ibid.*, 123; *ibid.*, xxxviii, 61.
171. *Ibid.*, 123; *ibid.*, xxxix., 7.
172. *Ibid.*, 123; *ibid.*, xliv., 68.
173. *Ibid.*, 123; *ibid.*, li., 77.
174. *Ibid.*, 123; *ibid.*, li., 87.
175. *Ibid.*, 123; EZ., I, 92.
176. *Ibid.*, 123; *ibid.*, I, 218, 219, 233.
177. *Ibid.*, 124; *ibid.*, I, 217.
178. *Ibid.*, 124; *ibid.*, I, 230.
179. *Ibid.*, 124; Mhv., xxxv, 89.
180. *Ibid.*, 124; *ibid.*, xxxvi, 31.
181. *Ibid.*, 125; Mhv., xxxvi, 104., xxxvii, 15, 31, 123, 174, 183, 201, *ibid.*, xxxviii, 61-68, 78., xxxix., 6, 7, 13, 45-46; *ibid,* xli, 29; xlii, 57; *ibid.*, xlii, 57; xliv, 68; xlv, 60-61; xlix, 49; xlviii, 137, 139; *ibid.*, xlix, 14, 17; I, 66; li, 69, 77, EZ., II, 18; III, 264.
182. *Ibid.*, 130; Mhv., xxxiv. 30; xxxv. 85. xxxvi, 16-17, 107.
183. *Ibid.*, 130; *ibid.*, xxvii, 4.

184. *Ibid.*, 130; *ibid.*, xxxvi, 107.
185. *Ibid.*, 130; *ibid.*, xxxvii, 15; xlvi, 29.
186. *Ibid.*, 131; EZ., I, 228; III, 227; Mhv., xxxvi, 7.
187. *Ibid.*, 131; Mhv, xv, 205; xx, 23; xxxvi, 12.
188. *Ibid.*, 131; *ibid.*, xx, 23., DPV., xvii, 92.
189. *Ibid.*, 131; RSV. II, 51; Fa Hien, 105; Hiuen Tsiang, 250.
190. *Ibid.*, 132; Mhv., xlii, 67.
191. *Ibid.*, 132; *ibid.*, xv. 205; xxxvi, 74; xlix, 32.
192. *Ibid.*, 132; Mhvg., 91, 164, 165, 216, 258; Mhv., xlvi, 31; Vsm 67.
193. *Ibid.*, 132; f.n. 5.
194. *Ibid.*, 132; RSV., II, 12-123.
195. *Ibid.*, 132; Nks., 12.
196. *Ibid.*, 132; EZ., III, 223.
197. *Ibid.*, 133; MHv., xxxvii, 232.
198. *Ibid.*, 133; Smp. III (Col. 1900), 334.
199. *Ibid.*, 133; MA. 65.
200. *Ibid.*, 133-134.
201. *Ibid.*, 134, f.n. 1.
202. *Ibid.*, 134., f.n. 1.
203. *Ibid.*, 134.
204. *Ibid.*, 134.
205. *Ibid.*, 153.
206. *Ibid.*, 153.
207. *Ibid.*, 153.
208. *Ibid.*, 153.
209. *Ibid.*, 153.
210. *Ibid.*, 154; Mhvg., 337. Cīvarakuhandhaka.
211. *Ibid.*, 154; Pācit. Ganabhajana sikkhāpada, 74.
212. *Ibid.*, 154; Mhvg., 242.
213. *Ibid.*, 155; Mhvg., 260, 288-289.
214. *Ibid.*, 155; *ibid.*, 260, 288-289.
215. *Ibid.*, 155.
216. *Ibid.*, 155, f.n. 3.
217. *Ibid.*, 156.
218. *Ibid.*, 156, f.n. 1.
219. *Ibid.*, 156., CHI, I, 290.
220. *Ibid.*, 157-158.
221. *Ibid.*, 158.
222. *Ibid.*, 158; Smp. (SHB), 503.
223. *Ibid.*, 158.
224. *Ibid.*, 158, f.n. 3; AA., 52.
225. *Ibid.*, 158.
226. *Ibid.*, 158.

227. *Ibid.*, 158; AA., 52-53.
228. *Ibid.*, 58; *ibid.*, 52-53.
229. *Ibid.*, 158-159.
230. *Ibid.*, 159; f.n. 1; AA., 53.
231. *Ibid.*, 159.
232. *Ibid.*, 159; f.n. 2., DA, 654; MA, 881.
233. *Ibid.*, 159; VbhA, 336; Smp. III, (1990), 92.
234. *Ibid.*, 160.
235. *Ibid.*, 160; DhpA., 4.
236. *Ibid.*, 160; *ibid.*, 4.
237. *Ibid.*, 160; f.n. 1.
238. *Ibid.*, 160.
239. *Ibid.*, 160, f.n. 2.
240. *Ibid.*, 160.
241. *Ibid.*, 159; DhpA., 4.
242. *Ibid.*, 159, f.n. 5., AA, 22.
243. *Ibid.*, 165.
244. *Ibid.*, 165.
245. *Ibid.*, 165; Smp. II (Colombo 1900), 260.
246. *Ibid.*, 165, f.n. 2; *ibid.*, III (Columbo 1900), 260.
247. *Ibid.*, 166; EZ., I, 167-168; Iripinniyāra Pillar Inscription, 173; Rambāra Pillar Inscription, III, 103-105; Manner Kacceri Pillar Inscription.
248. *Ibid.*, 166.
249. *Ibid.*, 167; Pācit., 37; Yo pana bhikkhu paṭhaviṃ khaneyya vā khaṇāpeyya vā pācittiyaṃ.
250. *Ibid.*, 167.
251. *Ibid.*, 167.
252. *Ibid.*, 167.
253. *Ibid.*, 167.
254. *Ibid.*, 167; EZ., I, 211; EZ., III, 116; EZ, IV, 123.
255. *Ibid.*, 168.
256. *Ibid.*, 168, f.n. 1.
257. *Ibid.*, 168.
258. *Ibid.*, 168.
259. *Ibid.*, 168.
260. *Ibid.*, 168.
261. *Ibid.*, 168-169.
262. *Ibid.*, 172.
263. *Ibid.*, 172.
264. *Ibid.*, 172.
265. *Ibid.*, 173.
266. *Ibid.*, 173.
267. *Ibid.*, 173.

268. *Ibid.*, 173.
269. *Ibid.*, 173.
270. *Ibid.*, 173; Mihintale Tablets of Mahinda IV, EZ, I, 85; AA, 351.
271. *Ibid.*, 173-174.
272. *Ibid.*, 174, f.n. 1.
273. *Ibid.*, 174.
274. *Ibid.*, 174; AA., 351.
275. *Ibid.*, 174; *ibid.*, 351.
276. *Ibid.*, 174.
277. *Ibid.*, 174.
278. *Ibid.*, 174.
279. *Ibid.*, 174.
280. *Ibid.*, 174-175; MA., 100.
281. *Ibid.*, 175.
282. *Ibid.*, 175.
283. *Ibid.*, 175; Fa Hien, 105.
284. *Ibid.*, 175; Hiuen Tsiang Bk XI, 250.
285. *Ibid.*, 175; RSv., II, 51.
286. *Ibid.*, 175-176; Vsm, 16.
287. *Ibid.*, 176, f.n. 1.
288. *Ibid.*, 176; DA., 133; MA., 210.
289. *Ibid.*, 176; Vsm., 67.
290. *Ibid.*, 176; Rsv, II, 176.
291. *Ibid.*, 176; Tonigala Inscription mentions it atarakaja, EZ., III, 178.
292. *Ibid.*, 176.
293. *Ibid.*, 176.
294. *Ibid.*, 176; Rsv. II. 128; MT., II, 519; Prmj. II (PTS), 104.
295. *Ibid.*, 176; EZ. III, 178.
296. *Ibid.*, 176-177.
297. *Ibid.*, 17; DA., 57.
298. *Ibid.*, 177; Vsm., 67.
299. *Ibid.*, 177; AA., 820; MA, 548.
300. *Ibid.*, 177.
301. *Ibid.*, 177; AA, 709.
302. *Ibid.*, 177; Smp. III (Colombo, 1900), 299.
303. *Ibid.*, 177.
304. *Ibid.*, 177-178; AA. 23.
305. *Ibid.*, 178.
406. *Ibid.*, 178; Vsm. 254.
407. *Ibid.*, 178.
408. *Ibid.*, 179.
309. *Ibid.*, 179; M.A. 150, 214, 354, 698.
310. *Ibid.*, 179; AA., 422.
311. *Ibid.*, 179; DA., 495; MA., 530.

312. *Ibid.*, 179., MA., 187; DA., 535, 758; AA. 23.
313. *Ibid.*, 179; AA., 385-386.
314. *Ibid.*, 180; Mhvg, 60, 44.
315. *Ibid.*, 180; Mhvg., 60.
316. *Ibid.*, 180; *ibid.*, 44.
317. *Ibid.*, 180; *ibid.*, 42.
318. *Ibid.*, 180; Vsm., 14, 74.
319. *Ibid.*, 181; AA, 708-709.
320. *Ibid.*, 182.
321. *Ibid.*, 182.
322. *Ibid.*, 182.
323. *Ibid.*, 182.
324. *Ibid.*, 183; MA, 65-66.
325. *Ibid.*, 183; DA., 752.
326. *Ibid.*, 183; Pācit, 39.
327. *Ibid.*, 183.
328. *Ibid.*, 183.
329. *Ibid.*, 183.
330. *Ibid.*, 183; VbhA., 335, 342.
331. *Ibid.*, 184; DA., 575; MA., 241; VbhA., 200.
332. *Ibid.*, 184; EZ., I, 4-5, 86.
333. *Ibid.*, 184; EZ., III, 258: Kaludiya-pokuṇa Cave Inscription.
334. *Ibid.*, 184; f.n. 3.
335. *Ibid.*, 185; Ez., 1, 4.
336. *Ibid.*, 185; f.n. 1.
337. *Ibid.*, 185.
338. *Ibid.*, 185, f.n. 2; Vsm. 88-89.
339. *Ibid.*, 185; *ibid.*, 88.
340. *Ibid.*, 185; AA., 707.
341. *Ibid.*, 185; Mhv, xxvii, 9-20.
342. *Ibid.*, 185; *ibid.*, xxx, 98.
343. *Ibid.*, 185; *ibid.*, xxx, 19-41.
344. *Ibid.*, 185; MA., 549.
345. *Ibid.*, 185; EZ., III, 215.
346. *Ibid.*, 185; f.n. 9.
347. *Ibid.*, 186; EZ., III, 132.
348. *Ibid.*, 186; Mhv, xxii, 25-28.
349. *Ibid.*, 187; AA, 26-27.
350. *Ibid.*, 187; Vsm., 70.
351. *Ibid.*, 187; VbhA., 318., Vsm., 54.
352. *Ibid.*, 187.
353. *Ibid.*, 188.
354. *Ibid.*, 188; MA., 353-354; AA. 13.
355. *Ibid.*, 188; AA. 13.

356. *Ibid.*, 188; *ibid.* 13.
357. *Ibid.*, 188.
358. *Ibid.*, 188, f.n. 3; EHBC., 127.
359. *Ibid.*, 188-189; M.A., 354-355, 214; DA., 137; VbhA., 282; AA., 16.
360. *Ibid.*, 189; MA., 354.
361. *Ibid.*, 189-190; Dharmapradīpikā, 322.
362. *Ibid.*, 189, f.n. 6.
363. *Ibid.*, 190.
364. *Ibid.*, 190., Rsv., II, 128; VbhA, 323.
365. *Ibid.*, 190-191; *ibid.*, II, 150; II, 17; *ibid,* 207; AA., 653; MA., 545; DA., 368.
366. *Ibid.*, 191; AA., 489, 277.
367. *Ibid.*, 191; Rsv., II, 124-125.
368. *Ibid.*, 191, f.n. 3.
369. *Ibid.*, 191; VbhA, 204; Vsm, 106.
370. *Ibid.*, 191; DA., 368; MA., 545; AA. 653.
371. *Ibid.*, 191; AA., 227.
372. *Ibid.*, 191; Rsv., II, 17; VbhA., 207.
373. *Ibid.*, 191; Rsv., II, 17.
374. *Ibid.*, 192.
375. *Ibid.*, 192; Vsm, 68, 74; AA., 708-709.
376. *Ibid.*, 192; MA., 312.
377. *Ibid.*, 193.
378. *Ibid.*, 194; Saddharmālaṅkāraya, 523.
379. *Ibid.*, 194.
380. *Ibid.*, 194; D., III, 117.
381. *Ibid.*, 194.
382. *Ibid.*, 194; DA., 750; MA., 237; AA., 276, 278; VbhA., 196., Rsv., II, 143.
383. *Ibid.*, 194; Smp (SHB), 335.
384. *Ibid.*, 194; Mhv., xli, 97; xliv, 131; xlv., 16; xlvi, 16; xlviii, 73; li, 14, 64, 113; lii, 10, 12, 35, 80.
385. *Ibid.*, 194; *ibid.*, xli, 95, 97.
386. *Ibid.*, 194.
387. *Ibid.*, 195.
388. *Ibid.*, 195.
389. *Ibid.*, 195; Mhv., V. 13; xxxix, 41; xlii, 43; xlvii, 1-2; lii, 17.
390. *Ibid.*, 195; *ibid.*, xlvi, 15-16.
391. *Ibid.*, 195; f.n. 2; *ibid.*, xlvi, 15-16.
392. *Ibid.*, 195; clv., Fr. I, 99, n. 2.
393. *Ibid.*, 195; AA., 52-53.
394. *Ibid.*, 196; Vsm., 47-48.
395. *Ibid.*, 196; Mhv., xlviii, 16; lii, 27; liii, 48; liv., 25.
396. *Ibid.*, 196; AA., 489., Mhv., xlvii, 66., li. 52.

397. *Ibid.*, 196; Mhv., li 52.
398. *Ibid.*, 196; AA, 489; Mhv., xlvii, 66; xlviii, 4; xlix, 81; I, 63; liii, 25.
399. *Ibid.*, 196; Mhv, xli, 99; lii, 22; liii, 14; liv., 20.
400. *Ibid.*, 196; *ibid.*, lii, 22.
401. *Ibid.*, 196; *ibid.*, lii, 22.
402. *Ibid.*, 196; *ibid.*, xli, 99; liv, 20.
403. *Ibid.*, 197.
404. *Ibid.*, 197; Mhv, liii, 14.
405. *Ibid.*, 197; Vsm., 45.
406. *Ibid.*, 197.
407. *Ibid.*, 197; Vsm., 45.
408. *Ibid.*, 197; f.n. 1., Nks., 20, 22, 24.
409. *Ibid.*, 197; f.n. 1.
410. *Ibid.*, 197; Mhv., liv., 27; lx, 68, 72.
411. *Ibid.*, 195; Smp (SHB), 220.
412. *Ibid.*, 195; Rsv, II, 51.
413. *Ibid.*, 195, f.n. 4.
414. *Ibid.*, 197; EZ., II, 22.
415. *Ibid.*, 198; Mhv., xxxix, 43; xlvi, 27; xlix, 25; EZ., I, 44.
416. *Ibid.*, 198; DpV., xviii, 20-23, 27-35.

8

The Arahants in Sri Lanka

The original meaning of the word arahant was "worthy" or "deserving."[1] It derives from the Vedic root arh.[2] In pre-Buddhist times, the term was used to signify an horrific title of high officials.[3] But the term was taken by the Buddha. According to him, the term indicates one person who had reached the highest stage in the realization of Nibbāna.[4] Likewise, the Buddha mentioned the term Brāhmaṇa to inform one who was free from evil, one not one born in the Brahamin caste.[5] A very common and popular term for arahant is Khīṇāsava (Skt. Kṣīṇāśrava) "One whose āsavas (defilements) have been destroyed."[6] There are three āsavas: kāmāsava "lust for sense-pleasure", bhāvāsava "desire for existence", and avijjāsava "ignorance" or "delusion". Sometimes diṭṭhāsava "group of false theories" is included, making them four.[7]

From the Tipiṭaka we learn that the arahants stated this supreme attainment in the following standard formula: *Khīṇā jāti, vusitaṃ brahmacariyaṃ, kataṃ karaṇīyaṃ, nāparaṃ, itthattāyāti* ("destroyed is birth, lived is the holy life, done is what should be done, there is no beyond hereafter."[8]) In the Chabbisodhana-sutta of the Majjhima-nikāya, the Buddha told his disciples that if a Buddhist monk stated this, then it was neither accepted nor rejected, but he was questioned with regard to certain points. These questions dealt with as to how his mind was liberated with regard to the four common usages (*Cattāro*

Vohāra), viz., the seen (*diṭṭha*). The heard (*suta*), the sensed (*muta*) and the apperceived by the mind (*Viññāta*); the five aggregates of clinging (*pañca-upādānakkhandhā*): matter (*rūpa*), feeling (*vedanā*), perception (*saññā*), mental formations (*saṅkhārā*) and consciousness (*viññāṇa*); six elements (*cha dhātu*): extensions (*paṭhavī*), cohesion (*āpo*), heat (*tejo*), motion (*vāyo*), space (*ākāsa*), and mind (*Viññāna*); the six inner and outer spheres (*cha ajjhattika-bāhirāni āyatanāni*): eye and visible objects (*cakkhu-rūpa*), ear and sound (*sota-sadda*), nose and odour (*ghāna-gandha*), tongue and taste (*jivhā-rasa*), body and tangible objects (*kāya-phoṭṭhabba*), and mind and cognizable objects (*mano-dhamma*); and this animate body and all external objects (*imasmiñ ca saviññāṇake kāye bahiddhā ca sabbamimittesu*). When his answers were satisfactory, than he would be an arahant.[9] Then as an arahant he was accepted. The *Chabbisodhana-sutta* indicated that at the time of the Buddha there were some Buddhist monks who falsely claimed arahantship or through halluciation.[10]

Several suttas in the *Nikāyas* mention that "an arahant was a person who practised the seven bojjhangas: mindfulness (*sati*), investigation (*dhammavicaya*), energy (*viriya*), joy (*pītti*, serenity (*passaddhi*), concentration (*samādhi*), and equanimity (*upekkhā*); who had got rid of the five *nīvaraṇas* (hindrances); sensuality (*kāmacchanda*), hatred (*vyāpāda*), sloth and torpor (*thīnamiddha*), worry-and-flurry (*uddhacca-kukkucca*) and doubt (*vicikicchā*); who had eradicated the three roots of evil (*tini akusamūkāṁ*): desire (*lobha*), hatred (*dosa*) and delusion (*moha*); who had cultivated various conduct (*sīla*), concentration (*samādhi*) and wisdom (*pañña*); who had no craving or attachment to the five aggregates (*khandhas*) that constitute human personality; who had cut himself away from the ten *saṃyojanas* (fetters); belief in a permanent self (*sakkāyadiṭṭhi*), doubt (*vicikicchī*), superstition (*sīlabbataparāmāsa*), sense-desire (*kāma-rāga*), hatred (*vyāpāda*), lust for material (*ruparāga*) and non-material things (*arūparāga*), pride (*māna*), excitement (*uddhacca*) and ignorance (*avijjā*); who was pure in deed, word and thought; who was free from lust for sense-pleasures (*kāmataṅhā*), desire for existence (*bhavataṇhā*) and desire for non-existence (*vibhavataṇhā*) — in short one who had won emancipation from all evil dispositions (*kilesā*)."[11] The Sāmañña-phala-sutta of the Dīgha-nikāya, the Sabhāsava, the Mahāsakuludāyi, the Cetokhila and the Chabbhisodhana suttas of the Majjhima-mikāya and the āseṭṭha-sutta of the Sutta Nipāta described the above mentioned matters. But the conception of the arahantship varied later at different times and in different places. Some stories and statements of the Pāli commentaries and chronicles throw flood of light to form an idea as to who were in ancient Sri Lanka regarded as arahants.[12]

From the commentaries we learn that in Sri Lanka at one time there was not a single puthujjana monk (a bhikkhu of the common sort).[13] "Imasmiṃ yera dīpe ekavāre puthujjana bhikkhu nāma vāhasi."[14] It shows that all Buddhist monks at that time in Sri Lanka had reached one of the four stages of the realization of Nibbāna, i.e. they were sotāpanna, sakadāgāmi, anāgāmi or arahant. The commentarial statement further narrated that, at another time, puthujjana monks were so are that they we mentioned as ceriosities.[15] "Ekasniṃ hi kāle paṭivedhakarā bhikkhū bahū honti; esa bhikkhu puthujjaroti aṅguliṃ pasāretvā dassetabbo hoti."[16] It is also stated that there was not a single seat in ȧny refectory in the villages of Sri Lanka on which some Buddhist monks, after his meal of rice gruel, had not obtained arahantship.[17] The Saṃyutta commentary[18] records that about 30,000 Buddhist monks stood at the southern gate of the Mahāvihāra and by looking at the Mahācetiya (Ruvanvali-saya), they had attained arahantship. In the same way, 30,000 Buddhist monks attained arahantship at each of the other three gates of the Mahāvihāra and also at Pañhamaṇḍapa, at the gate of the Thūpārāma, at the sourthern gate of the city and on the banks of the Abhaya tank and the Anurādhapura tank.[19] A mahāthera who was a preacher of the Ariyavaṃsa-sutta (Mahā-

Ariyavaṃsabhāṃka thera), describes: "what are you talking? It is possible to say that wherever two feet could be evenly placed within the space visible from the lower terrace of the Mahācetiya, 30,000 bhikkhus have attained arahantship at each of these feet."[20] Another Mahāthera spoke that the number of those who obtained arahantship was greater than grains of sand scattered on the coutyard of the Mahācetiya.[21] These figures only show that those who attained arahantship within the area of the Mahācetiya at Anurādhapura.[22] The Vibhaṅga commentary relates that during the time of the Brāhmaṇa Tissa famine about 24,000 arahants stayed at the Tissamahārāma and the Cittala-pabbata.[23] All these informations indicate that many arahants used to live in Sri Lanka.

Generally, the arahants lived in quiet place and they were fond of solitude. Dhammadinna of Talaṅgera was induced by arguments and advices with great difficulty to leave his place for Tissamahārāma to go there to discuss with the Buddhist monks for their subjects of meditation.[24] The arahants never welcomed visitors. Khujja-Tissa of Maṅgana did not like the king's coming to see him.[25] The arahants also went on pilgrimage to holy places such as the Mahācetiya and the Mahābodhi at Anurādhapura. But they avoided crowds as far as possible. An arahant came to Anurādhapura late in the evening to worship the Mahācetiya when all monks and laymen had left the place. He did not like crowds. He wished to avoid them.[26]

An arahant was always free from fear. This can be accepted as one criterion of an arahant. The Samantapasādikā mentions that an arahant would not be frightened if on his head a thunderbolt fell. There was no disturbance in his mind at that time. If he was frightened then he should not be an arahant. For this reason be should be rejected to become an arahant. He should be rejected "as no arahant."[27] "Khiṇāsavassa nāma asaniyāpi matthhake pataya mānāya bhayaṃ vā chambhitattaṃ vā lomahaṃso vā na hoti. Sacassa bhayaṃ vā chambhitataṃ vā lomahaṃso vā uppajjati, na tvaṃ arahāti apanetabbo."[28]

Dhammadinna gave a topic of meditation to Mahānāga and Mahānāga became an arahant immediately.[29] Dhammadinna of Talaṅgara was a famous arahant. Under his supervision Mahādatta of Haṅkana became an arahant. Dhammadinna made him an arahant.[30]

Another criteron of arahants was that they were free from misconduct or wanton behaviour with their hands and feet. They were not guilty of miscondut or wanton behaviour with their hands and feet.[31] Khujja-Tissa Thera was a famous arahant. He was an old man. He was fond of solitude. He stayed in a place called Maṇgaṇa abut five yojanas from Anurādhapura. He did not like to see anyone. When he know that king Saddhā-Tissa (77-59 B.C.) was coming to meet him, he then deliberately was on a bed and in order to disturb the king he started scrawling on the ground.[32] When the king saw this childish behaviour of the thera, he then left the place without saluting him and he remarked that "no arahant would be guilty of such wanton behaviour with his hands."[33] "Khīṇāsavānaṃ nāma hatthakukkuccaṃ natthi."[34]

Mahā-Saṃgharakkhita was a holy man. He became well-known for his great devotion to Buddhism. At the age of over 70, he did not feel well and he was lying on his deathbed. At this time the Buddhist monks wanted to know his spiritual attainments. He told them that he was a putujjama. Then his attendant monk stated him: "Sir, people from 12 yojanas how assembled, thinking that you had entered parinibhbāna (i.e., died as an arahant). If you die as a puttujjana, there will be great disappointment."[35] The old monk then answered: "with the idea of seeing the Buddha Matheya I did not cultivate meditation (vipassanā). If it is as you say, help me to sit up, and leave me alone."[36] The attendant monk helped him to sit up and left him alone. Before the attendant went far away, Mahā-Saṃgharakkhita obtained arahantship and showed him a sign by snapping his fingers.[37]

Another Mahāthera of Kaṇthakasāla Pariveṇa at the age of 80 was on his death-bed and in severe pain he was groaning.

King Vasabha arrived there to see the thera, but he was very much disappointed when he heard his groans. The king then at the door remarked that he did not like to worship a monk, who even after 60 years in the Buddhist Saṃgha, was unable to bear a little pain. The attendant monk then told the dying thera that the king was very much disappointed and went away when he had heard his groans. The thera then said, "Then leave me alone." The thera suppressed his pains and obtained arahantship. He informed the attendant to tell the king to come and worship him.[38]

These examples indicate that arahantship was a thing that one had the power and capacity to attain it, if necessary, at almost a moment's notice. The 5th century commentators opined it.[39]

In a certain village an arahant thera and a young Buddhist monk went out for piṇḍipāta. They got some hot rice-gruel at the very first house. The thera suffered from flatulence, and it was in his mind that the hot rice-gruel would be good for him. Then after sitting on a log of wood he drank it immediately. But the young monk did not like it and said that the hungry old man had disgraced them.[40] The Vinaya rule does not prohibit a monk from sitting down on a log of won near the road and drinking rice-gruel. But socially, this was not good and it did not look nice and for this reason the young monk did not appreciate the elder's behaviour and it was very disgraceful. The arahants were well-known for their go behaviour and they were well-mannered and were very careful in etiquette.[41]

At the time of the Buddha there were arahants who were guilty of improprieties. All arahants were not equally over careful about proprieties of behaviour and they sometimes commit a minor "offence." The Buddha prohibited the Buddhist monks from showing superhuman mirceles to laity, as well as from using wooden bowls.[42] From the Culavagga we learn that an arahant was not perfect in all matters of conduct and was not above committing petty mistakes. This was the opinion of those who compiled the Cullavagga.[43] The Mahāvaṃsa mentions that the arahants were not free from religious and national prejudices.[44] Some arahants consoled king Duṭṭa-Gāmaṇī when he was repenting over the destruction of many thousands of human lives in the war.[45] "When the arahants in Piyaṅgudīpa knew his thought they sent eight arahants to comfort the king. And they, coming in the middle watch of the night, elighted at the palace-gate. Making known that they were come thither through the air they mounted to the terrace of the palace. The great king greeated them, and when he had invited them to be seated and had done them reverence in many ways he asked the reason of their coming. "We are sent by the brotherhood at Piyaṅgudipa to comfort thee, O Lord of men." And thereon the king said again to them: "How shall there be any comfort for me, O venerable Sirs, since by me was caused the slaughter of a great host numbering millions?"

"From this deed arises no hindrance in the way to heaven. Only one and a half human beings (diyaḍḍha-manujā) have been slain here by thee, O lord of men. The one had come into the (three), refuges, the other had taken on himself the five precepts. Unbelivers and man of evil life were the rest, not more to be esteemed than beasts. (micchādiṭ-ṭhī ca dussīlā sesā hasu-samā matā.") But as for thee, thou wilt bring glory to the doctrine of the Buddha in manifold ways. Therefore cast away care from thy heart, O ruler of men." Thus exhorted by them the king took comfort."[46]

The Mahāvaṃsa informs that eight arahants gave the above advice. But it was against the spirit of the Buddha's teaching. According to the teaching of the Buddha, destruction of life even for the propagation or establishment of Buddhism can never be justified or accepted. It is difficult to understand whether the arahants who belonged to the second century B.C. ever opined such views. The author of the Mahāvaṃsa of the fifth century A.D. wrote these statements in the Mahāvaṃsa and this signifies that the Mahā-Thera and other responsible persons at that time took this statement to be worthy of arahants and that was reason in the chronicle it was included. They stated that the arahants for the progress of the Buddha's religion justified killing.[47]

The above facts give us an idea that at the time of the Pāli commentaries the conception of arhantship was ill-defined. The Arahants were not free from some of the minor human blemishes, such as pride and love of display. They had their own weakneses and idiosyncrasies. What was needed was that an arahant "should have a reputation for deep piety and scrupulousness" in following the prepts.[48]

The Puthujjan monks like the arahants used to lead a holy life. Their way of life was almost like that of the arahants. For this reason the common people took them as the arahants.[49] The topics of meditation (Kammaṭṭhāna) were given by some Buddhist monks and they were often mistaken by ordinary monks and laymen for the arahants.[50] The Buddhist monks used to live in caves at Cetiyagiri (Mihintale), Cittalapabbata (Situlpavva), Dakkhiṇāgiri and Hatthikuchi (not yet identified) and generaly by the undiscriminating they were considered as the arahants.[51] The commentary on the Majjhima Nikāya says that it was difficult for an ordinary man to make out an arahant.[52] A Khīṇāsara thera (arahant) used to live at Cittaba-pabbata and he had as his personal attendant a monk who in his old age joined the Buddhist Saṃgha. One day, this old attendant asked the arahant: "Sir, what sort of people are the ariyas?" Then the arahant told, "The ariyas are difficult to know, my friend. Some old people even while attending on the ariyas, moving with the carrying their alms-bowls and robes, do not know the ariyas."[53] The word ariya mean "noble one", and the term was used in opposition to puttujjama."[54]

NOTES

1. HBC., 217.
2. *Ibid.*, 217.
3. *Ibid.*, 217; Sat. Br. III., 4, 1, 3; 4.1.6; 4.1.8., SBE, xxvi.

4. *Ibid.*, 217.
5. *Ibid.*, 217.
6. *Ibid.*, 217.
7. *Ibid.*, 217.
8. *Ibid.*, 217.
9. *Ibid.*, 217-218, f.n. 4.
10. *Ibid.*, 218, f.n. 1.
11. *Ibid.*, 218.
12. *Ibid.*, 219.
13. *Ibid.*, 219; MA, 881; DA., 654.
14. *Ibid.*, 219.
15. *Ibid.*, 219.
16. *Ibid.*, 219; MA, 881; DA, 654.
17. *Ibid.*, 219; *ibid.*, 208; *ibid.*, 131.
18. *Ibid.*, 219; SA. III, 151.
19. *Ibid.*, 219.
20. *Ibid.*, 219.
21. *Ibid.*, 219-220.
22. *Ibid.*, 220.
23. *Ibid.*, 220; VbhA., 314.
24. *Ibid.*, 220; MA., 149.
25. *Ibid.*, 220; AA., 384.
26. *Ibid.*, 220; MA., 698; VbhA., 204.
27. *Ibid.*, 220; Smp (SHB), 350.
28. *Ibid.*, 220, f.n. 5; Smp (SHB), 350.
29. *Ibid.*, 221; Vsm, 476.
30. *Ibid.*, 221; Ma., 150.
31. *Ibid.*, 222.
32. *Ibid.*, 222.
33. *Ibid.*, 222; AA., 384-385.
34. *Ibid.*, 222, f.n. 4, AA., 384-385.
35. *Ibid.*, 223.
36. *Ibid.*, 223.
37. *Ibid.*, 223; Vsm. 36.
38. *Ibid.*, 223; DA., 205.
39. *Ibid.*, 223.
40. *Ibid.*, 225-226; Smp (SHB), 109; Vsm. 318.
41. *Ibid.*, 226.
42. *Ibid.*, 227; Clvg. 203-205.
43. *Ibid.*, 227.
44. *Ibid.*, 227; Mhv, xxv, 98-112.
45. *Ibid.*, 227-228.
46. *Ibid.*, 228; Mhv., xxv, 98-112.

47. *Ibid.*, 228-229.
48. *Ibid.*, 229.
49. *Ibid.*, 229; Vsm., 36, 37, 476; MA., 150, 535, 869; Smp (SHB), 350.
50. *Ibid.*, 229; MA., 833.
51. *Ibid.*, 229; Vsm., 89.
52. *Ibid.*, 229; MA., 18.
53. *Ibid.*, 229; MA., 18.
54. *Ibid.*, 229, f.n. 4.

Bibliography

CHAPTER ONE

A History of Indian Literature. M. Winternitz, 2 vols. Calcutta.

A Record of Buddhist Kingdom : An Account of Chinese Monk Fa Hien of his Travels in India and Ceylon (A.D. 399-414), by J. Legge, Oxford, 1886.

Aṅguttara Nikāya, ed. by Devamitta Tera, Samayawardhana Press, Colombo.

Aṅguttara-nikāyaṭṭha Kathā Manorathapūraṇī) commentary on the Aṅguttara-nikāya, 2 parts (SHB).

Abeyasinghe, Tikiri, Portuguese Rule in Ceylon, 1594-1612, Colombo, 1966.

Amaradasa Liyanagamage, The Decline of Polonnaruwa and the Rise of Dambadeniya, Colombo, 1968.

Banerjee, A.C., Buddhism in India and Abroad, Calcutta, 1973.

Barros, Joao de and Cuto, Diogo de. The History of Ceylon from the earliest times to 1600 A.D. Translated and edited by Donald Ferguson, Journal of the Ceylon Branch of Royal Asiatic Society, XX, 60, 1908, Colombo.

Bett, H.C.P., Report on the Kāgalla District of the Province of Sabaragamuva, Colombo, 1872.

Buddhist Records of the Western World, translated from the Chinese of Hiuen Tsiang (A.D. 629), by Samuel Beal....(London, Kegan Paul, Trench, Trubner & Co.).

Cūlavaṃsaa (Pāli Text), ed. W. Geiger, 2 vols. PTS, London, 1925, 1927. Eng. Tr. by W. Geiger, 2 Parts, PTS, London,

1929, 1930. Tr. from the German into English by C. Mahal Rickmers, 2 pts, Colombo, 1953.

Codrington, H.W., Notes on the Danbadeniya Dynasty, Ceylon Antigquary and Literary Register, X, Colombo, 1914.

Codrington, H.W., Notes on the Kandyan Dynasty in the Fifteenth and Sixteenth Centurise, Ceylon Literary Register, II, July 1932, No. 7, Third Series.

Culture of Ceylon in Mediaeval Times, ed. by Heinz Bechert, Wiestaden, 1960.

Dambadeṇi Asha, Kuveṇi Sihabā Saha Dambadeṇi Asha, ed. Kirialle Ñāṇavimala Thera, Colombo, 1960.

Dambadeṇi Katikāvata, ed. D.B. Jayatilaka in his Katikāvat Saṅgarā, 6-21, reprinted Kalaniya, 1955; first published 1922.

Daḷadā Sirita, ed., Valivitiye Sorata, Colombo, 154.

Dāṭhāvaṃsa, ed. by Silālaṅkāra Thera, Alutgama, 1914.

Dīpavaṃsa, ed. and Tr. into English by H. Oldenberg, London, 1879.

Dutt, Sukumar, Buddhism in East Asia, New Delhi, 1966.

Epigraphia Zeylanica, 4 vols. (Oxford University Press), 1904-55.

Geiger, Wilhelm, Culture of Ceylon in Mediaeval Times, ed. by Heinz Bechert, Wiesladen, 1960.

Glass Palace Chronicle, tr. by Pe Manng Tin and G.H. Luce, London, 1923.

Godakumbura, C.E., Kadadera Grant. An ola leaf manuscript from the Kadadora vihāra in Central Province, Journal of the Ceylon Branch of the Royal Asiatic Society, II, 2 parts, New Series, Colombo, 1952.

Godakumbura, C.E., Postscript to the Kadeadora Grant, Journal of the Ceylon Branch of the Royal Asiatic Society, III, Part I, New Series, Colombo, 1953.

Godakumbura, C.E., Sinhalese Literature, Colombo, 1955.

Hall, D.G.E., A History of South-East Asia, London, 1964.

Hatthavanagallavihāravaṃsa, ed. C.E. Godakumbura, PTS, London, 1956.

Hazra, Kanai Lal, History of Theravāda Buddhism in South-East Asia with special reference to Ceylon, New Delhi, 1982.

Hazra, Kanai Lal, The Introduction and Development of the Sīhala Saṇgha, the Mahābodhi, Calcutta, 1972.

Journal Royal Asiatic Society, Ceylon Branch, New Series, VI, Colombo.

Katikāvat Saṅgarā, ed. D.B. Jayatilaka, reprinted Kalaniya, 1955., first published Colombo, 1922.

Ko, Taw Sein, A Preliminary Study of the Kalyani Inscriptions of Dhammaceti, 1476 A.D., IA., xxii, Bombay, 1893.

Mahāvaṃsa (including Cūlavaṃsa), ed. by W. Geiger, PTS, London, 1908; Eng. Tarns, by W. Geiger, PTS, London, 1934.

Mahāvaṃsa, ed. by Sumaṅgala and Batuwantudawa, Colombo, 1908.

Majjhima Nikāya, 3 parts, ed. by K. Ñāṇavimala Thera, Colombo.

Majjhima Nikāya, Part I, Vidyālaṅkāra Tripiṭaka Publication, Kalaniya, 1946.

Malalasekera, G.P., The Pāli Liteature of Ceylon, Colombo, 1928.

Nicholas, C.W. and Paranavitana, S., A Concise History of Ceylon, Colombo, 1961.

Nikāyasaṅgrahaya, ed. by Simon de Silva, A Mendis Gunasekera and W.F. Gunawardhana, (Ceylon Government Press, 1907).

Nīlakanta Sastri, K.A., Vijaybāhu I the Literature of Lanka, Journal of the Ceylon Branch of the Royal Asiatic Society, New Series, IV, 1955.

Pandita, Vincent, Buddhism during the Polonnaruva Period, Ceylon Historical Journal, IV, 1954-1955.

Paramavitana, S., Poḷonnaruva Inscription of Vijayabāhu I, Epigraphia Indica, XVIII, 1925-26, parts 7-8, July-October, 1926, Calcutta.

Paramavitana, S., Poḷonnaruva Slab Inscription of the Velaikkaras, C. 1137-1153 A.D., Epigraphia Zeylanica II, part 6, 1927.

Pūjāvaliya ed. Bentara Śraddhā Tisya, Pānadura, 1930.

Pūjāvaliya ed. D.E. Heṭṭiāracci and D.C. Disānāyaka, chapters I-II, Colombo, 1936; Chapter, 12-16, ed. by D.E. Heṭṭ iāracci, Colombo, 1948.

Pūjāvaliya, 33-34 Pariccheda, ed. A.V. Suravira, Colombo, 1961.

Pūjāvaliya, chapter XXXIV, ed. Mābopitiyā Medhumkera, Colombo, 1932.

Pūjāvaliya, ed. B. Gunasekera Mudaliyar, Colombo, 1895.

Perera, E.W., The Age of Parākramabāhu VI, Journal of the Ceylon Branch of the Royal Asiatic Society, XXII, no. 10, 1910.

Perera, H.R., Buddhism in Ceylon, Its Past and its Present, Kandy, Ceylon, 1966.

Pieris, P.E., Ceylon, The Portuguese Era, I. Colombo, 1913.

Rahula, Walpola, History of Buddhism in Ceylon, the Anurādhapura Period 3rd century B.C.-10th century B.C. colombo, 1956.

Rasavāhinī, ed. by Saraṇatissa Thera (Part I, 1913, Part II 1920, Jināloka Press, Colombo).

Ray, H.C. & Paramavitana, S., History of Ceylon, Vol. I, 2 parts, Colombo, 1959, 1960.

Rājāvaliya, ed. B. Gunasekera, reprinted, Colombo, 1953.

Rājāvaliya, Tr. into English by B.Gunasekera, reprinted Colombo, 1954., first published 1980.

Sandeśakathā, ed. Prof. Minayeff of St. Petersburg, Journal of the Pāli Text Society, London, 1895.

Sāsanavaṃsa, ed. M. Bode, PTS., London, 1897.

Sāsanvaṃsa, ed. B.C. Law, London, 1952.

The Way of the Buddha, Publications Division, Ministry of Information and Broadcasting, Government of India.

Universities of Ceylon Review, Colombo.

Vaṃsatthappakāsiṇī (Mahāvaṃsa-Ṭikā), 2 volumes, ed. by G.P. Malasekera (PTS).

Vibhaṅgaṭṭhakathā (Sammohavinodani) commentary on the Vibhaṅga (SHB).

Vimalananda, Tennakoon, Buddhism in Ceylon under Christian Powers, Colombo, 1963.

Wickremasinghe, Sirima, Successors of Parākramabāhu I, Downfall of the Polonnaru Kingdom, University of Ceylon History of Ceylon, I, Part II.

CHAPTER TWO

A Concise History of Ceylon, by C.W. Nichloas and S. Paranavitana, Colombo, 1961.

A Memoir by Dr. S. Paranavitana on the God of Adam's Peak, Artibus Asiac, Ascona, Switzerland.

Adikaram, E.W., Early History of Buddhism in Ceylon or "State of Buddhism as Revealed by the Pāli commentaries of the 5th century A.D.", Colombo, 1946.

Buddhism in Ceylon, Its Past and its Present, H.R. Perera, Kandy, 1966.

Buddhism in India and Abroad, Anukul Chandra Banerjee, Calcutta, 1973.

Ceylon Journal of Science, II, Colombo.

Codrington, H.W., A Short History of Ceylon, Macmillan & Co., 1926.

Dīpavaṃsa, ed. and tr. into English by H. Oldenberg, London, 1879.

Dīpavaṃsa, ed. and tr. into Sinhalese by P. Ñāṇānanda Thera, Star Press, Panaduras, 1927.

Dr. S. Paranavitana, Upulvan, Archaelogical Survey of Ceylon Memoir, VI, Ceylon.

Eliot, Charles, Hinduism and Buddhism, Vol. III.

Foucher, M., L'iconographic bondhighe de l'Inde.

History of Buddhism in Ceylon, Walpola Rahula, Colombo, 1956.

Kern, H., Manual of Indian Buddhism, 1896.

Mahāvaṃsa (including Cūlavaṃsa) edited by W. Geiger, PTS., London, 1934.

Mahāvaṃsa, ed. by Sumangala and Batwantudewa, Colombo, 1908.

Mahāvaṃsa, tr. by W. Geiger, 1934. London.

Majjhima-nikāyaṭṭakathā (Papaṃcarūdaṁ), commentary on the Majhima-Nikāya (Aluvihāra edition), ed. by Siri Dhammārāma (Vidyāsāgara Pres, Colombo, Vol. I, 1917, Vol. II, 1926).

Mendis., G.C., The Early History of Ceylon, Calcutta, 1935.

Nikāyasaṅgrahaya, ed. by Simon de Silva, A. Mendis Gunasekera and W.F. Gunavardhana, Ceylon Government Press, 1907, Colombo.

Nikāyasaṅgrahaya, tr. into English by C.M. Fernando, Ceylon Government Press, Colombo, 1908.

Paṃcappakaraṇa ṭṭhakathā I (Kathāvatthuppakaraṇavaṇṇanā).

Paramavitana, S., Mahāyānism in Ceylon, The Ceylon Journal of Science, Vol. II, Part I, Section G., Ceylon, 1920.

Pradhan, Abhidharma-Samuccaya, Santiniketan, 1950.

Tenent, Sir James Emerson, Ceylon, London, 1859.

The Ceylon Journal of Historical and Social Studies, Vol. 9, No. 1. January-June, 1966: R.A.L.H. Gunavardana, Buddhist Nikāays in Mediaeval Ceylon.

The Journal of the Bengal Asiatic Society, 1915, Plate xx, Calcutta.

The Mahābodhi 1891-1991 centemary Volume, The Mahābodhi Society of India, Calcutta, 1991: Dr. S. Paramavitana: Mahāyānism in Ceylon.

Vibhaṅgaṭṭhakathā (Sammohavinodanī), commentary on the Vibhaṅga.

Winternitz., M., History of Indian Literature, 2 Vols., Calcutta.

CHAPTER THREE

Aṅguttara-Nikāya, ed. Devamitta Thera, Samayawardhana Press, Colombo.

Aṅguttara-Nikāyaṭṭakathā (Manorathapūraṇī), Commentary on the Aṅguttara-Nikāya, 2 parts (SHB).

Beal, Samuel, Buddhist Records of the Western World, Translated from the Chinese of Hiuen Tsiang (A.D. 629) by Samuel Beal, London, Kegan Paul, Trench, Trubner & Co.

Beal, Samuel, The Life of Hiuen Tsiang, London, 1911.

Coomaraswamy, Ananda K., History of Indian and Indonesian Art, London, 1927.

Coomaraswamy, Ananda K., Mediaeval Sinhalese Art, Second Edition, New York, 1956.

Cullavagga (of the Vinaya), ed. by Saddhātissa Thera, Alutgama, 1915.

Dhammapada (with old Sinhalese Sanmya), ed. by K. Dhammaratana Thera, Colombo, 1926.

Dhammapadaṭṭhakathā, Commentary on the Dhammapada (SHB).

Dīgha Nikāya, 3 parts ed. by Welitara Siri Ñāṇāvāsa Thera, Vidyāsāgara Press, Colombo.

Dīgha-Nikāyaṭṭhakathā (Sumaṅgalavilāsin¤), Commentary on the Dīgha Nikāya, 2 perts (SHB).

Dīpavaṃsa, ed. and tr. into English by H. Oldenberg, London, 1879.

Epigraphia Zeylanica, 4 vols., Oxford University Press.

Kotahence Prajmākīrti: Śrī Dharmāloka Caritaya, 1937.

Mahāvaṃsa, ed. by Sumaṅgala and Batuwantudewa, Colombo, 1908.

Mahāvaṃsa, tr. into English by Geiger, London, 1934.

Mahāvagga (of the Vinaya) ed. by B. Saddhātissa Thera, Alutgama, 1922.

Majjhima-Nikāyaṭṭhakathā (Papaṃcasūdanī, Commentary on the Majjhima Nikāya (Aluvihāra Edition) ed. by Siri Dhammārāma (Vidyāsāgara Press), Colombo, Vol. I, 1917, Vol. II, 1926.

Mookerji, Radha Kumud, Ancient Indian Education, Macmillan and Co., London, 1947.

Nattana Katz and Judith Simmer, Buddhist Perspectives on Education, Mahabodhi Centenary Commemorative volume Sambhasha, Volume I, No. 2, 1991, Culcutta.

Paranavitana, S., Sīgiriya Graffiti, Journal of the Royal Asiatic Society, Ceylon Branch, XXXIV, No. 92, 1939, Colombo.

Rahula, Walpola, History of Buddhism in Ceylon, Colombo, 1956.

Samantapāsādikā, Vinaya Commentary, 3 parts (SHB), 1900.

Tennant, Sir J.E., Ceylon—An Account of the Isalnd, Physical, Historical and Topographical, 2 Vols., London, 1859.

Vibhariganhakathā (Sammohavinodanī) Commentary on the Vibhaṅiga (SHB).

Visuddhimagga (SHB) 1920

CHAPTER FOUR

Anesaki, M., Buddhist Art, London, 1916.

Brown, Percy, Indian Architecture (Buddhist and Hindu Periods), Bombay, 1942.

Ceylon, The Ceylon Tourist Board, Colombo.

Commaraswamy, Anand, K., Mediaeval Simhalese Art, New York, 1956.

Coomaraswamy, Ananda, K., History of Indian and Indonesian Art, London, 1927.

Fernando, P.E.E., 'Tantric Influence on the Sculptures of Gal Vihāra, Poḷonnaruva', U.C.R., XVIII, 1960.

Foucher, A., Baginnings of Buddhist Art, London, 1918.

Godakumbura, C.E., 'Bronzes from Poḷonnaruva', J.R.A.S., Cey. Br. NS. VII, 1961.

Goloulew, Victor, 'The Art of India and Indo-China with special reference to Ceylon'. J.R.A.S. Cey. Br. XXXI, No. 83, 1930.

Levi D'ancous, Mirella, 'Anarāvati, Ceylon and Three "Imported" Bronzes, Art Bulletin, XXXIV, 1-17.

Marshal, Sir John, The Monumetns of Sanchi, 3 Vols., London.

Marshall, Sir John, Mohenjo-daro and the Indus Civilisation.

Nicholes, C.W. and Paramavitana, S., A Concise History of Ceylon, Colombo, 1961.

Pachori, Dr. L.N., The Splendours of Buddhist Art in Asia, The Mahā Bodhi Centenary Volume, 1891-1991, The Maha Bodhi Society of India, Calcutta, 1991.

Paramavitana, S., The Stūpa in Ceylon (Memoirs of the Archaeological Survey of Ceylon, Vol. V).

Paranavitana, S., 'The Art and Architecture of the Poḷonnaruva Period', reprinted in C.H.J., IV, 1954-1955.

Smith, V.S., History of Fine Art in India and Ceylon, Oxford, 1930.

The Maha Bodhi Centenary Volume, 1891-1991, The Maha Bodhi Society of India, Caclutta, 1991.

The Mahabodhi Centenary Commemorative volume, Sambhasha, Volume 1, No. 2-1991, Sri Lanka.

Wijesekara, N.D., Sinhalese Sculpture, Colombo, 1963.

Zimmer Heinrich, The Art of Indian Asia, New York, 1955.

CHAPTER FIVE

Aṅguttara-nikāya, edited by Devamitta Thera (Samaya-wardhana Press, Colombo), ed. by R. Morris, E. Hardy, C.A.F., Rhys Davids, P.T.S., London, 1855-1910, Vols. I-VI.

Aṅguttara-nikāyaṭṭhakathā (Manorathapūraṇī), Commentary on the Aṅguttara-nikāya, 2 parts (SHB), ed. by M. Walleyer, H. Kopp, vols. 1-4, P.T.S., London, 1924-56.

Buddhist Records of the Western World, Translated from the Chinese of Hiuen Tsiang (A.D. 629) by Samual Beal, London, 1911.

Catubhāṇavāraṭṭhakathā (Sāratthasamuccaya) (SHB).

Cūlavaṃsa, tr. by Geiger, Part I, 1929; Part II, 1930.

Culavaṃsa, ed. by W. Geiger, 2 Vols., London, 1925, 1927; Tr. Eng. by C. Mabel Rickmero, 2 perts, Colombo, 1953.

Dāṭhāvaṃsa, ed. by Sīlālaṅkāra Thera, Alutgama, 1914; ed by T.W. Rhys Davids, and R. Morris, Journal of the Pāli Text Society, London, 1884.

Dhātuvaṃsa, Colombo, 1914.

Dīgha-mikāyaṭṭhakathā (Sumaṅgalavilāsinī), Commentary on the Dīgha-nikāya, 2 parts (SHB), ed. by T.W. Rhys Davids, J.E. Carpenter, W. Stede, P.T.S., London, 1866.

Dīpavaṃsa, ed. and tr. into English by H. Oldenberg, London, 1879.

Legge, J., A Record by Buddhist Kingdom: An Account of Chinese Monk Fa Hien of his Travels in India and Ceylon (A.D. 399-414 A.D.) by J. Legge, Oxford, 1886.

Mahāvaṃsa (including Cūlavasa), Eng. Tr. by W. Geiger, assisted by M.W. Bode, Colombo, 1950.

Mahāvaṃsa, ed. by Sumaṅgala and Batuwantudewa, Colombo, 1905 and 1908.

Majjhima-nikāyaṭṭhakathā (Papaṃcasūdanī), Commentary on the Majjhima-nikāya (Aluvihāra Edition), edited by Siri Dhammārāma, Vidyāsāgar Press, Colombo, Vol. I, 1917, Vol. II, 1926; ed. by J.M. Woods and D. Asambi, P.T.S., London, 1922-38.

Milinda-Paṃha, ed. by Piyaratana and Gunaratana Theras, Cclombo, 1927; ed by V. Trenckers London, 1928.

Rahula, Walpola, History of Buddhism in Ceylon, Colombo, 1956.

Rahula, Walpola, The Significance of "Ariyavaṃsa", University of Ceylon Review, Vol. I, No. 1.

Rasavāhinī, ed., by Saraṇatissa Thera, Part I, 1913, Part II, 1920, Jinãloka Press, Colombo.

Saṃyutta-nikāyaṭṭakathā (Sāratthappakāsini), Commentary on the Saṃyutta-nikāya, ed.by F.L. Woodward, P.T.S., London, 1929-37.

Suttanipātaṭṭhakathā (Paramatthajotikā), Commentary Lon the Sutta-nipāta (SHB), ed. by Helmer Smith, P.T.S., London, 1916-18., by Welipitiya Dewamuda Thera and revised by Mahagoda Sri Nanissara Thera, Colombo, 1922.

The Toṇigala Inscription, Epigriphia Zeylanica, III.

Vibhaṅgaṭṭhakathā (Sammohavinodanī), Commentary on the Vibhaṅga (SHB), ed. by A.P. Buddhadatta Thera, P.T.S., London, 1923.

Visuddhimagga (SHB), 1920, ed. by C.A.F. Rhys Davids, 2 Vols., P.T.S., London, 1920-21., ed. by H.C. Warren and D. Kosambi, Harvard Oriented Series, 41, New York, 1950.

CHAPTER SIX

Adikaram, E.W., The Early History of Buddhism in Ceylon, Colombo, 1953.

Banerjee, A.C., Buddhism in India and Abroad, Calcutta, 1973.

Cūlavaṃsa, ed. by W. Geiger, 2 vols., London, 1925, 1927, tr. by W. Geiger, tr. Eng. by C. Mabel Rickmero, 2 pts., Colombo, 1953.

Childers, R.C., A Dictionary of the Pāli Language, London, 1875.

Dambadeṇi Asna, Kuveṇi Sihabā Saba Dambtadeṇi Asna, ed., Kirialle, Nanavimala Thera, Colombo, 1960.

Daḷadā Pūjavāliya, ed. by Kanadulle Ratanaramsi Thara, Columbo, 1954

Daḷadā Sirita, ed. by Valivitiya Sorato, Colombo, 1954.

Dāṭhāvaṃsa, tr. by M. Coomaraswamy, London, 1874.

Dāparaṃsa, ed. and tr. by H. Oldenberg, London, 1879.

Dāthāvaṃsa, ed. by T.W. Rhys Davids and R. Morris, Journal of the Pāli Text Society, London, 1884.

Dīpavaṃsa, ed. by B.C. Law, Ceylon Historical Journal, Colombo, VII, July 1957, April 1958, Nos. 1-4, Ceylon, 1959.

Dīpavaṃsa, tr. by M. Coomaraswamy, London, 1908.

Elu Attanagaluramsasaya, ed. by P. Ariyaratana, Colombo, 1932.

Geiger, W., 'The Trustworthiness of the Mahāvaṃsa', in Indian Historical Quarterly, VI, 1930, reprinted in Ceylon Historical Journal, Colombo, IV, 1954-55.

Geiger, W., The Dīpavaṃsa and the Mahāvaṃsa and their Historical Development in Ceylon, tr. Eng. by M. Coomaraswamy Colombo, 1908.

Godakumbura, C.E., "The Cūlavaṃsa", Journal of the Ceylon Branch of the Royal Asiatic Society, Colombo, XXXVIII, 1949.

Godakumbura, C.E., Sinhalese Literature, Colombo, 1955.

Haldar (De), Manikuntala, A Study on the Hatthavanagallavihāravaṃsa, Calcutta University, 1988-89.

Haldar (De), Manikuntala, The Hatthavanagallavihāravaṃsa in Bengali, Pāli Department, Calcutta University, 1998.

Hatthavanagallavihāravaṃsa, ed. by C.E. Godakumbura, P.T.S., London, 1956.

Hazra, K.L., History of Theravāda Buddhism in South-East Asia, New Delhi, 1982.

Hazra, K.L., Pāli Language and Literature, Vols. I and II, New Delhi, 1994.

Hazra, K.L., The Buddhist Annals and Chronicles of South-East Asia, New Delhi, 1986.

Law, B.C., A History of Pāli Literature 2 vols., London, 1933.

Law, B.C., On the Chronicles of Ceylon, Calcutta, 1947.

Liyannagamage, Ameradara, The decline of Polonnaruwa and the Rise of Dambadeniya, Ceylon, 1968.

Mahābodhivaṃsa, ed. by S.A. Strong, P.T.S., London, 1891.

Mahāvaṃsa, ed. and tr. by G. Turnour, Colombo, 1837.
Mahāvaṃsa, ed. by W. Geiger, P.T.S. London, 1905.
Mahāvaṃsa, Eng. Tr. by W. Geiger, assisted by M.H. Bosle, Colombo, 1950.
Mahāvaṃsa, H. Sumangala and Batuwantudewe, Colombo, 1905.
Mahīvaṃsa, Eng. Tr. by L.C. Wijesinha, Colombo, 1909.
Malalasekera, G.P., The Pāli Literature of Ceylon, Colombo, 1958.
Nicholas, C.W. and Paranavitana, S., A Concise History of Ceylon, Colombo, 1961.
Nikāya Sangralaya, ed. by D.P.R. Samaranayaka, Colombo, 1960.
Nikāya Sangralaya, Eng. Tr. by C.M. Fernando, revised edition by Mudaliyar D.F. Gunavardhana, Colombo, 1908.
Perera, H.R., Buddhism in Ceylon, Kandy, Ceylon, 1966.
Pūyāvaliya, ed. by Bentara Sraddha Tisya, Panadura, 1930.
Rahula, Walpola, History of Buddhism in Ceylon, Colombo, 1956.
Ray, H.C., and Paranavitana, S., History of Ceylon, Vol. I, 2 parts, Colombo, 1959-1960.
Rājaratnākaraya, ed. by Simon de Silva, Colombo, 1907.
Rājāvaliya, ed. by B. Gunasekera, reprinted, Colombo, 1953.
Rājāvaliya, tr. Eng. by B. Gunasekera, Colombo, 1954.
Samanakūṭavaṇṇā, ed. by C.E. Godakumbura, P.T.S., London, 1958.
Siṃhala Bodhivaṃśaya, ed., by Baddegama Kirtisiri Dhammaratna, Matara, Ceylon, 1911.
Siṃhala Thūpavaṃśaya, ed. by D.E. Hettiaracci, Colombo, 1947.
Thūpavaṃsa, ed. by B.C. Law, P.T.S., London, 1935.
Wickremasinghe, D.M. de 2., Catalogue of the Siṃhala Manuscripts in the British Museum, London, 1960.
Winternitz, M., A History of Indian Literature, Vol. II, Calcutta, 1933.

CHAPTER SEVEN

A Record of Buddhist Kindom: An Account of Chinese Monk Fa Hien of his Travels in India and Ceylon (A.D. 399-414) by J. Legge, Oxford,1886.

Aṅguttara-nikāyaṭṭhakathā CManorathapūraṇī), Commentary on the Aṅguttara-nikāya, I-V, ed. by M. Walleser, H. Kopp, PTS., London, 1924-1956.

Adikaram, E.W., Early History of Buddhism in Ceylon or "State of Buddhist as Revealed by the Pāli Commentaries of the 5th century A.D.", Colombo, 1946.

Anāgatavaṃsadesanāva, Colombo.

Buddhist Records of the Western World, Translated from the Chinese of Hiuen Tsiang (A.D. 629) by Samuel Beal, London.

Cūlavaṃsa, translated by W. Geiger, Part I, 1929; Part II, 1930.

Ceylon Journal of Science.

Dhammapadaṭṭhakathā, Commentary on the Dhammapada (SHB). ed. by H.C. Norman, H. Smith and L.S. Talaing, PTS., London, 1966-1915., tr. by E.W. Burlingame. "Buddhist Legends" in three parts, Harvard Oriental Series, vols. 28-30. Cambridge, Man., 1821., C. Durieselle, tr. in Buddhism, II, Rangoon, 1905-08.

Dharmapradīpikā, ed. by Śrī Dharmārāma, Sri Lanka, 1915.

Dīgha-nikāya, 3 parts ed., by Welitara Siri Ñāṇāvāsa Thera, Vidyasāgara Press, Colombo.

Dīgha-Nikāya, ed. by T.W. Rhys Davids and J.E. Carpenter, 3 Vols. London, 1889-1910. Tr. by T.W. Rhys Davids and Mrs. Rhys Davids, Dialogues of the Buddha, Sacred Books of the Buddhists, London, 1899-1921.

Dīgha-vikāyaṭṭhakathā (Sumaṅgalavilāsinī), Commentary on the Dīgha-nikāya, 2 parts (SHB), ed. by T.W. Rhys Davids and J.E. Carpenter, W. Stede, P.T.S., London, 1866.

Dīpavaṃsa, edited and translated by H. Oldenberg into English,

London, 1879.

Dutt, Nalinaksh, The Cultural Heritage of India, Vol. I.

Epigraphia Zeylanica, I, Buddhannchala Pillar Inscription, Oxford University Press.

Īripinniyāra Pillar Inscription.

Kaludiya-pokuṇa Cave Inscription, EZ, III, 258.

Mahāvaṃsa (including Cūlavaṃsa), ed. by W. Geiger, Colombo, 1950.

Mahāvaṃsa, ed. by Sumaṅgala and Batuwantudewa, Colombo, 1905.

Mahāvagga (of the Vinaya), ed. by B. Saddhātissa Thera, Alutgama, 1922.

Majjhima=nikāyaṭṭhakathā (Papaṃcasūdanī), Commentary on the Majjhima-nikāya Aluvihāra Edition). ed. by Siri Dhammārāma (Vidyāsagara Press, Colombo, Vol. I, 1917, Vol. II, 1926).

Majjhima-Nikāya, 3 parts edited by K. Ñāṇavimala Thera, Colombo.

Majjhima-Nikāya, Part I, Vidyālaṅkāra Tripiṭaka Publication, Kalaniya, 1946.

Malalasekera, G.P., Dictionary of Pāli Proper Names, Vols. I & II, London, 1960.

Manner Kacceri Pillar Inscription.

Mihintale Tablets of Mahinda IV, EZ, I.

Nicholas, C.W. and Paramavitana, S., A Concise History of Ceylon, Colombo, 1961.

Paramatthajotikā (11) PTS. (Suttanipāta Commentary), by Welipitiya Dewananda Thera and revised Mahagooda. Sri Namissara Thera, Colombo, 1922.

Pācittiya Pāli (of the Vinaya) ed. by Medhā Siri Ariyavaṃsa Thera, Colombo, B.E. 2472.

Rahula, Walpola, History of Buddhism in Ceylon, Colombo, 1956.

Rambhāva Pillar Inscription, III.

Rasavāhinī, edited by Saraṇatissa Thera (Part I, 1913, Part II 1920, Jināloka Press, Colombo).
Saddharmālaṅkāraya, ed. by Ñāṇavimala Thera.
Samantapāsādika, Vinaya Commentary III (Granthaloka Press, Colombo, 1900).
Samantapāsādika, Vinaya Commentary, PTS, ed., by J. Takakusu, assisted by M. Nagai, 1, 1924, II, 1927, London.
Thera-gāthā CVimānavatthu-Petarathu-Thergāthā-therīgāthā in one volume), edited by M. Dhammānanda Thera, Colombo, 1930.
Vaṃsatthappakāsinii (Mahāvaṃsa-Tikā), 2 Vols., ed. by G.P. Malalasakera (PTS), London, 1935.
Vibhaṅgaṭṭhakathā (Sammohavinodanī), Commentary on the Vibhaṅga ed by A.P. Buddhadatta Thera, P.T.S., London, 1923.
Vinaya Pitaka, ed. by H. Oldenberg, Vol. I, London, 1879.
Visuddhimagga (SHB), 1920.
Visuddhimagga, ed. by A.C. Warren and D. Kosambi, Harvard Orinetal Series, 41, New York, 1950.
Visuddhimagga, ed. by C.A.F. Rhys Davids, 2 Vols. P.T.S., London, 1920-21.
Warnasuriya, W.M.A., Inscriptional Evidence bearing on the Nature of Religious Endowments in Ancient Ceylon, UC., Vol. I, Nos. 1, 2; Vol. II, Nos. 1, 2.

CHAPTER EIGHT

Aṅguttara-nikāyaṭṭhakathā (Manorathapūraṇī), Commentary on the Aṅguttara-nikāya, 2 parts (SHB).
Cullavagga (of the Vinaya), ed. by Saddhātissa Thera, Alutgama, 1915.
Dīgha-nikāyaṭṭhakathā (Sumaṅgalavilāsini), Commentary on the Dīgha-nikāya, 2 parts (SHB).
Śatapatha Brāhmaṇa (SBE).

Mahāvaṃsa (including Cūlavaṃsa), ed. by W. Geiger, P.T.S., London, 1908.

Mahāvaṃsa, ed. by Sumaṅgala and Batuwantudewa, Colombo, 1908.

Mahāvaṃsa, Eng. Tr. by W. Geiger, assisted by M.H. Bode, reprinted in Colombo, 1950, first published 1912.

Majjhima-nikāyaṭṭhakathā (Papaṃcasūdanī), Commentary on the Majjhima-nikāya (Aluvihāra Edition), ed. by Siri Dhammārāma (Vidyāsāgara Press, Colombo, Vol. I, 1917, Vol. II, 1926).

Rahula Walpola, History of Buddhism in Ceylon, Colombo, 1956.

Saṃyutta-nikāyaṭṭhakathā (Sāratthappakāsinī), Commentary on the Sanyutta-nikāya, 3 parts, (SHB).

Sacred Books of the East.

Samantapāsādika, Vinaya Commentary, III. (Granthaloka Press), Colombo, 1900.

Samantapāsādikā, Vinaya Commentary, 3 parts (SHB).

Vibhaṅgaṭṭhakathā (Sammohavinodanī), Commentary on the Vibhaṅga (SHB).

Visuddhimagga (SHB), 1920.

Index

S

T

U

V

Pictures

Standing Buddha at Galvihāra, Polonnaruva

Buddha on the Outer Circular Road at Anurādhapura

The Samadhi Buddha: unique example of ancient sculpture

Ruvanvaliseya built by Duttha Gamani (161-137 B.C.)

Seated Buddha, Vatadage, Polonnaruwa